"Dennis Johnson leads us by the hand [...] Ethiopian eunuch met Philip in the b[...] understanding the Bible's message. Like Philip, Dr. Johnson focuses our gaze on the crucified, risen, and glorified Messiah, Jesus, as the central message of the Scriptures. In the process, he teaches us how to trace these biblical connections with greater skill, both for our own personal benefit and so that we can better teach others."

—**Iain Duguid**, Professor of Old Testament, Westminster Theological Seminary

"*Redemptive-historical hermeneutics* has been a major topic among Reformed scholars. What it means is simply that every part of the Bible teaches Christ, and that the most important thing about every passage is what it teaches us about Christ. Many pastors interpret biblical texts this way in their sermons, but they don't always explain to the congregation what they are doing. Dennis Johnson's *Walking with Jesus through His Word* explains the concept well. Johnson shows us how we can read the Bible ourselves in a Christ-centered way, and how this approach enriches our understanding of the Word of God."

—**John M. Frame**, J. D. Trimble Professor of Systematic Theology and Philosophy, Reformed Theological Seminary, Orlando

"Experiencing Dennis Johnson's instruction firsthand as a seminary student was an enormous privilege. But in this book he has poured his decades of research, teaching, and life into one volume that reignites our passion for Bible study. The Bible itself tells us how to read it. Professor Johnson not only believes this, but displays it on every page. For anyone wanting to see how the Bible fits together, this book is a treasure."

—**Michael S. Horton**, J. Gresham Machen Professor of Systematic Theology and Apologetics, Westminster Seminary California

"The invitation given by Dennis Johnson to walk through the whole Bible with Jesus is challenging and exciting. Anything written by Dr. Johnson is bound to be theologically sound and intellectually stimulating. This book is more than that. It comes from the heart of a man who has walked with Jesus in his personal life as well as in his study of the Scriptures. Dennis Johnson knows Jesus and knows how to help others to know him."

—**Rosemary Jensen**, Founder and President, Rafiki Foundation

"Like every other Christian, I long to walk more closely and constantly with Jesus. This book helped me to refine my walk by showing me more of Jesus throughout the Bible. It was an easy and delightful read, and it's sure to ignite many hearts."

—**David Murray**, Professor of Old Testament, Puritan Reformed Theological Seminary; Pastor, Grand Rapids Free Reformed Church

Walking with Jesus through His Word

Walking with Jesus through His Word

Discovering Christ in All the Scriptures

Dennis E. Johnson

PUBLISHING

P.O. BOX 817 • PHILLIPSBURG • NEW JERSEY 08865-0817

© 2015 by Dennis E. Johnson

All rights reserved. No part of this book may be reproduced, stored in a retrieval system, or transmitted in any form or by any means—electronic, mechanical, photocopy, recording, or otherwise—except for brief quotations for the purpose of review or comment, without the prior permission of the publisher, P&R Publishing Company, P.O. Box 817, Phillipsburg, New Jersey 08865–0817.

Unless otherwise indicated, all Scripture quotations are from the ESV® Bible (*The Holy Bible, English Standard Version*®), copyright © 2001 by Crossway, a publishing ministry of Good News Publishers. Used by permission. All rights reserved. All quotations are from the 2007 text edition of the ESV.

Scripture quotations marked (NASB) are taken from the New American Standard Bible®, copyright © 1960, 1962, 1963, 1968, 1971, 1972, 1973, 1975, 1977, 1995 by The Lockman Foundation. Used by permission.

Scripture quotations marked (NIV) are from the HOLY BIBLE, NEW INTERNATIONAL VERSION®. NIV®. Copyright © 1973, 1978, 1984 by International Bible Society. Used by permission of Zondervan Publishing House. All rights reserved.

Italics within Scripture quotations indicate emphasis added.

ISBN: 978-1-59638-220-6 (pbk)
ISBN: 978-1-62995-121-8 (ePub)
ISBN: 978-1-62995-122-5 (Mobi)

Printed in the United States of America

Library of Congress Cataloging-in-Publication Data

Johnson, Dennis E. (Dennis Edward)
  Walking with Jesus through his word : discovering Christ in all the scriptures / Dennis E. Johnson. -- 1st ed.
    pages cm
  Includes bibliographical references and index.
  ISBN 978-1-59638-220-6 (pbk.)
  1. Bible. Old Testament--Introductions. 2. Jesus Christ. I. Title.
  BS1140.3.J63 2015
  220.6--dc23
                          2015001737

To Our Children:

Eric and Susanne
Christina and Julien
Peter and Mandi
Laurie and Daniel

And Their Children:

Jonathan, Simeon, Andrew, Gabriel
Kellen, Zane, Logan, Maya
Naomi, Peyton, Sophia, Carter
Finnan, Keziah, Iain, Claire

He commanded our fathers
to teach to their children,
that the next generation might know them,
the children yet unborn,
and arise and tell them to their children,
so that they should set their hope in God
and not forget the works of God,
but keep his commandments.
(Psalm 78:5–7)

Contents

Contents

Foreword

THERE ARE MANY books about how to read and interpret the Bible. This volume stands out because it offers us a key to the way in which Jesus himself interpreted the Old Testament. Understanding how the Old Testament relates to the New is one of the most important things that Christians need to understand about the Bible. Jesus' first followers initially had a difficult time understanding how and where the Old Testament books prophesied about the Messiah. As Jesus taught them how to find him in the Scriptures, however, they began to understand the diverse ways in which the Old Testament looked forward to him. Likewise, the better we know how Jesus interpreted and applied the Old Testament, the better we can emulate his methods.

Dennis Johnson will ably and clearly explain why and how Jesus understood that "all the Scriptures" point to Christ. We may well think that naturally *Jesus* could properly see how this was so. But we ourselves might not have the confidence to find him in the Old Testament beyond the New Testament passages that cite messianic verses from the Old. Johnson's work will help us to gain that confidence. It will also aid us in not finding Jesus in the Old Testament where he is not.

Thus, this volume will help us to see the proper ways in which the Old Testament is Christ-centered. It will enable us to read the Old Testament Christianly. I eagerly commend this book to readers, who are sure to benefit from following Jesus' approach to interpreting the Old Testament. In doing so, they will discover the many glorious ways in which the Old Testament points to Jesus and sees him as its goal.

G. K. Beale
J. Gresham Machen Chair of New Testament and
Professor of New Testament and Biblical Theology
Westminster Theological Seminary

Acknowledgments

PLEASE DO NOT BE MISLED by the fact that there are hardly any footnotes in this book. The truth is that whatever you might find useful in these pages for your study of God's Word I have learned from others. I have spared you a flood of footnotes to make *Walking with Jesus through His Word* more accessible and to make it feel less "academic." (If you happen to thrive on delving into documentation and checking sources, feel free to start with my *Him We Proclaim* and the other resources listed in "For Further Reading" at the end of this book.)

I am glad to acknowledge those through whom I have come to see more of how the tapestry of Scripture and the history of redemption find their focus and coherence in the Lord Jesus Christ. Some have taught me in person, through formal instruction and informal conversation: Derke P. Bergsma, Edmund P. Clowney, Raymond B. Dillard, Iain M. Duguid, Bryan D. Estelle, John M. Frame, Mark D. Futato, Richard B. Gaffin Jr., Robert H. Gundry, Michael S. Horton, Vern S. Poythress, and O. Palmer Robertson. Others have taught me primarily through their publications and correspondence: G. K. Beale, Bryan Chapell, Sinclair Ferguson, R. T. France, Graeme Goldsworthy, Leonhard Goppelt, Sidney Greidanus, Meredith G. Kline, Tremper Longman III, Geerhardus Vos, and Christopher J. H. Wright. From many of these I have learned both in person and in print.

My colleagues on the faculty of Westminster Seminary California were kind enough to read and discuss a couple of these chapters with me. Their comments have helped to improve clarity at various points, and for those observations I am thankful. I'm even more grateful for our shared commitment across our various disciplines—biblical studies, theology, homiletics—to point students to Christ as the center of God's Word.

As they have for my previous work, the editorial staff of P&R Publishing have improved this book in the process of preparing it for publication. John J. Hughes has not only managed the editorial process adroitly, but also recommended additions to the work that will make it, I expect, more useful to readers. Copyeditor Karen Magnuson's sharp eyes and mind caught and corrected errors; and she raised questions that astutely diagnosed obscurity and suggested remedies, resulting in greater clarity, for which every reader should join me in thanksgiving.

I thank God that for decades my family and I have been well fed spiritually, week by week, by hearing Christ preached from all the Scriptures in our congregation, New Life Presbyterian Church in Escondido, California. For over a decade now, our present pastor, Ted Hamilton, has shown us how to walk with Jesus through his Word and the difference it makes in the joys and struggles of everyday life.

I am especially grateful for Jane, my beloved *'ēzer kenegdô* ("helper who fits" me just right, Gen. 2:18) for over four decades. For this project, as for every previous one, she has been my first sharp-eyed reader, my insightful editor, and my constant encourager.

Finally, human words—even the best of them—fail to express the thanks that I want to offer to the triune God, who revealed himself to us and reconciled us to himself through the incarnation of the Son, Jesus the Christ, and through his redemptive achievement on our behalf. My prayer is that you will be drawn to praise him with me as we walk with Jesus through his Word, from Genesis through Revelation.

PART 1

Beginning the Journey

1

The Walk through the Bible
That Sets Hearts Afire

THE TITLE OF THIS BOOK implies an audacious claim. The claim is that the sixty-six books contained in the Christian Scriptures, the Bible, which were written by dozens of people in many different centuries, are bound together by a central theme, a single plotline, and a unique Hero, Jesus the Messiah. Admittedly, two-thirds of these Scriptures were given long before Jesus was born in Bethlehem, and do not even mention him by name. To be sure, these documents come in different forms: historical narratives, law codes, wisdom aphorisms, theological discourses, poems, letters, symbolic visions, and more. Still, this study seeks to persuade you that Jesus is the central figure in the outworking of God's plan for human and global and cosmic history, the divine agenda that unifies everything in the Bible, from Genesis to Revelation. Moreover, this study proposes a way of reading Scripture that is, I believe, rooted in Scripture itself and that will equip you to appreciate more fully how the whole Bible reveals Christ and his mission of rescue and renovation.

Readers might have several reactions to the claim on which this book is built. If you are a believer in Jesus, a follower of Jesus, you might be excited by the prospect of learning more about how to read your Bible in such a way that each text shows you more of his glory and grace. Yet you might have encountered approaches that connect the Bible's diverse pieces to Christ in ways that seem far-fetched and unpersuasive, twisting texts in ways that suggest more about the interpreter's creativity

3

than about the meaning and message that the Holy Spirit intended to convey. Implausible links between far-flung Bible passages and Jesus' person and mission make us justifiably cautious, even suspicious. I share your concerns, but invite you to explore a sounder way of connecting all the Scriptures—especially the Old Testament in all its diversity—to Christ, the approach that we see applied by the inspired authors of the New Testament itself. Since the Bible is God's Word, we can and must let it teach us how to read its constituent books. Let's learn from the Bible how to read the Bible.

If you are not a Christian, you might find highly dubious the claim that so many documents, produced by so many people in so many venues over so many centuries, could possibly have the sort of unity that I am affirming. But that is only one of many things about Christianity that you find hard to accept. Perhaps you question whether everything in the universe could have been created by an invisible, all-powerful, personal God. Maybe you have trouble with the Bible's insistence that what is wrong in this world is attributable, in the end, to the fact that we and our ancestors have broken this God's moral law. If these biblical teachings bother you, you probably balk at the Bible's insistence that Jesus is the only way to find peace with God (John 14:6; Acts 4:11–12). I invite you to keep an open mind about all these aspects of the Bible's teaching and to consider the possibility that they all—including the claim that the whole story finds integral unity in Jesus of Nazareth—actually fit together into a coherent view of reality and human experience. Let me go a step further and challenge you to compare your own way of making sense of life to the Bible's perspective, which has captivated millions of people over thousands of years. I believe you will find that the Bible's diagnosis of our human condition and the remedy it prescribes—Jesus' sacrificial death on behalf of others and his powerful resurrection—are both intellectually cogent and personally transforming.

In this introductory chapter, we will ask the Bible to answer two questions:

(1) Should we expect to "walk with Jesus through his Word"—that is, throughout the whole span of the Scriptures?

(2) If we should, why is it important for us to expect to "walk with Jesus through his Word"?

In the last chapter, we will look more fully at the second question, why it is important to link the Bible's every passage to Jesus. But you have every right to expect a preliminary answer to the "why?" question up front, before you invest your time in chapters 2 through 10. Happily, the answer to the first question will, in itself, begin to help us with the second. Why should we read the whole Bible, Old Testament as well as New, in connection with Christ? Because that is the way Jesus himself taught his closest followers to read the Bible.

As you see in the table of contents, we are using the metaphor of taking a journey from a point of origin to a destination to represent the process by which careful readers discover the routes that God's Spirit embedded in the Scripture to lead us through the diverse terrain of the Bible toward its center, the person and saving mission of Jesus the Messiah. This analogy is suggested, in part, by an illustration given by Charles Spurgeon, the great nineteenth-century preacher, which will open chapter 2. It also echoes the way in which God's Word evokes the Israelites' forty-year pilgrimage from Egypt through wilderness to the Promised Land as an illustration of believers' whole life in this world (Heb. 3–4), imagery that John Bunyan turned into one of the world's all-time best sellers, *The Pilgrim's Progress*. I am suggesting that learning to trace the lines, to follow the paths, that link passages throughout the Scriptures to Jesus at the center is comparable to a traveler's task of finding the way to a desired destination. Sometimes the "navigation" is an easy matter of following clear and unmistakable road signs on highways. At other times, it will demand a more experienced explorer's skills to discern "the lay of the land" and to identify landmarks that subtly signal paths to our destination.

In this first chapter, we join a group of three travelers as they walk together the seven-mile (11 km) journey from ancient Jerusalem to a small town called Emmaus. As we eavesdrop on their conversation, recorded in Luke 24, we will see that the answer to our first question must be "Yes, we should definitely expect to hear every text of Scripture as a witness that points us to Jesus Christ." And one answer to our second question ("Why is it important?") is simply: "Because that is the way Jesus taught his apostles to read the Word." As we walk alongside Cleopas and a colleague—two disillusioned, downcast disciples—and a mysterious stranger, as we overhear him lead them through a survey of Israel's ancient Scriptures, I hope you will find your heart, as they did theirs, burning with hopeful wonder.

5

Jesus' Sluggish Students "Before" and "After"

Before we set out from Jerusalem with Cleopas and his companion and before the stranger joins them, we should take one step back for perspective. Consider the contrast between what we see and hear in Jesus' disciples throughout the four Gospels, on the one hand, and the way they behave and speak in the book of Acts, after Jesus' resurrection from the dead and ascension to heaven, on the other.

The Apostles' "Before"

The apostle Paul wrote to the church in Ephesus that "the mystery of [God's] will, according to his purpose," was "set forth in Christ as a plan for the fullness of time, to unite all things in him, things in heaven and things on earth" (Eph. 1:9–10). You can't get much clearer than that: God has one plan for history. That plan finds its climax in "the fullness of time," and its unifying focus in Christ. But the Gospels show that Jesus' disciples simply did not get the point that he tried repeatedly to impress on them throughout his earthly ministry: that the whole Scriptures—the Old Testament books that had been given hundreds of years before he was born in Bethlehem—are all about one redemptive plan of God, which reached its fulfillment in the life, death, and resurrection of Jesus the Messiah.

Often, Jesus' followers could not accept his ominous prediction that what lay ahead of him was not the military victory over Rome's armies for which oppressed Israelites longed, followed by his accession to a throne, a crown, and the adulation of his adoring subjects. Rather, he bluntly predicted that he would be repudiated by Israel's leaders, tortured, and delivered over to suffer a shameful execution. After Simon Peter confessed that Jesus was the Messiah, Jesus confirmed that God the Father had given Peter that insight. But then he went on to explain his messianic mission: "that he must go to Jerusalem and suffer many things from the elders and chief priests and scribes, and be killed, and on the third day be raised." Peter found this agenda unthinkable and began to correct Jesus, whereupon Jesus sharply rebuffed his loyal but misguided disciple: "Get behind me, Satan! You are a hindrance to me. For you are not setting your mind on the things of God, but on the things of man" (Matt. 16:21–23). Again and again en route to Jerusalem, Jesus prepared his friends for the worst, reinforcing his predictions from Israel's ancient Scriptures:

6

> See, we are going up to Jerusalem, and everything that is written about the Son of Man by the prophets will be accomplished. For he will be delivered over to the Gentiles and will be mocked and shamefully treated and spit upon. And after flogging him, they will kill him, and on the third day he will rise. (Luke 18:31–33)

This cruel mistreatment was foretold in "everything that is written . . . by the prophets"—that is, in the Old Testament Scriptures. But still, Jesus' disciples "understood none of these things. This saying was hidden from them, and they did not grasp what was said" (Luke 18:34).

They seemed to have as much trouble accepting Jesus' promise that he would rise from the dead as they did his dire predictions of his violent death. Even after the third day arrived and heavenly messengers sent by God announced to women that Jesus was risen, as he had said he would, the apostles dismissed the women's report as "an idle tale, and they did not believe them" (Luke 24:1–11). Their confusion and despair seemed incurable.

The Apostles' "After"

When we turn the page from the four Gospels to the book of Acts, suddenly we hear Peter and other apostles confidently connecting Old Testament Scriptures to the sufferings of Christ and his resultant resurrection glory. For forty days after his resurrection, Jesus had appeared to his apostles to give them intensive instruction about God's kingdom (Acts 1:2–5). Then he ascended to heaven. As a result of Jesus' teaching, in the ten-day interim between Jesus' ascent to heaven and the promised outpouring of the Holy Spirit (Luke 24:49), Peter addressed those gathered to await the Spirit's arrival, speaking with the authority of one who had learned to read the Bible as it is meant to be read: "Brothers, the Scripture had to be fulfilled, which the Holy Spirit spoke beforehand by the mouth of David concerning Judas" (Acts 1:16). He went on to quote statements from the Psalms (Pss. 69:25; 109:8) that described the punishment that would befall a close confidante who presumed to betray God's Anointed King. The traitor's disloyalty "had" to happen—it was "necessary" (Luke 24:26)—because it was purposed by God, who had revealed this part of his divine plan by foreshadowing it in ancient psalms. In the Scriptures that Simon Peter had heard in synagogues for years, at last he was beginning to see the shape of a greater plan, the pattern into which God had woven even the sobering reality that his beloved Messiah would be mistreated not only by open enemies but even by one near and dear to him.

A few days later, when God's Spirit came down in revitalizing presence and power, Peter again proclaimed the fulfillment of centuries-old prophetic promises in Jesus the Christ. God had promised through the prophet Joel that in the last days the Spirit would come on men and women, opening their mouths to speak God's Word. Those last days had now arrived, as Jesus poured out the Spirit from his throne at God's right hand in heaven and his people proclaimed God's mighty deeds (Acts 2:16–21, 33, quoting and interpreting Joel 2:28–32). Jesus is the Holy One whose deliverance from the grave David foresaw and foretold (Acts 2:24–33, quoting and explaining Ps. 16:8–11). Jesus is the Lord and Christ to whom the Lord has said, "Sit at my right hand, until I make your enemies your footstool" (Acts 2:33–36, quoting and interpreting Ps. 110:1). We could go almost chapter by chapter through Acts and the same portrait would emerge in the sermons of Peter and John, in Stephen's speech in Acts 7, and finally in the most unlikely gospel preacher, the persecutor turned propagator of Christian faith, Saul/Paul of Tarsus.

The Difference between the Apostles' "Before" and Their "After"

What transformed Jesus' followers from confused, cowering, intimidated, hopes-dashed, defeatist doubters into confident, joyful, hopeful, bold heralds?

Certainly the outpouring of the Holy Spirit on the day of Pentecost was *one* decisive factor. At the end of Luke's Gospel, Jesus predicted that the Father's promise—that is, the life-renewing Spirit of God—would soon engulf his followers in unparalleled power (Luke 24:49). The same promise reappears as we open Luke's "volume 2," the Acts of the Apostles: "wait for the promise of the Father . . . . You will receive power when the Holy Spirit has come upon you" (Acts 1:4, 8). We can never overestimate the unleashing of new-creation power that Jesus brought about when he took his seat at the right hand of God the Father and then celebrated his enthronement by lavishing the great gift, the Holy Spirit of God, on the small and fragile gathering of his friends in Jerusalem.

Notice, however, that in Acts 1:15–22, *before the Holy Spirit is poured out* on the church, Peter's remarks to the waiting congregation exhibit a new confidence and hope, a new perspective on Jesus' sufferings, and a new insight into the ancient Scriptures that Peter and his fellow Jews had heard, no doubt, many times before. Peter now echoed Jesus' assertion that "it was necessary" for the Scripture to be fulfilled, even those troubling texts that portrayed the suffering of God's faithful Servant. Judas's treachery and Jesus' death were necessary because they were intrinsic to God's plan to rescue his people and his universe. Peter now knew that these events were key elements in that plan because God had announced them—sometimes overtly and sometimes subtly—in the Old Testament Scriptures.

What made the difference in the apostles' "before" and "after," then, was not only the bestowal of God's Spirit but also a new way of reading the Bible. Who taught Peter to read the Bible this way? Luke has shown us the answer in the last chapter of his Gospel: Jesus himself!

Bible Studies with the Risen Lord Jesus

We return now to the road leading from Jerusalem to the small town of Emmaus, to eavesdrop on the first of two Bible studies that, as Luke recounts, Jesus conducted on the very day that he rose from the dead. Remember the background: It was the third day after Jesus' brutal, bloody execution by crucifixion. Some women came to the tomb in which his body had been placed in haste before the Sabbath fell at sundown two days earlier, hoping to express their love and grief by preparing his body for burial more adequately. At the tomb, now empty, they saw angels, who announced that Jesus was risen, as he had foretold. Immediately the women carried the word to the apostles and others (Luke 24:1–12). Hearing the women's report but not believing it, Cleopas and a colleague set off for Emmaus. They were discussing the heartbreaking events of the past week—Jesus had received a royal welcome as he entered David's city just a week earlier, but had been repudiated by his people and their leaders and executed by the Roman authorities.

A stranger joined them on the road—a stranger to them, not to us the readers, for Luke identifies him as Jesus but observes that "their eyes were kept from recognizing him" (Luke 24:16). When he asked what they had been discussing, they poured out their disillusionment and confusion. Then the stranger, who seemed so ignorant of recent events, replied: "O foolish ones, and slow of heart to believe all that the prophets have spoken! Was it not necessary that the Christ should suffer these things and enter into his glory?" (vv. 25–26).

We might expect that such an abrupt rebuke from a stranger would halt the conversation, but the mysterious stranger kept right on talking: "And beginning with Moses and all the Prophets, he interpreted to them in all the Scriptures the things concerning himself" (Luke 24:27). Jesus traced both their dismay over their Master's suffering and their doubt about his resurrection to unbelief, a foolish and sluggish reluctance to trust what God had spoken through Israel's ancient prophets. The ancient Scriptures given through Moses and the Prophets—our Old Testament—showed that God had planned all along for the Messiah to suffer a humiliating and violent death, but then to "enter into his glory"—a reversal that would be explained more fully in Luke's narrative of a second Bible study later that evening.

The unrecognized traveler's explanation of Scripture set their hearts afire with hope and joy; so when they reached Emmaus, Cleopas and his companion prevailed on him to join them for supper. As he took the role of the dinner host, breaking the bread (as he had done just a few evenings before, instituting the Lord's Supper), suddenly they recognized Jesus. Then he vanished. They immediately returned to Jerusalem, where they found that the risen Lord Jesus had appeared to Simon Peter, as he had to them. Then, in the midst of this larger group of disciples, Jesus appeared again, demonstrated the physical reality of his risen body, and gave an even fuller exposition both of the breadth of Old Testament books that announce his saving work and of the specifics of his mission revealed in those ancient Scriptures. He said:

> "Everything written about me in the Law of Moses and the Prophets and the Psalms must be fulfilled." Then he opened their minds to understand the Scriptures, and said to them, "Thus is it written, that the Christ should suffer and on the third day rise from the dead, and that repentance and forgiveness of sins should be proclaimed in his name to all nations, beginning from Jerusalem. You are witnesses of these things. And behold, I am sending the promise of my Father upon you. But stay in the city until you are clothed with power from on high." (Luke 24:44–49)

What do these almost back-to-back accounts of the risen Lord's exposition of the Scriptures teach us about the Old Testament and how to interpret it? As we reflect on the conversations recorded in Luke 24, several truths emerge.

The Timing and Placement of These Conversations Show the Importance of Having Jesus Teach Us How to Interpret the Scriptures

Of the writers of the four canonical Gospels, only the author of the Third Gospel (whom early tradition identifies as Luke the physician) went on to tell the story of Jesus' words and deeds through his apostles and his church, after his ascension to heaven. Luke's second volume is known to us as the Acts of the Apostles. The events recounted in Luke 24 constitute the "hinge," the crucial transition and turning point between Jesus' ministry through his personal presence on earth, to which Luke's Gospel testifies, and Jesus' ministry from heaven through his Spirit's presence in the church, described in the book of Acts. These resurrection appearances and the teaching that Jesus offers in them are the climax of "all that Jesus began to do and teach, until the day when he was taken up" to heaven (as Luke sums it up in Acts 1:1–2). At the same time, these postresurrection, preascension Bible studies show the source of the apostles' life-transforming preaching that we hear in Acts. In Acts 1:3, we read that Jesus appeared to his apostles over forty days to prepare them for their mission as his witnesses, "speaking about the kingdom of God." That is Luke's shorthand for these longer summaries of Jesus' instruction, recorded in the last chapter of his Gospel. In other words, Jesus' instruction in biblical interpretation, provided over that intensive forty-day period, set the stage for the apostles' preaching of Christ from the Old Testament as we find it in the pages of Acts.

Jesus Connected the Whole Old Testament Canon to His Redemptive Mission

To appreciate this point, we need to understand that the order of the Old Testament books as they are found in the Hebrew Scriptures differs somewhat from the order to which we are accustomed in our English versions. Our structuring of the Old Testament is derived from that of the Septuagint, the ancient Greek translation of the Scriptures. In our translations, we have four divisions: (1) the Pentateuch (Genesis through Deuteronomy, the "five books" of Moses); (2) the historical books (Joshua, Judges, Ruth, Samuel, Kings, Chronicles, Ezra, Nehemiah, Esther); (3) the poetical books (Job, Psalms, Proverbs, Ecclesiastes, Song of Songs); and (4) the Prophets (Isaiah through Malachi). In the *Hebrew canon*, however, the Scriptures are grouped into three sections:

11

(1) Torah (Law or Instruction) (Genesis through Deuteronomy, the books of Moses);

(2) Prophets, which include two subdivisions: (a) the "former prophets" (Joshua, Judges, Samuel, Kings); and (b) the "latter prophets" (Isaiah, Jeremiah, Ezekiel, and the Minor Prophets);

(3) Writings (Psalms, Job, Proverbs, Song of Songs, Ecclesiastes; some "historical books" such as Ruth, Esther, Ezra, Nehemiah, Chronicles; and some that we categorize as prophetic, such as Daniel and Lamentations).

Now, keeping in mind the way in which first-century (and later) Jews would view the subdivisions of the Hebrew Scriptures, look again at the portions of the Old Testament that Jesus used to teach the two disciples en route to Emmaus, and then the larger group of his followers later in Jerusalem. To the two, we read, Jesus expounded from "Moses and all the Prophets" the things concerning himself (Luke 24:27). Thus he took them through passages in the Pentateuch, in which *Moses* told of creation and the fall, human sin and the flood, Abraham and other patriarchs, the exodus from Egypt and pilgrimage through the desert, commandments pertaining to holiness and justice, the sanctuary and its sacrifices, and so on. Jesus also opened to them passages that spoke of himself in *"all the Prophets."* To the Jewish mind, "the Prophets" would include not only the sermons and predictions of prophets such as Isaiah, Ezekiel, and Hosea, but also the covenantal history of Israel's life in God's land, narrated in the books of Joshua, Judges, Samuel, and Kings.

Although we do not know which specific passages Jesus expounded, Luke's summary suggests that he might have sketched out for these two disciples how the whole history of Israel—the creation of the universe, the flood, the patriarchs, Moses and the exodus, the giving of the law at Sinai, wilderness wandering, to the conquest of Canaan, chaotic years of the judges, the monarchy under Saul, David, Solomon, to the subsequent fracturing of the kingdom, exile, and return from exile—contained glimpses of and longings for the arrival of the perfect King, the ultimate Rescuer, the faithful, covenant-keeping Israel. Then Jesus moved on to the latter prophets, such as Jeremiah, Joel, Micah, and Malachi, who expressed God's promise that he would bring salvation even to unfaithful Israel, offering increasingly specific profiles and predictions of the coming Rescuer and

Redeemer: Immanuel, the Suffering Servant of the Lord, the son of David, the Branch who will make a new covenant between God and his wayward people, the Lord who will replace his people's hearts of stone with hearts of flesh by his life-giving Spirit, Israel's God himself coming to his temple as a refiner's fire, preceded by the messenger who prepares the way for the Lord, and so on.

Later, to the larger group that included his apostles and other followers, Jesus explained "the Law of Moses and the Prophets and the Psalms" (Luke 24:44). Again we should think of our Pentateuch ("Law of Moses") and historical books and Prophets ("Prophets"); but now a third section appears: "the Psalms." The book of Psalms—the 150 poems of praise, thanksgiving, lament, and instruction composed by David and others for use in Israel's worship—is the first book in "the Writings," the third division of the Hebrew Old Testament canon. It is probably mentioned here in Luke's summary to indicate that this whole section of the Scriptures (other wisdom books, historical narratives, etc.) was included in the "curriculum" that Jesus taught that evening. In other words, Luke's summary is shorthand for the *whole* Old Testament—"from Genesis to Malachi," as we might say.

Jesus Showed How Various Dimensions of His Redemptive Mission Were Forecast and Foreshadowed in the Old Testament

To the downcast disciples on the road to Emmaus, Jesus said that Scripture shows that it was "necessary" for the Christ to "suffer these things" and then to enter his glory (Luke 24:26). Some years later, Peter would use the same two categories to sum up what the Spirit of Christ foretold through the Old Testament prophets: "the sufferings of Christ and the subsequent glories" (1 Peter 1:11).

Within these two rather general categories—suffering, followed by glory—are many more specific themes and events in the life and saving mission of the Christ to which the ancient Scriptures testify. Luke shows that Jesus expounded many of these details when he appeared to the apostles and others in Jerusalem (Luke 24:44–49). He showed them that "it is written" in God's Word (the Scriptures given through Moses, the prophets, and other inspired authors):

- That the Christ would suffer;
- That he would rise from the dead on the third day;

- That repentance and forgiveness would be proclaimed in his name;
- That this proclamation would go not only to Israel, but to all other nations;
- That the preachers' mission would begin from Jerusalem.

In fact, there is good reason to add at least two more items to this list:

- That the apostles would be witnesses, testifying to the truth of Christ's works and words;
- That the apostles would be "clothed with power from on high," in fulfillment of "the promise of my Father"—the promised outpouring of God's Spirit, as we have seen.

In the prophecy of Isaiah, the Lord called his people to be his witnesses, testifying that he alone is God and Savior (Isa. 43:9–12; 44:6–8); and he promised to pour out his Spirit to empower them for this task (44:3–5). The book of Acts shows both of these prophetic promises coming to fulfillment in the Spirit's descent at Pentecost and the apostles' resultant boldness as witnesses to Jesus' resurrection (Acts 1:4, 8; 2:1–11, 32–33; 3:15; 5:30–32; etc.).

This shows us that to walk with Jesus through the varied terrain of his Word and the diverse eras of God's redemptive history is not to strum a one-stringed guitar! To be sure, Jesus' cross and resurrection take center stage in the true, historical drama of God's great and costly rescue adventure. But just as Jesus traveled the breadth of the Bible—Law, Prophets, Writings—to show his friends its disclosure of his person and saving mission, he showed them the fullness of blessing that would flow from his sacrificial death and resurrection triumph. The multidimensional effects of his accomplishment of redemption are reflected throughout Israel's Scriptures. We are rebellious and guilty, needing repentance and forgiveness. Both are found in Jesus' name, through faith in him. The human race is a beautiful rainbow of many nationalities and ethnic groups, yet our sinful pride and suspicion turn our diversity into a breeding ground for division and conflict. Israel's Scriptures forecast the fulfillment of God's ancient promise to Abraham, to bring blessing and unity to "all the families of the earth" (Gen. 12:3), in a glorious reconciliation effected by Christ. Through Isaiah, the Lord enlisted his people as his witnesses, but they (and we all) suffered from spiritual blindness and deafness (Isa. 42:18–20). Yet Jesus showed that the Scriptures anticipated a new company of witnesses, renewed and empowered by God's promised Spirit. When we read the Bible through the lens of Jesus Christ, we begin to glimpse an astonishing display and array of wisdom, mercy, and power. We see how "the manifold grace of God" (1 Peter 4:10 NASB; see Eph. 3:10) radiates in all directions from the beloved eternal Son who became the well-pleasing incarnate Son, who was rejected as the curse-bearing Son for others, and who now lives and rules in glory as the exalted Son and who dwells with his people by his Spirit.

Bible Studies with Jesus before His Death

From the fact that Jesus' approach to the Old Testament in Luke 24 seemed so foreign to his followers, we might be tempted to think that those conversations were exceptions to the rule, anomalies from the way in which Jesus had previously interpreted the Bible. In fact, as we survey Jesus' teaching earlier in his ministry, we see that the Bible studies summarized in Luke 24 do not stand alone. The four Gospels provide ample evidence that throughout his ministry on earth, Jesus saw the whole Old Testament as pointing to himself, as anticipating and promising his coming as the long-awaited Redeemer of God's people.

In other words, even before his death and resurrection, Jesus taught people to read the ancient Scriptures in connection with himself and his messianic mission. In John 5:46–47, for example, he told the experts in the law of Moses and honored tradition, "If you believed Moses, you would believe me; for he wrote of me. But if you do not believe his writings, how will you believe my words?"

Or consider the Scripture with which Jesus clinched his announcement that Israel's leaders were like evil tenant farmers, plotting to get rid of him, the beloved Son of the Owner of the vineyard that is Israel (an allusion to Isaiah 5): "He looked directly at them and said, 'What then is this that is written: "The stone that the builders rejected has become the cornerstone"?'" (Luke 20:17). He was quoting Psalm 118:22, a statement that, as its context in the psalm shows, is not about evaluating building materials, but rather concerns the Lord's selection and exaltation of his righteous Champion, the One "who comes in the name of the LORD" (Ps. 118:26), just as David the anointed had done against the Philistine Goliath (1 Sam. 17:45). This psalm had been echoed by the crowds that welcomed Jesus to Jerusalem just a few days before (Luke 19:38), although it was Jesus who called attention to its motif of rejection by Israel's experts and leaders.

Later that same week, Jesus would dine in one last supper with his closest disciples. After soberly announcing that they would abandon him and one would deny him repeatedly that very night, he assured them that their failure and his suffering were all part of the Father's plan, revealed in his Word. Quoting Isaiah 53:12, he said: "I tell you that this Scripture must be fulfilled in me: 'And he was numbered with the transgressors.' For what is written about me has its fulfillment" (Luke 22:37).

To these and other passages in which Jesus explicitly quotes Old Testament passages that were coming to fulfillment in his mission, we could add the almost countless echoes and allusions to Old Testament texts and themes that recur repeatedly in Jesus' description of himself and his mission:

- "Destroy this *temple*, and in three days I will raise it up" (John 2:19, referring to the sanctuary that was the center of Israel's worship).
- "I am the *bread of life*, that comes down from the Father" (John 6:35, alluding to the manna that sustained Israel in the wilderness [Ex. 16:4; Ps. 78:24]).
- "I am the *light of the world*," better than the pillar of fire that lit Israel's camp in the wilderness (John 8:12, alluding to the light-giving pillar of fire that was remembered at the Feast of Booths [John 7:2; see Ex. 14:19–20; 40:38]).
- "I am the *good shepherd*" (John 10:11, alluding to Ezek. 34).

The list could go on and on, and the following chapters will explore these and many other passages in which Jesus and the inspired authors of the New Testament show the many ways in which the Old Testament pointed ahead to the Christ.

How Can We Learn to Read the Bible from Jesus?

Don't you envy Cleopas and his traveling companion, and Peter and Andrew and James and John and Thaddeus and the rest? Don't you wish you could have eavesdropped on Jesus' Bible expositions on the road or in the upper room? To which Old Testament texts did he take his listeners? How did he trace the right routes, draw the correct lines, to connect those ancient Scriptures with himself as the Great Fulfiller and with the current events that they had experienced and would experience in the coming weeks and months and years? If only Matthew's "lecture notes" from that Easter evening and the forty days that followed had survived, so that we could see the passages in Moses, the Prophets, and the Psalms for which Jesus gave them the interpretive key to unlock their meaning—himself!

Then again, even without transcripts or audio recordings, perhaps we do have access to those historic studies in Scripture that Jesus conducted. After all, as we glimpsed earlier and will see more fully in later chapters, the sermons of Peter and others in the book of Acts exhibit not only a new confidence (replacing the old discouragement) but also a new insight into Scripture and God's redemptive plan revealed in the Word. It is not too far a stretch to infer that among the texts that Jesus interpreted over the forty days between his resurrection and his ascension were those to which the apostolic preachers turned as they bore witness to the facts and the significance of his death and his resurrection: Joel 2, Psalm 16, and Psalm 110 on the day of Pentecost (Acts 2); Isaiah 52–53, Deuteronomy 18, and Genesis 12 in Solomon's Portico (Acts 3); and so on. Moreover, the same Spirit of Christ who predicted the sufferings of Christ through the Old Testament prophets (1 Peter 1:11) later inspired the apostolic authors of the New Testament (1 Cor. 2:10–13; 2 Cor. 3:5–11; 1 Thess. 1:5; 2:13). We have reason to read the whole New Testament as the commentary given to us by Jesus, our risen Lord, to help us grasp the message of the Old Testament as it leads us to him.

Before we leave Luke 24, however, we should learn from Jesus two lessons about how to attune our hearts to hear in the ancient Scriptures given to Israel the Holy Spirit's testimony about the coming Rescuer. Two appearances of the word *opened* in verses 32 and 45 show what we need from Jesus, if we want to grow in our sensitivity to how the Bible in all its variety keeps pointing us, from countless angles, to its one and only Hero: We need Jesus to open our minds and hearts, and we need him to open the Scriptures.

We Need Jesus to Open Our Minds and Hearts

Returning to the road to Emmaus, let us listen again, carefully, to Jesus' abrupt response to his fellow travelers' heartbroken confusion: "O *foolish ones, and slow of heart* to believe all that the prophets have spoken!" (Luke 24:25). His reaction to their dashed hopes and downcast demeanor seems insensitive at best and rude at worst.

But Jesus was not going out of his way to be offensive or insulting when he called these men foolish and slow-hearted to believe God's Word through his prophets. Rather, by those labels Jesus was showing them and us that discovering each passage's link to Scripture's focal point, Christ, is not just a matter of learning a technique, of mastering principles and practices that yield a desired outcome, whatever the spiritual condition of the interpreter who processes the biblical text. Jesus' rebuke implied that when we fail to see how the whole Bible finds its integrating unity in Christ at the center, part of our problem—not the whole problem, as we will see, but part of it—could be that our hearts are sluggish, slow, and unbelieving. It could be that we are not coming to our Bibles with the anticipation and expectation that everything between these covers is given to us by our loving Creator and Redeemer to draw our hearts more firmly to himself in confident trust, humble repentance, grateful love. It could be that disastrous circumstances around us loom larger in our minds than the sure promises that God has spoken in his Word, as they did in the lives of Cleopas and his companion. It could be that we are repulsed by the pathway that Scripture lays out for the Messiah—first suffering, then glory and joy—and for those who follow the Messiah (Acts 14:22; 2 Cor. 4:17), as Simon Peter found that route unthinkable and intolerable (Matt. 16:21–23). When we have trouble seeing how the whole Bible centers on Christ, the problem may well be not in the Bible or in our Bible-study strategies, but in us.

Jesus had been telling his disciples for weeks, perhaps months, what was going to happen when they got to Jerusalem. Not only had he been preparing them for the bad news—his rejection and gruesome execution—but he had also been telling them the good news of his resurrection. Yet when what Jesus had told them would happen *did actually happen*, they were first shattered by his death and then dubious about the reports of his resurrection. These men were not in the same spiritual state of outright rebellion as the Jewish leaders whom Jesus confronted in John 5. Those leaders, despite their boasts about being Moses' heirs and defenders, had resisted Jesus tooth and nail because they had never really believed Moses and his prophecies about the Messiah. By contrast, in Luke 24 we are reading about Jesus' friends and followers, not his enemies. Nonetheless, these weak believers deserved Jesus' rebuke. So do we, when we do not trust deeply what God has said in his Word—not believing "down deep enough" to have that faith transform our feelings and perceptions about the all-too-visible circumstances around us.

The wonderful thing is that Jesus did not merely express frustration and rebuke over his followers' obtuseness and resistance to God-centered, Scripture-secured hope. He kept on talking (whether they wanted him to or not). And as he talked, their hearts, previously chilled by disappointment and confusion, got warmer and warmer, to the ignition point: "Did not our hearts burn within us while he talked to us on the road, while he opened to us the Scriptures?" (Luke 24:32). Luke later describes this inner spiritual dynamic, which comes at God's initiative rather than through our intellectual effort, in these simple terms: Jesus *"opened their minds* to understand the Scriptures" (v. 45).

So here is the first key to our seeing Christ in the entire Bible: We need him to open our minds, to ignite our hearts, to take away the foolishness and sluggishness and unbelief and low expectations with which we approach his holy written Word. Since we need *Jesus* to do this for us, one indispensable key to walking with Jesus through the pages of Scripture is simply this: Pray! Face the sobering fact that, left to yourself, you will not "get" what God designs to show you of his Son in his Word by your own research and analysis and ingenuity. Pray that as you read the Word, his Spirit will remove the veil of misunderstanding that keeps you from seeing Jesus' ever-increasing glory (2 Cor. 3:14–18)—in fact, that "God, who said, 'Let light shine out of darkness,'" will shine with increasing radiance "in our hearts to give the light of the knowledge of the glory of God in the face of Jesus Christ" (4:6).

We Need Jesus to Open the Scriptures

Not only do we need Jesus to open our minds and hearts, but we also need Jesus to open the Scriptures to us. Luke 24 uses several words to describe the process by which Jesus disclosed the real meaning of Old Testament passages. We read that he *"interpreted"* to the two on the road in all the Scriptures the things concerning himself (v. 27), and that they recalled how he had *"opened* to us the Scriptures" (v. 32). When he opened the minds of the larger group that evening, they were able to *"understand* the Scriptures" (v. 45). In this way, Luke quietly shows that we not only need God's Spirit to give us the grace to repent of our unbelief and spiritual sluggishness, but also need Jesus to teach us how to read the Bible, to show us a sound method of interpreting God's written Word that honors its origin and its authors (given by God through human authors controlled by his

Spirit), its unity (revealing consistent truth and a single redemptive plan), its variety (constituted of many books given over many centuries), and its purpose (to lead to God's glory and our salvation). In the following chapters, we will explore more deeply the strategy for reading Scripture that Jesus, the Author and Subject of Scripture, taught his church through his apostles.

Another Road, Another Heart Set Afire

Let us consider one more account recorded by Luke, which also concerns a Bible study conducted on the road. The conversation recorded in Acts 8:26–35 gives us a taste of how the Christ-centered way of reading Scripture that Jesus taught his apostles was passed along to another generation of Christians.

The Philip in this passage is not one of the twelve apostles, but rather one of the seven men chosen by the church in Jerusalem to care for the material needs of widows. When his colleague Stephen was martyred for being a bold and effective witness for Jesus, Philip and many others were scattered by persecution away from Jerusalem. So he ended up in the territory once occupied by the Philistines, toward the Mediterranean coast. In God's flawless planning, Philip encountered an African governmental dignitary, a eunuch who served as the secretary of the treasury for the queen of Ethiopia (probably not the modern state, but the Nubian kingdom located in what is now Sudan). In another divine coincidence, the Ethiopian was reading a scroll of the prophecy of Isaiah. In an age long before the printing press, such a long scroll, copied by hand, would have been an expensive treasure. For a foreign dignitary to invest both the time and effort to travel and the expense to obtain this document shows that he had a ravenous hunger to know the true and living God, the God of Israel. This is even more remarkable because his physical condition of being a eunuch had excluded him from entering the Lord's temple in Jerusalem. Ethiopia (Nubia) was ruled by a dynasty of queens, who had male officials castrated to prevent any sexual misconduct; but the surgery that qualified him to wield power in Ethiopia disqualified him from entering the courts of the Lord (see Deut. 23:1).

We are not told whether he had learned of his outcast status during his pilgrimage to Jerusalem or had known of it before he set out from his homeland in Africa. In any case, as he returned in his private coach, he was reading aloud the song of the Suffering and Exalted Servant of the Lord in Isaiah 53. Philip, traveling on foot, overheard him, and asked, "Do you understand what you are reading?" (Acts 8:30). With humility born of puzzlement, the eunuch replied, "How can I, unless someone guides me?" (v. 31).

Christian readers might marvel that the Ethiopian had trouble discerning whether Isaiah was describing his own experience of shameful suffering leading to vindication, or the trajectory of another individual, a Suffering Servant who was yet to come, from the prophet's perspective. We might have trouble connecting Israel's wilderness itinerary in Numbers 33, for example, with the messianic mission of Jesus; but in our believing eyes (thanks to other New Testament passages, e.g., Matt. 8:17; Luke 22:37; 1 Peter 2:22) the route from Isaiah 53 to Christ's cross looks like a superhighway that no one could miss (though it does not look this way in many eyes even today). Yet the Ethiopian asks, "How can I, unless someone *guides* me?" The Greek word, *hodēgeō*, evokes the image of one who leads another along a road, as a blind person needs one who has sight to be his guide (Matt. 15:14).

Philip did not rebuke him, "O foolish one and slow of heart to believe all that the prophet has spoken!" No, patiently he started from that Scripture, prepared for that very rendezvous by the Sovereign God, and he told him the good news about Jesus, the Lamb of God who takes away the sin of the world. When they came to water, the Ethiopian asked to receive baptism, that outward sign of the washing away of sin's defilement through faith in the Suffering Servant-Messiah. From there he went home to the queen's court full of joy, and Nubia became one of the earliest Christian communities in Africa (or anywhere else outside Palestine).

I suspect (don't you?) that as his coach rumbled south after his baptism, the eunuch continued reading Isaiah's prophecy, but now with new eyes. If he did, he soon came to chapter 56, where he found the prophecy of a coming day when God would welcome both foreigners and eunuchs into his sanctuary, to worship in the midst of the Lord's holy assembly (vv. 3–7). We know that this text was dear to Jesus, who appealed to it to explain his outrage at the greedy, commercial desecration of the temple's courts, obstructing the temple's true purpose (Mark 11:17). Through Isaiah, the Lord had said of Gentile foreigners, "These I will bring to my holy mountain, and make them joyful in my house of prayer; . . . for my house shall be called a house of prayer for all peoples" (Isa. 56:7). Surely this African leader, previously excluded as both a foreigner and a eunuch but now welcomed by God's grace in Jesus, was a firstfruit fulfillment of Isaiah's prophecy!

21

The Ethiopian needed a guide, someone to lead him by the hand, as it were, through the pages of the Scriptures and to point out the landmarks and the road signs that God had installed over the centuries to keep his people facing forward, moving forward toward the coming of their true King and supreme Rescuer, Jesus the Messiah. Did he personally attend Jesus' forty-day crash course in biblical interpretation? No, not in person. Yet he did hear Jesus open the Scriptures, through Philip, who in turn had heard Peter and John and other apostles. We, too, can eavesdrop on the apostles' forty days of intensive Bible study with Jesus by paying attention to the way that they and the other inspired New Testament writers read the wide spectrum of Old Testament passages in light of their fulfillment in Jesus.

Questions for Reflection and Discussion

1. From what you know of the Old Testament, for which books or types of Old Testament literature is the claim hardest to support that they are "bound together by a central theme, a single plotline, and a unique Hero, Jesus the Messiah"? Why is this "audacious claim" so hard to believe for those parts of the Bible?

2. What is the significance of the fact that in Acts 1:16—even *before the outpouring of the Holy Spirit at Pentecost*—the apostle Peter was interpreting the Psalms as fulfilled in Jesus' suffering? From whom did Peter learn to read the Bible in that way?

3. Which sections of the Old Testament did Jesus explain to the two disciples on the road to Emmaus? To the larger group of disciples in Jerusalem later in Luke 24?

4. What books are included in "the Prophets"? What books should probably be inferred in the reference to "the Psalms" (Luke 24:44)? What do these terms show about the breadth of the Old Testament in which Jesus showed his disciples "the things concerning himself" (Luke 24:27)?

5. In Luke 24:44–49, what events and truths about Christ were "written" in the Old Testament Scriptures? Can you identify one or more Old Testament passages that reveal each of these events and truths? (If not, don't be discouraged: you will meet them in chapters 2 through 10!)

6. In which passages from the account of Jesus' ministry *before* his death and resurrection did he teach explicitly that portions of the Old Testa-

ment, or specific Old Testament texts, were now being fulfilled in him and his mission?

7. What Old Testament institutions and events are alluded to in some of the symbolic ways that Jesus referred to himself (e.g., "bread of life")?

8. As you compare the Old Testament foreshadows with Christ and his redemptive fulfillment, how does each Old Testament passage enrich the meaning and vividness of the New Testament's revelation of Jesus? How does the New Testament fulfillment in Christ reveal the richer significance of the Old Testament texts?

9. How can the book of Acts help to satisfy our curiosity about which Old Testament passages Jesus may have explained to his followers during the forty-day interim between his resurrection and his ascension?

10. How do Jesus' two acts of "opening" (the Scriptures, Luke 24:32; "their minds," v. 45) show us what we will need if we are to learn to read the Bible as the apostles learned to read it? Why is it not enough simply to learn an interpretive technique or "key" to "open the Scriptures"? Why must we also have our minds opened, our hearts set afire, by the risen Christ? How does this happen today? What should we do to seek this opening of our minds?

PART 2

"You Are Here"

2

Learning to Read the Bible from the Bible: Biblical Texts in Their Contexts

IN THE FIRST CHAPTER, we joined Jesus and two of his disciples on a journey that was both short and long. In geography, the distance between Jerusalem and Emmaus is short, only seven miles, or eleven kilometers—a few hours' walk. But along the way, Jesus led them on a long trek through the ancient Word of God, from the books of Moses to those written by prophets centuries later. All along the way, in every text he touched, Jesus pointed out "the things concerning himself" (Luke 24:27). Another story that draws an analogy between understanding the Bible and taking a trip brings up a problem that makes many people uneasy when they encounter the idea of walking with Jesus through every passage of God's Word, hearing his Spirit speaking his testimony to the coming Redeemer. This story was told over 150 years ago by Charles Spurgeon, one of the most powerful preachers ever to proclaim the good news of Jesus in the English language.

All Roads Lead to London, but If Necessary, Climb Hedges and Ford Ditches!

In a sermon on 1 Peter 2:7, entitled "Christ Precious to Believers," Spurgeon attributed this story to a Welsh preacher: A young preacher had preached in the presence of a respected older pastor. Afterward, he asked what the old minister thought of his sermon. The old preacher said that it was "a very poor sermon indeed." The young man had worked a long time on the sermon and was shocked to be told that it was so poor. Perhaps a little defensively, he asked where the problem lay: Did he not explain the text well? Yes, said the seasoned pastor, his explanation was "very good indeed." Weren't his metaphors appropriate and his arguments conclusive? They, too, were "very good as far as that goes," but still it was "a very poor sermon." Finally the young man asked what the defect was that made his sermon so poor, and the answer came back: "*There was no Christ in it.*"

Now the young man began to defend himself, objecting, "Well, Christ was not in the text; we are not to be preaching Christ always, we must preach what is in the text." In response, the older pastor drew this analogy: "Don't you know, young man, that from every town, and every village, and every little hamlet in England, wherever it may be, there is a road to London?"

> "Yes," said the young man.
>
> "Ah!" said the old divine, "and so from every text in Scripture, there is a road to the metropolis of the Scriptures, that is Christ. And my dear brother, your business is when you get to a text, to say, 'Now what is the road to Christ?' and then preach a sermon, running along the road towards the great metropolis—Christ. And," said he, "I have never yet found a text that had not got a road to Christ in it, and if I ever do find one that has not a road to Christ in it, I will make one; I will go over hedge and ditch but I would get at my Master, for the sermon cannot do any good unless there be a savour of Christ in it."[1]

Often when Spurgeon's story is retold, attention is drawn to the statement about going "over hedge and ditch" to reach Christ, whatever it takes to get there. Those who have read Spurgeon's sermons might even think to themselves that they have seen him climbing hedges and fording ditches, sometimes overlooking the meaning of a passage in its original context, in order to make some sort of connection between the biblical text he was expounding, on the one hand, and the person and redeeming work of Jesus, on the other. When we sense that some interpreter's clever ingenuity has "blazed the trail" from an Old Testament passage to Christ, we get suspicious of the idea that we can find a route to Christ from passages written centuries before his birth in Bethlehem.

---

1. Charles H. Spurgeon, "Christ Precious to Believers" (March 13, 1859), available at http://www.spurgeon.org/sermons/0242.htm.

But let me say two things in defense of Spurgeon's little parable. First, the old minister was correct to say that unless our engagement with Scripture enables us to taste the "savour"—the flavor or aroma—of the Savior, it cannot do us any substantial spiritual good. In the Bible, God speaks truth and defines the standards for goodness. Many people use it merely as a manual of doctrine or a guidebook for living. But our minds will remain blind to God's truth and our wills resistant to his commands unless his Holy Spirit intervenes to transform us; and that transformation occurs only when we encounter the astonishing good news about the undeserved mercy that God has shown toward us in his Son. So the seasoned pastor's passion to bring his hearers to Jesus at all costs is exactly right.

Second, notice the main point of the old preacher's analogy between the Bible and the English road system. Every hamlet in England, no matter how small or remote, is linked, somehow or other, to London, the capital of the kingdom. If a bewildered tourist asks directions to the great metropolis, no honest villager would ever say, "Sorry, you cannot get there from here." So also the Bible tells one coherent story that, despite all its diversity in details, is focused on one majestic Hero and directed toward the climax of one cosmic conflict. We should therefore approach every text in the Bible expecting that God has actually laid out a path, a lane, an avenue, or a superhighway by which we can travel from that passage, with its unique message in its distinctive location in the history of redemption and revelation, to its fulfillment in Christ. Our challenge, then, is not to hack our way through dense forest, but to discern the routes that the Bible's Designer has already embedded in its landscape.

In other words, we need the divine Author of the Bible to teach us how to read the Bible. The means by which he does this is, of course, the Bible itself, since it is in the pages of Scripture that God speaks infallibly, inerrantly, and most clearly. As wise shepherds and theologians stated several centuries ago, "The infallible rule of interpretation of Scripture is the Scripture itself: and therefore, when there is a question about the true and full sense of any Scripture (which is not manifold, but one), it must be searched and known by other places that speak more clearly" (Westminster Confession of Faith [WCF] 1.9). As I said in the previous chapter, we want to learn a sound method of interpreting God's written Word that honors its origin and its authors (given by God through human authors controlled by his Spirit), its unity (revealing consistent truth and a single redemptive plan), its variety (constituted of many books given over many centuries), and its purpose (to lead to God's glory and our salvation).

Our starting point is the observation that the true and living God who speaks in the Bible is the preeminent Communicator. He is so effective in getting his message across to his hearers and readers because he knows his audience as no other speaker could know an audience. When he speaks, he draws on his exhaustive, infinite understanding of our past experience and present situation, our language and culture, our areas of knowledge and of ignorance and of misunderstanding and confusion. Every book of Scripture, from the time of Moses to the completion of the New Testament books, was a flawless "fit" for its location in history and an exact "fit" to its original hearers' needs and capacities. That means that whenever we make the journey from a distant passage of the Bible to Christ, the metropolis of Scripture, we must begin by orienting ourselves to the passage's meaning as God expected its first recipients to receive and understand it.

Our movement toward Christ at Scripture's center must therefore begin with the message and meaning of a passage in its original context—the life experience of its first readers and hearers, their era in the unfolding of God's redemptive plan through history, the words that God had already given by that point. How you reach a desired destination depends on understanding your current location, as well as the terrain between where you are and where you want to go. Large shopping malls often aid disoriented customers by posting a map at each entrance with a bright arrow bearing the words "You Are Here," pointing to the location of that doorway. The screen of a GPS (global positioning system) unit helps travelers to get their bearings by showing their "present location" as well as their desired destination.

Letting the Bible Interpret the Bible

One of the great commitments of the Protestant Reformation was *sola Scriptura*—that the Scripture *alone* is the supreme standard and judge for our beliefs about God and our relationship to him, and for our behavior in response to his majesty as Creator and his mercy as Redeemer. That meant that the Scripture itself, as God's own Word, has the authority to teach and show us how to understand the Scripture. If the Bible itself is the ultimate norm that God has given for our belief and our life, our thinking and our doing, it follows that the Bible itself is the ultimate norm to direct us how to read and understand the Bible.

The early Reformers reflected deeply on how the Bible itself teaches us to read the Bible, how we can let Scripture interpret Scripture, rather than imposing our own inventive ideas or treasured traditions on the text of God's Word. The times in which they lived required them to spell out what they meant when they affirmed that Scripture is its own interpreter. Opponents of the Reformation who revered church tradition and ecclesiastical hierarchy were charging that when the Reformers insisted on reexamining long-held beliefs and practices through a fresh study of the Scriptures themselves, they were throwing the door wide open to every kind of strange, subjective way to read the Bible. Unless the church and its tradition tell us what the Bible means, said the critics, we will be back in the chaos of the time of Israel's judges, when "everyone did what was right in his own eyes" (Judg. 21:25). At another extreme were those who claimed that the Holy Spirit revealed Scripture's meaning directly to them through various mystical experiences, so that they did not need to pay attention to what words or phrases or sentences meant to their original audience in their original context. The Reformers had even less confidence in an individual's private experience than they did in a church's long-held and widespread consensus. They were confident that God's voice speaking in his written Word held the remedy to both extremes, so they took pains to clarify the factors that enable us to interpret the Bible as its divine Author intends us to understand it.

One clear, concise, and yet comprehensive summary of what it means to let Scripture show us how to read Scripture is the Second Helvetic Confession of 1566. This expression of biblical conviction was composed by Heinrich Bullinger, a colleague of John Calvin, to express what the Protestant churches of Switzerland believed to be the teaching of Scripture. In chapter 2, "Of Interpreting the Holy Scriptures; and of Fathers, Councils, and Traditions," these Reformed Christians explained what they meant when they said that we must let Scripture interpret Scripture:

> We hold that interpretation of the Scripture to be orthodox and genuine
> which is gleaned from the Scriptures themselves (from the nature of the
> language in which they were written, likewise according to the circum-
> stances in which they were set down, and expounded in the light of like
> and unlike passages and of many and clearer passages) and which agrees

with the rule of faith and love, and contributes much to the glory of God and man's salvation.[2]

I marvel that so few words could express so fully what it means to listen attentively to the way in which the Scriptures interpret themselves. Four factors are identified here as helping us to "glean" the meaning of any biblical passage faithfully and accurately:

- Language
- Circumstances
- Canonical Contexts ("like and unlike passages," "many and clearer passages")
- Purpose (directing our response of "faith and love," contributing to "the glory of God and man's salvation")

As we read a passage of God's Word, then, the starting point for our understanding is the text's meaning in its original and closest contexts. Because God condescends to speak our human languages, this means paying attention to the roles and relationships of the words and grammar of the *language* in which God gave it (Hebrew, Aramaic, or Greek) and, by extension, to the literary forms familiar to the first audience. Because our personal God addresses us personally in the setting of our experience, we also need to attend to the *circumstances* of those to whom the text was first written and spoken: their history, their culture, and their present problems and opportunities.

Because every part of Scripture fits perfectly into a consistent and unified whole, we must interpret each text in the *canonical context* of the system of truth revealed in other Old and New Testament passages. (*Canon* comes from a Greek word meaning "measuring rod" and refers to the entire Bible as the standard for our belief and behavior.) This canonical context is implied when the Second Helvetic Confession mentions "like and unlike passages" and "many and clearer passages," and when the Westminster Confession recommends consulting "other places [in the Bible] that speak more clearly." This process begins by paying attention to the sentences and paragraphs before and after the passage. Then

2. Arthur C. Cochrane, ed., *Reformed Confessions of the 16th Century* (Philadelphia: Westminster, 1966), 226–27.

32

it widens out to consider teaching elsewhere in that specific book, and to other passages that are connected to the text being studied thematically in earlier or later Scriptures.

Finally, because our God always speaks to us for a *purpose*, to achieve specific wise and holy goals, we need to ask what our consideration of a passage's language, circumstances, and canonical context tells us about the spiritual need that the passage was given to address and the redemptive agenda that it was intended to accomplish. In general, God's purpose is to evoke faith and love in us, thus advancing his glory and our salvation. Each passage is aimed toward a specific form of faith-and-love response, and discerning the circumstances of the original audience and the spiritual needs that we share with them across the centuries will help us to pinpoint God's particular agenda for that text in their lives and in ours.

Let us now survey in a little more detail what each of these four aspects of Bible study involves, using a well-known New Testament text to illustrate what types of questions to consider as we explore the language, circumstances, canonical contexts, and purpose of a passage. I hope to show you how each contributes to our understanding of a passage in its original setting, and then opens the way to our hearing its message in the wider horizon of the whole Bible and the whole redemptive plan of God. Then, to conclude this chapter, we will put into practice what we have learned, to begin reflection on an early and intriguing Old Testament prophecy.

Language

Most of us live day by day surrounded by an atmosphere of language. We "breathe in" others' words through our ears (hearing) and eyes (reading), and we "breathe out" through our mouths (speaking) and fingers (writing). Words surround us so pervasively that they become as invisible as air. From early childhood, we start absorbing words and how they work: their meanings, their forms, their relationships. Long before we have grammatical terms to label words, we have mysteriously discovered that nouns and pronouns represent things (persons, places, objects, concepts), and that verbs represent actions or states, and that adjectives and adverbs describe nouns and verbs, and that conjunctions connect items and ideas, and so on. It might be only when schoolteachers compel us to study grammar or when we first tackle a foreign language that we start paying attention to all that we know, but did not know that we knew, about our own language.

When we study the Bible, even when we do so in a translation in our own language, we need to approach it with the careful attention that we would devote to a foreign language. We want to discover, as well as we can, what idea each word would evoke in the minds of those who first heard or read a biblical text. We want to notice how words are connected to each other in phrases, and phrases linked to each other in clauses, and clauses in sentences, and sentences in paragraphs, and paragraphs in longer discourses such as stories or doctrinal explanations or commands (or stanzas linked to each other to form poems). We will ask questions such as these: Which noun or pronoun stands for the agent of an action, and which for the action's object? What does the choice of one noun in contrast to another reveal about how the author wants us to view that person, place, object, or idea? Do the verbs represent actions that follow and precede each other, or that happen at the same time? Do the conjunctions signal contrasts between ideas, or causation between events, or some other relationship?

For example, consider Paul's well-known summary about God's surprising grace in Ephesians 2:8–10:

> For by grace you have been saved through faith. And this is not your own doing; it is the gift of God, not a result of works, so that no one may boast. For we are his workmanship, created in Christ Jesus for good works, which God prepared beforehand, that we should walk in them.

At the level of individual words, we want to understand what Paul means, and what he wanted the Ephesian Christ-followers to understand, by such key terms as *grace*, *saved*, *faith*, and *works*. Within these few sentences, we notice that "by grace" is in contrast to "your own doing" and "a result of works," on the one hand, and coincides with "the gift of God," on the other. Looking at the sentences just before verse 8, we notice that grace belongs in the company of God's rich mercy, "the great love with which he loved us," and his kindness (2:4–6). We observe that "you have been saved" is a verb in the passive voice, meaning that *you* is not the agent performing the action but rather the object of an action performed by someone else. Again, the preceding verses identify the Agent who saves and show some aspects of the plight from which he saved us: "But God, . . . even when we were dead in our trespasses, made us alive together with Christ . . . and raised us up with him and seated us with him in the heavenly places" (vv. 4–6). So we move through the passage, noticing how the relationships between

34

other key terms—"through faith" and "not a result of works"—unveil their meaning. A Bible concordance will help us to find and read other passages in which Paul uses these words, and a Bible dictionary will sum up their significance throughout Scripture.

We also want to see the relationship between ideas in the text, and here is where conjunctions, though so humble, prove their worth. In the midst of Ephesians 2:9, we read that salvation is God's gift, not the product of our works, "*so that*" no one may boast. The result of the free and gracious rescue performed by God—to which we contributed nothing but our guilt and helplessness—is to squelch in us any inclination to take any credit whatsoever for our salvation. Paul reinforces this point—that God, not we, gets the glory for our salvation—with the conjunction that opens verse 10: "*For* we are his workmanship, created in Christ Jesus for good works." Even the tiny prepositions deserve our attention. Since Paul just said that God shows us grace and kindness "*in* Christ Jesus" (v. 7), we want to grasp what he meant when he mentioned that we are "created *in* Christ Jesus." And though verse 9 stresses that our salvation was not "a result of" our works, we cannot miss the statement in verse 10 that God created us "*for* good works." Although our salvation does not *result from* our obedient actions, God's saving grace does *result in* our obedient actions—and even those good works were prepared by God, and so display his glory.

As we take a step back from the specific words, phrases, clauses, and sentences in this passage to see it in a larger perspective, we realize that another dimension of its "language" concerns the type (genre) of document in which it appears. It is part of an epistle, a letter, written to a first-century congregation. In a sense, it is an interpersonal conversation, so Paul speaks naturally of *you* and *we*. Its readers would recognize its use of terms as straightforward, relatively free of symbolism, unlike Jesus' parables or the visions in the book of Revelation. In this early part of the letter, as is customary for Paul, the function of the verbs is primarily to present things as they are (the indicative mood, as grammarians would say). Later on (at Eph. 4:1), the "mood" will turn "imperative": then the apostle will spell out in specific commands how we should respond to the gospel truth that he told in the first three chapters.

These are at least some of the issues and questions that emerge from the language of a biblical text, and that help us to get acquainted with the meaning that its first recipients would have taken away when they heard it read.

Circumstances

Because we use language in the context of our personal experience and social relationships, in many respects the meaning of words and sentences varies, depending on who says them to whom, as well as when and where. Years ago, I noticed that a certain pattern of conversational exchange in our home might strike a houseguest as slightly strange. As we each read on a quiet evening, my wife would say, "Would you like a cup of coffee?" I would reply in the affirmative. Now, at this point our guest might infer that she had asked out of idle curiosity about my present desires, which my "Yes" satisfied—if we simply returned to our books. Then again, perhaps it was more than a question seeking information. Our guest might interpret my wife's question as an implicit offer to fix me a cup of coffee, expecting her to rise and head for the kitchen. (She is kind like that, after all.) Her reply to my reply, however, would make clear the real meaning and purpose of her question. To my "Yes" she might (not always, but sometimes) respond sweetly, with a smile, "Will you make me one, too?" Smiling back, I would rise from my easy chair and head for the kitchen! Our circumstances—how long we have known each other, how much we love each other, the patterns of interaction that have developed over the years, so that we can often "read between the lines" in everyday conversation—affect the meanings of the words we share.

The living God who speaks in the Bible knows the circumstances of his audience and speaks in ways that make sense in their situation. In fact, he not only knows but also controls our circumstances. And his speech not only makes sense in our setting but also meets our need in that setting. Even his choice of the languages in which he gave us the Bible showed his gracious willingness to meet us where we are, as WCF 1.8 implies:

> The Old Testament in Hebrew (which was the native language of the people of God of old), and the New Testament in Greek (which, at the time of the writing of it, was most generally known to the nations), being immediately inspired by God, and, by His singular care and providence, kept pure in all ages, are therefore authentical.

God gave the Old Testament in Hebrew because the Israelites spoke that language. He gave the New Testament in Greek because Greek was widely spoken throughout the Roman Empire.

When we think of the diverse circumstances in which God spoke Scripture, different languages are just the tip of the iceberg. The Old Testament was addressed to Israelites who, on the whole, worked as herdsmen and farmers, so they easily grasped references to agriculture and weather. Many of Jesus' parables likewise drew on the experience of common, rural folk. Paul's letters, on the other hand, were addressed to city dwellers, some of whom were acquainted with Roman law and Greek athletics and most of whom were exposed to idolatry and religious pluralism. Rarely, God's people enjoyed a measure of political independence and influence, such as during the reign of Solomon. In such circumstances, God gave wisdom books to instruct leaders of the nation as well as families in prudent and just decision-making. More often, however, people in power suppressed and harassed them, or worse: bondage in Egypt, homeless pilgrimage after the exodus, frequent invasions in the era of the judges, defeat and exile, and persecution by Jewish and pagan opponents in the days of the apostles. In circumstances of suffering, Scripture calls God's people to courage, endurance, and hope.

Since God perfectly shapes his words to the needs of his audience, as we seek to hear any Scripture as though we were standing alongside its first recipients, we need to ask and answer questions about their background, experience, and situation: When and where did they live—in the ancient Near East during the time of Abraham or Moses or David or Daniel? In first-century Galilee or Philippi or Rome? Were they pilgrims in the wilderness, shepherds settled in the Promised Land, exiles in Babylon, or a tiny pocket of slaves and laborers in a cosmopolitan city such as Corinth? What kind of work did they do? Were they farmers, craftsmen, shepherds, slaves, or politicians? Were they so poor that starvation constantly threatened them, or so rich that their comfortable affluence blinded them to their poverty of spirit? What religions did their neighbors practice? Did they worship Baal in Canaan, practice rabbinic Judaism in Judea, or practice pagan idolatry in Corinth or mystery religions in Colossae?

When we try to understand Ephesians 2:8–10 in the context of the original readers' circumstances, we are helped both by other passages in the epistle and by other books in the New Testament. In the paragraph following our text, Paul addresses his readers as "you Gentiles" and calls attention to their lack of circumcision and previous alienation from God's community and covenant (2:11–12). He goes on to refer to the high wall separating Israel as the people in covenant with the Lord, on the one hand, from all the other nations in their allegiance to empty idols—a metaphorical wall that also found expression in a physical wall in the Jerusalem temple, which excluded uncircumcised Gentiles from the inner courts (v. 14; see Acts 21:28–29). Acts 19 shows the spiritual darkness that Paul encountered as he brought God's Word to that prominent city in Asia Minor. Even Revelation 2, written after Paul's letter to the Ephesians, fills out the picture of the doctrinal challenges that confronted the church at Ephesus in the first century.

As we bring to our text these aspects of the circumstances, we naturally identify the *you* whom Paul addresses as Gentile believers in Jesus, who were once dead in sin (Eph. 2:1) and alienated from Israel (v. 12). But it is not as though Paul is carrying over into the church the sharp disjunction that first-century Jews drew between themselves and the other nations (rather, that they saw that God had drawn between Israel, his covenant people, and the idol-worshiping nations). In the sentences leading to our passage, Paul said not only that the Gentiles had been dead in sin but also that "we all"—we Jews, too—lived in evil passions and deserved God's wrath, so "we were dead in our trespasses" includes the whole human race and the "us" whom God made alive and saved by grace includes believers of every race and nation (vv. 3–5). In Christ's cross, the ancient dividing wall between Jew and Gentile has been demolished (vv. 13–16). So Paul meets the circumstances of the Gentile Christians in Ephesus, as he does elsewhere, by emphasizing the abundance of God's grace, in order to protect them from Judaizers' emphasis on keeping the works of the law as a basis for acceptance by God or a ground for boasting (see Rom. 3:17–28; Gal. 3:1–18; Phil. 3:3–11). At the same time, he also stresses that God in grace has created them *for good works*, in order to dispel the illusion that faith in Christ will leave their desires unchanged—still enslaved to "the spirit that is now at work in the sons of disobedience," captivated by "the passions of our flesh, . . . the desires of the body and the mind" (Eph. 2:2–3). Seeing the circumstances in which a biblical text was given unlocks its background in the experience of its original audience, but it also exposes the spiritual purposes for which God gave that passage.

Canonical Contexts

When the Second Helvetic Confession mentions considering "like and unlike passages" and "many and clearer passages" as we interpret any text of the Bible, it assumes that because all sixty-six books of the Bible were given by God the Holy Spirit and because the God who speaks in Scripture is the One who sets the standard for truth, we can expect that the meaning of each text, as we come to grasp it, will be consistent with what the rest of the Bible teaches. This does not mean, of course, that our tiny, finite minds will be able to comprehend the whole network of interlocking truth that God has revealed in his Word. We might find some parts of Scripture and their interrelationships mystifying to our dying day.

Nor does it mean that the Bible contains only "like passages" and no "unlike passages." The Swiss pastors knew well that some biblical texts seem, at first, to contradict each other and challenge us to ponder more deeply how apparently conflicting Scriptures present varying perspectives on complex realities. Paul spoke God's truth when he wrote that we are saved "by grace . . . through faith" and "not a result of works" (Eph. 2:8–9). Elsewhere, Paul appealed to Abraham, the great father of Israel, whose experience showed that God justifies the ungodly through faith, not works (Rom. 4:1–5). But James also spoke God's truth (though Martin Luther had doubts about this) when he wrote, "You see" (from Abraham!) "that a person is justified by works and not by faith alone" (James 2:21–24). How can two such "unlike passages" both be true? Our confidence that God will not contradict himself invites and urges us to seek an answer, which we do by asking more questions. From Paul we learn to discern the difference between faithless (that is, self-trusting) works that cannot save and the good works that God prepared for those of us who are saved by faith, apart from our works (Eph. 2:10). From James we learn to distinguish a professed faith that leaves the heart unmoved and unchanged from the genuine, living trust that—as Paul himself says—works "through love" (Gal. 5:6).

You might have noticed that in our previous discussions of a biblical text's language and circumstances, we already invoked the principle of canonical context to shed light on Ephesians 2:8–10. We put these verses in their setting in this epistle, noticing significant features in the preceding and following paragraphs; and we touched on "like passages" in Paul's other letters, such as his teaching on justification by grace through faith in Galatians, Romans, and Philippians.

We even alluded, though subtly, to a more overarching dimension of "unlikeness" that cuts across the even more comprehensive unity of the whole Bible: the law that God gave through Moses had functioned as a wall to sequester Israel from the Gentiles, but now with the death of Christ, that divider had been shattered. Now through Jesus, believers from Israel and from all nations together "have access in one Spirit to the Father" (Eph. 2:18). In our next chapter, we will look more deeply at the way in which the Bible shows us, on the one hand, that God's plan to redeem his people and the universe from the effects of our sin is *unified*, and on the other, that his plan is worked out in a series of *different phases*. One aspect of reading every biblical passage in terms of both "like" and "unlike" passages is to notice that the Bible is structured not as an encyclopedia of articles on various topics, but as a collection that grew over many centuries, in which an unfolding succession of historical events is central. God revealed himself and his saving plan more clearly as history progressed, from a general promise in Genesis 3:15 that an offspring of the woman would someday crush the head of the serpent—of Satan—to more explicit prophecies that God would bless all nations through Abraham's family, that the Great Champion would arise from David's descendants, that his victory would entail his suffering, and more.

Realizing the variations introduced by the fact that God's words in Scripture kept in step with God's works in history, about any portion of the Bible we want to ask these questions: "At what time were the original readers of this text living? How much of God's big plan of redemption had he revealed when they first heard or read this passage?"

So much depends on where an event occurred or when a command was issued in God's redemptive agenda! When God made his covenant with Abraham, he commanded Abraham to circumcise his sons and all males in his household as a sign that they belonged to the people of God (Gen. 17:10). That sign continued under the covenant that God gave Israel at Sinai. But under the new covenant that Jesus inaugurated, Gentiles who submit to the God of Israel by trusting his Son must *not* be compelled to submit to circumcision anymore (Acts 15; Gal. 5:2). Instead, they are to be baptized. There remains a visible sign that sets God's people apart from others, but it no longer involves the shedding of blood, as circumcision did. The canonical context of each biblical passage reveals so much about how its message fits into the intricate tapestry of God's awesome revelation.

Purpose

Finally, the Swiss pastors confessed that when we rightly use Scripture to interpret Scripture, the result of our study will conform to "the rule of faith and love" and further "the glory of God and man's salvation." In his wisdom, God always speaks purposefully, with specific aims in view. At one level, God's purposes are as broad as the confession indicates: every passage in the Bible is designed, somehow or other, to evoke in us faith in God, his promises, and his beloved Son, and every passage is designed to elicit from us a fitting response of love for the Creator and Redeemer who loved us so sacrificially, and then love for our neighbors with whom we share his image. And when the Holy Spirit uses the Bible to draw us into faith and love, the result is that we experience the salvation that only Christ could accomplish, and therefore God receives all the glory for that salvation. As Paul wrote to the Corinthians:

> But God chose what is foolish in the world to shame the wise; God chose what is weak in the world to shame the strong; God chose what is low and despised in the world, even things that are not, to bring to nothing things that are, so that no human being might boast in the presence of God. And because of him you are in Christ Jesus, who became to us wisdom from God, righteousness and sanctification and redemption, so that, as it is written, "Let the one who boasts, boast in the Lord." (1 Cor. 1:27–31)

Here Paul was quoting Jeremiah 9:24, but throughout Scripture we read that God alone deserves to be glorified by his creatures. Consider, for instance:

> Not to us, O LORD, not to us, but to your name give glory,
> > for the sake of your steadfast love and your faithfulness! (Ps. 115:1)

> For from him and through him and to him are all things.
> > To him be glory forever. Amen. (Rom. 11:36)

As the Bible displays the majesty and mercy of God, displayed in the obedience and sacrifice of his Son, our self-focused boasting is silenced and our faith reaches out to rest in Christ and his achievement. Faith in so great a Savior overwhelms our hearts with responses of love toward him and toward others. We receive salvation as his free gift, and he receives the glory that he so eminently deserves. We can see all four of these purposes—faith, love, our salvation, and God's glory—in our sample text, Ephesians 2:8–10:

41

- "By grace you have been *saved*" ("man's salvation")
- "Through *faith*"
- "It is the gift of God, . . . so that no one may boast [except in God]. For we are *his* workmanship" (not our own, so "the glory of God" is displayed)
- "Created . . . for good works . . . , that we should walk in them" (*love*)

These four interrelated purposes of the Bible as a whole should function as "guardrails" as we study specific passages, keeping our interpretation from driving off the road and over cliffs. If our reading of a biblical text inclines us to imagine that we deserve spiritual credit rather than God's receiving all the glory, we are steering in a dangerous direction. If I come up with an interpretation that leads me away from trusting in God and toward relying on myself or any other creature, I know that I have missed the point of the text. If what I *think* I understand about a portion of the Bible does not challenge me to grow in love for the Lord and for others, again, I have not yet seen God's purpose for the passage.

These *overall purposes of the Bible*—to convey salvation by evoking our faith in Christ and then stimulating our love, to the ultimate end of God's glory—apply to every passage in the Scriptures. But for any particular passage, the purpose for which it was given is more precisely focused on some specific aspect or aspects of that comprehensive "big picture" purpose of the whole Bible. The purpose of some texts is to expose and rebuke their original readers' (and our) doubts or disobedience, turning hearts to Christ for forgiveness and for the power to break away from sin. Others are given to comfort and strengthen God's people in hard times, leading them then and us now to respond courageously and patiently to those who make our lives miserable, and to meet scary circumstances beyond our control with hope and trust. Whether a particular Scripture calls us to change or to hold fast, we can be sure that God's purpose for every passage of the Bible in our lives is accomplished as that passage leads us first of all to Jesus (as we will see in the following chapters). Then, in our dependence on his grace, the Bible leads us back into the present troubling circumstances, to which we must respond in faith and in love.

Conclusion

We want to travel across the landscape of the Bible—with all its variety of times and places and people and types of literature—noticing the scenery along the way as we always keep our destination in view. Because Jesus is Scripture's centerpiece and because, as the old preacher in Spurgeon's story rightly said, only reaching him can make our study of the Word worthwhile and spiritually nourishing, we want to tread the paths and lanes and roads that the Spirit of Christ himself embedded in the terrain of his Word until we reach the metropolis, Jesus. As we have seen, this means starting with Scripture's original audiences in their various locations along the route of redemptive history, listening with them to each passage's language and experiencing their circumstances, and then stepping back to listen to the Word that they heard in the wider context of "many and clearer passages," including those given centuries later, and submitting our hearts to the purposes that God's Spirit is pursuing through his Word: responses of faith and love, leading to our salvation and God's glory. Here is where we start our journey through Scripture to Jesus.

Putting It into Practice: Seeing a Star from Afar (Numbers 24:15–19)

The importance of beginning our study of a Bible passage in its original context—of paying attention first to the "You Are Here" sign that shows the passage's location in the wide landscape of Scripture—can be illustrated by a brief exploration of the fourth oracle of the prophet Balaam during Israel's wilderness wanderings. Balaam's fourth and final prophecy is this:

> The oracle of Balaam the son of Beor,
> > the oracle of the man whose eye is opened,
> the oracle of him who hears the words of God,
> > and knows the knowledge of the Most High,
> who sees the vision of the Almighty,
> > falling down with his eyes uncovered:
> I see him, but not now;
> > I behold him, but not near:
> a star shall come out of Jacob,
> > and a scepter shall rise out of Israel;
> it shall crush the forehead of Moab
> > and break down all the sons of Sheth.
> Edom shall be dispossessed;
> > Seir also, his enemies, shall be dispossessed.
> > Israel is doing valiantly.
> And one from Jacob shall exercise dominion
> > and destroy the survivors of cities! (Num. 24:15–19)

Two sets of *circumstances* help us to understand the significance of Balaam's words. First, there is the situation of Moses and the wilderness generation, moving slowly but surely toward the Promised Land (though none of that generation except Joshua and Caleb would enter it). The Lord had given his people victory over Sihon, king of the Amorites, and Og, king of Bashan. As a result, the leaders of Moab and Midian, led by King Balak, were terrified by Israel's advance. They bribed Balaam to invoke a curse that would weaken or destroy the people of Israel. Balaam was a strange character. Although he was willing to take money to try to curse the Lord's people, still God gave true prophecies through this corrupt prophet. Though warned by the Lord that he must not curse this people whom God blessed, Balaam tried repeatedly to earn the reward that Balak offered by speaking words of power to harm the Israelites. Each time Balaam tried to speak evil, Israel's divine Protector "overrode" his attempts and compelled him to speak further good instead. Balaam's fourth and final oracle previewed the Lord's greatest blessing to Israel, at the distance of many generations into the future. The *purpose* of these events, for those of that wilderness generation, untrained in warfare, was to strengthen their trust and deepen their allegiance to the Lord who sovereignly overruled Balaam's and Balak's malicious plot. Sadly, as subsequent events show, Balaam knew another way to separate Israel from the Lord: he advised Moab and Midian to seduce Israel into sexual immorality and idolatry, thereby affronting God's holiness and incurring his just wrath (Num. 25; 31:16).

The second situation to which this Scripture was addressed is that of the next generation of Israelites, who received the books of Moses (in which the account of Balaam is recorded) as they were about to enter and conquer the Promised Land under Joshua's leadership. For this "conquest generation," the *purpose* of Moses' written account of Balaam would be to bolster their confidence in the Lord's power to conquer the entrenched peoples of Canaan who stood before them, just as he had thwarted Balaam's efforts to curse their parents. The negative example of their fathers' physical and spiritual infidelity should serve a further purpose: to teach Joshua's contemporaries to stay pure in their allegiance to the Lord, who was giving them his land.

The *language* of Balaam's oracle identifies a king that would arise in Israel to conquer and wield sovereignty over other nations. A star (Isa. 14:12; Matt. 2:2) and a scepter (Gen. 49:10; Pss. 45:6; 60:7) are images of royal power. The use of the scepter to "crush the forehead of Moab," the nation that would pay Balaam richly if only he would (that is, could) say what it wanted him to say, brings into view the military victory of the ruler who would arise out of Israel. Perhaps the most striking thing about Balaam's language, however, is the way in which he contrasts his own time to the time of Israel's emergent and triumphant ruler: "I see him, but not now; I behold him, but not near." In the "geography" of the Bible's redemptive history, this strange prophet-for-hire somehow knew that his time and place were far, far away from the "metropolis," from the arrival of Israel's coming king, who would wield dominion over the nations of the world. Not surprisingly, at such a distance all that Balaam could decipher about the coming king's conquest was phrased in the terms of destruction and dispossession, without a hint of mercy or grace. Across Lake Hodges, near my home in southern California, are two bridges. One supports a six-lane superhighway, Interstate 15, which carries hundreds or thousands of vehicles daily, from motorcycles to semi-trucks, all traveling at high speed. The other, running parallel to the interstate perhaps two or three hundred yards to the west, is a footbridge for pedestrians. When hikers on the path around the lake reach its western shore and look back toward the east, they experience a bizarre optical illusion: the two bridges appear to be one, and walkers seem to be strolling only a few feet from trucks barreling south at sixty-five or seventy miles per hour! Only as you get closer can you see the distance between the bridges, and between the traffic that each is carrying. Balaam somehow sensed that he stood far from the fulfillment of God's words spoken through the prophet's reluctant mouth. Only the unfolding of history would bring the fulfilling figures close enough so that the distance, as well as the resemblance, between them would become clear.

When we step back and view Balaam's prophecy in relation to "like and unlike passages" and "many and clearer passages"—that is, in its *canonical context*—the big question is: "When and by whom was Balaam's prophecy fulfilled?" As we read further in biblical history, we find a first fulfillment in King David, who defeated the Moabites, made the whole Moabite army lie down on the ground, and killed two-thirds of them (2 Sam. 8:2). David went on to conquer other surrounding nations as well: Edom (whose dispossession Balaam predicted, Num. 24:19), Amalek (whose destruction Balaam foresaw, Num. 24:20), Syria, Ammon, and Philistia (2 Sam. 8:5–14). That might be as far as Balaam could see into the future, since his whole prophecy focuses on how Israel's king will defeat, destroy, and subdue other nations.

45

So as we interpret this prophecy, so early in the history of God's words to his people, we might need to recognize that Balaam's vision did not have a clear focus on details that would be revealed later on.

Then again, we can be grateful that we do not live in the days of Moses and Balaam, or even in the days of David. We start with the vague impression that Balaam had of a coming, conquering king in Israel; but then we can trace the theme forward in history, finding that later passages prove to be clearer passages, bringing into view glorious and gracious details that Balaam could not see from afar. Through the prophet Amos in the eighth century B.C., the Lord announced:

> "In that day I will raise up
>   the booth of David that is fallen
> and repair its breaches,
>   and raise up its ruins
>   and rebuild it as in the days of old,
> that they may possess the remnant of Edom
>   and all the nations who are called by my name,"
>   declares the LORD who does this. (Amos 9:11–12)

Amos pronounced woe on those who felt secure in their sin both in Zion, capital of Judah, and in Samaria, capital of the northern kingdom of Israel (Amos 6:1); and he foresaw the fall of Judah and the destruction of Jerusalem, which would occur in the sixth century B.C. (2:4–5). In those events the dynasty of David would be humiliated and deprived of royal power. But Amos also saw a day when God would reverse this judgment. The restoration of David's royal "booth" is described in terms that involve military power and the dispossession of Edom from its territory southeast of the Dead Sea, as we heard in Balaam's oracle. But Amos's mention of "nations who are called by my name" alludes to God's promise to Abraham—long before Balaam—that through Abraham's offspring the nations would be *blessed*, not merely destroyed, evicted, or enslaved (Gen. 12:3).

Another leap forward in biblical history brings us to the fulfillment of Amos's prophecy in the days of the apostles. Acts 15 reports that an assembly of apostles and church elders gathered in Jerusalem after the first missionary journey of Paul and Barnabas. As the council sought to discern how to regard Gentiles who trusted in Jesus, testimonies offered by Peter, Paul, and Barnabas showed that God had welcomed believing Gentiles without requiring that they be circumcised. James then put these testimonies into a biblical context, commenting, "Simeon [Peter] has related how God first visited the Gentiles, to take from them a people for his name" (Acts 15:14), and then showing that this development fulfilled Old Testament prophecy, citing Amos's prediction of the reconstruction of David's dynasty to rule over nations (that is, Gentiles) who would bear God's name. God's recent acts have shown James that David's Great Son, Jesus, would conquer Edom and other Gentiles not by violence and armies, but by the gospel of grace applied by the invincible power of the Holy Spirit to call Gentiles to bear the Lord's name, to constitute his willing and grateful possession.

Balaam could see that the King of Israel who would conquer Moab, Edom, and other nations was in the distant future, "not now; . . . not near." Despite his unworthy motives, by Christ's Spirit he spoke God's truth about "the sufferings of Christ and the subsequent glories," and he seemed to sense, as did more faithful prophets, that "they were serving not themselves but you" in the era in which the gospel is preached through the Holy Spirit (1 Peter 1:10–12). What Balaam glimpsed at a distance, James and the apostles eventually saw "up close," as the risen Messiah began to extend his reign across the world through the heart-captivating, life-transforming power of his grace—a kingdom expansion that has embraced even us, almost two millennia after God enthroned King Jesus at his right hand in heaven. When we begin our journey to Jesus from Numbers 24, standing with that strangely conflicted prophet Balaam on Moab's plains and catching the glimpse that he received of a future, conquering scepter-bearer, we respect the way that God gave his Word over many centuries. We marvel at the way he brought the image of the coming King into sharper and sharper focus until Christ made his appearance in human history and in human nature at the appointed moment.

Questions for Reflection and Discussion

1. In light of Charles Spurgeon's little parable, have you heard or read sermons that seemed to take you "over hedge and ditch" to bring you from a biblical passage to Christ? Can you discern a clearer "route"—actually embedded by God in his works of redemption and revelation—that connects that text to Jesus, just as England's network of roads links every hamlet to London? (If not, don't be discouraged: that's our agenda for chapters 3 through 10!)

2. Which is the most reliable authority for interpreting the Bible: (a) the consensus of the church's pastors and theologians over the centuries; (b) the Holy Spirit's impressions on the heart and mind of each reader; (c) other, clearer passages in Scripture and the inspired biblical authors' own example in showing the full meaning of earlier passages? Why is the authority that you chose preferable to the others? Is there *any* role for the options you bypassed in our study of Scripture?

3. Why is it important to anchor our understanding of any biblical text at the outset by trying to discover, as much as we can, how its first recipients (readers or hearers) should have understood it, in their own time and place?

4. According to the Second Helvetic Confession, to what four features of a biblical text will we give attention in order to "glean from the Scriptures themselves" an "orthodox and genuine" interpretation of any passage? How does attending to *each* of these features show our respect for the way that God has chosen to given us his written Word?

5. How does attending to *each* of these four features help to safeguard our study of any biblical passage from misinterpretation or misapplication?

6. What kinds of questions should we ask in order to get as complete a picture as possible of the circumstances in which a text of the Bible was given?

7. The Second Helvetic Confession says that we need to interpret a biblical text in the light of "unlike passages." How do Romans 4:1–5 and James 2:21–24 illustrate one aspect of taking account of "unlike passages" as we study the Bible? How does the difference between the requirement of circumcision for Abraham (Gen. 17) and the removal of that requirement today (Acts 15; Gal. 5:2) illustrate how *redemptive history* should control how we relate some "unlike passages" to each other?

8. What are God's purposes in giving us his Word? What "fruit" does his Holy Spirit intend to produce in us through the Bible? If we forget that our study of Scripture must align with God's purpose to make a difference in our hearts and lives, how will that forgetfulness distort or thwart our understanding of the Word?

9. How are we helped to understand the oracle of Balaam (Num. 24) by considering first the circumstances of the generation of Israelites who left Egypt with Moses, and then the circumstances of their children

who would grow to adulthood, receive the completed books of Moses, and finally enter the Promised Land? What were God's purposes for the prophetic words that he compelled Balaam to speak in the lives of those two generations?

10. What later passages in the Bible place Balaam's glimpse of a "star" emerging from Jacob at a distance in wider canonical contexts? What details do these later Scriptures fill in to clarify both the identity of the "star" and the form of his conquest over Moab, Edom, and other nations?

PART 3

Reading the Road Signs

3

Previews Embedded in Life: Types and Their Fulfillment in Scripture

IN THE PREVIOUS CHAPTER, we heard the story that Charles Spurgeon attributed to a Welsh preacher, in which a seasoned pastor compared the Christ-centered unity of the Bible to the English landscape, where every village is linked to London, somehow or other, by a network of roads and highways. Let's continue to use that analogy to explore the process of Christ-centered Bible study.

In overland travel, how you get from where you are to where you want to be depends on several factors: where you are starting from, the terrain that you need to cross (mountains, valleys, meadows, deserts, rivers), and the road system that links the village to the big city. So we saw that the first step in learning from the Bible itself how to read the Bible is to pay attention to our "point of origin," to the passage's meaning in its original and closest contexts, which include the background experience of its first audience, the sentences and paragraphs and chapters surrounding it, and earlier Scriptures that its original recipients would have or should have known. This is like standing at the map of a shopping mall and noticing its "You Are Here" arrow, or consulting a GPS to get our bearings in a wilderness. We want to discover, as much as we can, what a biblical passage meant to the folks who originally heard it, in their place and time in the history of God's redemptive plan. We want to stand beside them and listen to the text in the contexts that God had already provided for their understanding, both in the portions of his Word that he had already spoken and in his providential preparation of circumstances that were challenging their faith and faithfulness. In this way, we show respect for the fact that God decided to interweave his words of revelation with his works of creation and redemption, sovereignly and patiently revealing and enacting his plan to bring rescue to our race. As Hebrews 1:1–2 says, God previously spoke through prophets in many ways and many pieces, but now "in these last days" (which began with Jesus' birth at Bethlehem) he has spoken to us in his Son—his best and final Word. The words that those ancient prophets spoke piecemeal over centuries are like shadows: they show shapes but lack substance, when contrasted with the reality now revealed in the coming of Jesus Christ (10:1–18).

So we start studying Old Testament passages by trying to hear them as ancient Israelites should have heard them, but we also keep in mind that Israel's experience of God's works and words was the first phase of a larger rescue plan that would focus, finally, on Jesus and his mission. Reading any part of the Bible in all its appropriate contexts means placing that passage into the setting of the whole Bible ("like and unlike passages," "many and clearer passages," as stated by the Second Helvetic Confession). That is why I found it irresistible (as I hope you did, too) to unfold the truth expressed in Ephesians 2:8–10 not only by looking at the surrounding paragraphs in that letter, but also by looking back to Paul's ministry in the church of Ephesus (Acts 19–20) and looking around at Paul's other epistles. That is why, as Balaam surveyed Israel's camp in the wilderness (Num. 24), his glimpse of a coming king in a far-off future invited us to look ahead to later Scriptures—to David, to Amos's prophecy, and to James's commentary on the fulfillment that has arrived with Jesus, David's Son, now captivating the nations by his grace. These later words of God filled in the details of Balaam's oracle more fully than he himself could see at the time.

As we reflected on Spurgeon's story, however, we agreed that we do not want to travel from the Bible's far-flung texts toward Jesus by going "over hedge and ditch," blazing trails and inventing links that display our own ingenuity, instead of using the "road system" that God himself has embedded in his Word. Far-fetched allegorical explanations, in which some spiritual significance is injected into every tiny detail of the narrative, leave us thinking, "Well, what that author or preacher taught might be taught

somewhere in the Bible, but I can't see how he got it out of *this passage.*"
We are not persuaded, for example, when Augustine, the great North African pastor-theologian of the early church, observes that the dimensions of
Noah's ark—its length six times its breadth from side to side and ten times
its thickness—are the same as the dimensions of the human body . . . and
then concludes that the ark symbolizes the body of Christ (*City of God*,
bk. 15, chap. 26). When he compares the door in the ark's side to the spear
wound inflicted on Jesus and tells us that the wood anticipates Christ's
cross, we are dubious. When he reasons further that the church is "the
body of Christ" and so other details of the ark's blueprint preview aspects
of the church, we are even less convinced. Do the three levels inside the ark
(Gen. 6:16) really symbolize Noah's three sons, from whom all humanity
came after the flood? Or faith, hope, and charity? Or "the three harvests
in the gospel, thirtyfold, sixtyfold, an hundredfold"? Or the three states
of sexual purity among the church members: marriage (in the basement),
widowhood on the middle level, and virginity on the top story? Augustine
makes all these suggestions, but does not commit himself to any; and the
variety of these speculations makes us suspect that Augustine's meditation
has left far behind the meaning that Noah and his sons (or Moses and his
readers) were to find in Genesis 6. Presumably, Augustine's thoughts were
launched by 1 Peter 3:20–21, which presents the preservation of Noah and
his family through floodwaters in the ark as a preview of Christians' salvation through baptism. But we wonder: Was the elaborate symbolism that
Augustine developed actually a network of "roads" that the Spirit of God
himself placed in Scripture, leading us to Christ and his church? Or has
Augustine, whose brilliance and piety we admire, been "climbing hedges
and fording ditches"?

Our question, therefore, is: How can we follow the paths and roads and
highways that *God has actually embedded* in the Bible, rather than blazing
our own trails in flights of invention and imagination? I'm suggesting that
the avenues that connect various passages in the Bible to Christ come in
three general categories.

First, some routes are quite plainly labeled, like a major interstate
highway with mileage markers and illuminated exit signs, or like a crossroad
intersection of country lanes where a signpost stands, its arrows pointing
in various directions toward different destinations. The routes that lead
from many Old Testament passages to Jesus are marked with unmistakable

"road signs" when one or more New Testament texts explicitly interpret an ancient Scripture through quotation, allusion, or commentary. Students of the Bible call these road signs *types*, a term derived from a Greek word that means "pattern." The study of types—Old Testament individuals, events, institutions, and offices that are shown to foreshadow Christ and his mission by the way they are interpreted in the New Testament—is called *typology*. It is the subject of this chapter, to which we will return in a moment.

Second, suppose we expand the horizons of our travel metaphor and envision regions very different from the settled English countryside—for example, trekking through the forested mountains of North America or the tropical jungles of Africa. In such settings, finding the right route from our point of origin to our desired destination is more challenging. In pristine wilderness, we would look in vain for route markers and directional signs. Instead, we would need the skills of experienced explorers who find clues in the slant of the sunlight, the moss on tree trunks, the flow of a stream, and other subtle signals of geography and directionality. Even without the aid of compass or GPS, trackers who can read such clues discern what we might call "the lay of the land" and find a way to their destination. Similarly, there are passages in the Bible for which the route that leads to Christ is not explicitly marked. Many Old Testament texts are never quoted in the New Testament with a preface such as "this was to fulfill what the Lord had spoken by the prophet." To see the network of subtler connections by which the wide landscape of God's Word is linked to Christ at the center, we need to cultivate an experienced explorer's eye for Scripture's lay of the land. That is, we need to keep in mind that the whole assortment of sixty-six documents that have been given to us by God's Holy Spirit focuses on an amazing interpersonal relationship, the bond of loyal and loving commitment between God the Creator and human beings, whom he created in his image and for his friendship. The Bible's word for this relationship is *covenant*, so "getting the lay of the land" is tracing the covenant story of the Bible, from its inauguration at creation, through its disruption by human sin, to its restoration by God's promise and power and grace in Christ, and finally reaching its consummation in a new heavens and earth, purged forever of the poisons that pour from our cosmic treason. Since Jesus is the Mediator and Guarantor of the new and better covenant (Heb. 7:22; 12:24), paying attention to how biblical texts relate to that divine-human relationship will show us the lay of the land that leads to him. In chapters 4,

5, and 6, we will survey the themes of the covenant, its Lord, and its Servant. These categories will sharpen our eyesight, so that we can find those paths through the underbrush and follow their lead to Christ.

Finally, finding our way from some biblical passages to Christ, "the metropolis," is akin to travelers' experience when recognizable landmarks keep them oriented in the right direction as they progress toward their destination. The landmark might be a mountain such as Pikes Peak, which looms over Colorado Springs in the United States, or Mount Kilimanjaro, which dominates the horizon in northern Tanzania, or Mount Kinabalu in Malaysia, on the island of Borneo. Landmarks such as these might not offer the specific directions that road signs provide, but they enable us to get our bearings, even if we are not skilled adventurers attuned to subtle signals that suggest the lay of the land. In chapters 7 through 9, we will see how the three categories of leaders—prophets, priests, and kings—whom God gave to mediate his revelation, his presence, and his righteous rule among his people can guide us like landmarks, since their distinctive areas of responsibility in connecting God with his people beautifully sum up the work of Christ, the complete and climactic Mediator of the new covenant.

What Is Biblical Typology?

I have claimed that the connection between biblical types and Christ their Fulfiller is as plain to see as road signs on a highway, but you might still ask how such obvious, unmistakable foreshadowings of the Savior can be identified. Let me first describe what biblical types are, and, second, show the ways that the New Testament identifies features and figures of the Old Testament as types of Christ. Third, we will observe that the ancient types and Christ, who fulfills them, are linked through a blend of resemblance with contrast. We will see, fourth, that the typological way of viewing biblical history—that God's older acts provide previews of his coming events—is not a novelty invented by Jesus and his apostles, but a perspective on the unity of God's past and future interventions that was already visible in the Old Testament itself. We will see, fifth, how typology is grounded in the reality that the Creator and Redeemer who speaks sovereignly in Scripture also acts sovereignly in history. In other words, the typological interpretation of Scripture emerges from Scripture's doctrine of God, the Lord who acts in history, and it finds expression in the Old Testament as well as the New. The plainly labeled road signs are not exceptions to the rule for reading our

Bibles, but rather the most visible expressions of a deeply embedded pattern, the continuous interplay of God's works and words, which permeates God's Word. Thus, the road signs of biblical typology sensitize our eyesight to perceive the lay of the land and the landmarks that direct us to Jesus, as we will see in the following chapters. Finally, we will put into practice the road-signs route that leads us to Christ by looking briefly at an event during Israel's wilderness wanderings and Jesus' commentary on it in the Gospel according to John.

What Is a Type?

The English word *type* comes from the Greek *typos*, which was used in various ways to describe a visible mark, impression, pattern, or model. In the New Testament, *typos* refers to the shape of the scars (ESV: "marks") made by the nails in Jesus' hands (John 20:25) and to the heavenly "pattern" that Moses saw on Mount Sinai, the prototype (notice: "proto-*type*") or template that Israel's craftsmen were to follow in designing and constructing the earthly tabernacle (Acts 7:44; Heb. 8:5). Think of an ancient metal seal pressed into warm wax on an official document, so that the design on the seal is reflected in the wax. Or recall that, before computers took over most word processing, there were *typewriters*, which had tiny metal letters—type—mounted on slim metal arms, so that when you pressed a key, the arm rose until the type at its tip struck an inked ribbon, imprinting the shape of the letter onto a sheet of paper. The feature that links these various examples of *typos*/type is the resemblance between an original and its copy, between a pattern and the replica to which it gives shape.

That resemblance between an earlier exemplar and its later reflection is in view when Paul describes Adam as "a type [Greek *typos*] of the one who was to come" (Rom. 5:14). In following verses, Paul stresses how different Adam's original sin—"one man's trespass," "one trespass," "one man's disobedience"—was from the unified and flawless obedience of Jesus, whom Paul elsewhere calls the "last Adam" and the "second man" (1 Cor. 15:45, 47). Underlying the radical difference between Adam's and Christ's decisions and the outcomes of those decisions, however, lay a profound similarity: Adam and Christ each acted as a covenantal representative on behalf of others, so each man's response to God affected all those whom he represented. Adam made a choice, and many were affected. Because Adam disobeyed, all for whom he acted were constituted sinners, condemned to death. Christ made a choice, and many were affected. Because Christ obeyed, all for whom he acted are constituted righteous, vindicated in life (Rom. 5:15–21). Again and again we will find that the relationship between ancient types/patterns/previews and Christ, the reality whom they foreshadow, is characterized by this blend of resemblance with difference, of similarity with contrast.

Another passage in which Paul uses *typos* terms to connect the Old Testament to Christ is 1 Corinthians 10. Here the apostle warns the Christians of Corinth against getting entangled in the city's pagan idolatry and sensual immorality. He draws a sobering lesson from the Israelite generation who experienced God's liberation from Egypt and provision in the wilderness but who fell into sexual and spiritual infidelity, incurring God's judgment. Like those Israelites, the church at Corinth had experienced God's saving power and provision. Like that ancient generation, the Corinthians were tempted by sexual sin and pagan worship. Would they withstand the temptations to which the Israelites fell? They must, Paul argues, because those events so long ago "took place as examples *for us*" and were recorded in Scripture "*for our instruction*, on whom the end of the ages has come" (1 Cor. 10:6, 11).

At first glance, it might seem that Paul called those events "examples" (*typos*) merely to suggest that we should avoid imitating the Israelites' sins, lest we follow their footsteps into destruction. But Paul stresses that the ancient Israelites and the Christians of Corinth have a much closer bond than some generic principle such as: "Don't repeat their mistakes." He characterizes Israel's exodus and wilderness experience in theologically freighted terms that call to mind the Christian sacraments: "all were *baptized* into Moses in the cloud and in the sea, and all *ate* the same *spiritual food*, and all *drank* the same *spiritual drink*" (1 Cor. 10:2–4). Moreover, Paul says pointedly that the rock that spared the Israelites from dehydration and death "was Christ" (v. 4). Now, in this arresting statement, Paul is not suggesting that it was anything other than a boulder in the desert. But when life-giving refreshment flowed from the rock that had borne a judgment blow from God's rod, it became a preview of Christ, whose death is our fountain of life. When Paul says that those events long ago happened and were recorded "for us" and "for our instruction" (vv. 6, 11), he means that *God's purpose* both for the events themselves and for their record in Scripture was to guide and guard his *new covenant* church. In fact, the apostle explicitly mentions our privileged position in God's timeline: his readers are people "on whom *the end of the ages has come*" (v. 11). Along with other New Testament authors, Paul knew that Christ's appearing "at *the end of the ages* to put away sin" (Heb. 9:26) was the "hinge" on which all history turns, the dawn of the last days that were forecast by God's prophets and longed for by his people (see also Acts 2:17; Heb. 1:1–2; 1 Peter 1:10–12, 20–21).

Let me draw together what we have seen so far from Romans 5 and 1 Corinthians 10 to propose a description of biblical types. Biblical types are previews embedded by God, the Lord of history, into time and space, into the historical experience of his covenant people, in order to show the shape of things to come. Types may be individuals such as Adam or events such as Israel's exodus from Egypt and trials in the wilderness. As we will soon see, they may also be institutions such as the tabernacle and the temple; and they may be special offices occupied by chosen individuals: prophets, priests, judges, kings, and sages. Christ the coming Rescuer and King is the center toward which Old Testament types point forward and focus our gaze; but some types also bring into our view Christ's people, gathered around him.

How Can We Recognize Types?

Romans 5 and 1 Corinthians 10 have shown us one of the most obvious road signs that direct us from an ancient individual (Adam) or ancient events (Israel's exodus and its sequel in the wilderness) toward their fulfillment in Christ and his church. When inspired New Testament authors actually apply *type* (*typos*) terminology to individuals or incidents in the Old Testament, we can walk the roads that they have marked out with confidence. But frankly, the use of *type/typos* terminology in the New Testament is rare. Besides the passages that we have touched on (including 1 Peter 3:20–21 on Noah's ark), these terms themselves are used to describe the relationship between Old and New Testament realities only in Hebrews, where (unlike the usage of Paul and Peter) the type/pattern/exemplar is God's heavenly sanctuary and the antitype/copy/replica is the earthly tabernacle (Heb. 8:5; 9:24; see Acts 7:44). So if the only road signs to be seen in Scripture were those labeled with *type* terminology, this chapter could end here—and the "road signs" category would not help us very much to walk with Jesus through his Word in the Old Testament's vast array of events, individuals, commands, poems, proverbs, prophecies, and eras.

Happily, the Holy Spirit has provided several other signals to mark the route from ancient individuals, events, institutions, and offices to their fulfillment in Jesus, his work, and his people. Among the most obvious are Old Testament passages that New Testament writers explicitly quote and apply to Christ. Sometimes the Old Testament quotation is introduced with a formula such as "this was to fulfill," or "so it is written." In the early chapters of Matthew's Gospel, for example, "this was to fulfill" introduces not only promises expressed in words (prophecy) but also promises embodied in historical events (type). This formula introduces the *predictive words* of the prophet Micah, that Israel's future Ruler would come from Bethlehem (Mic. 5:2, quoted in Matt. 2:6). But it also prefaces the words of Hosea, "Out of Egypt I called my son" (Hos. 11:1, quoted in Matt. 2:15), which look back to a *past event*, Israel's exodus from Egypt through Moses. Some scholars accuse Matthew of taking Hosea's words out of context, forcing them to predict an event that was future to the prophet, when Hosea himself was looking back to the exodus long before his time. What such critics do not see is the deeper matrix that links God's protection of Israel, his adoptive son, at the exodus to his preservation of Jesus, the Father's unique Son. Matthew's point is that Jesus fulfills Israel's early history because he is the true Israel, delivered from death as an infant, brought out of Egypt, and tested in the wilderness (and successfully passing the test that Israel had failed). By affirming that Hosea's words are "fulfilled" in the young Jesus' return from Egypt with his parents, Matthew does not claim that Hosea's words fit Jesus *instead of* Israel, but rather that they fit Jesus *because he himself is Israel's fulfillment.*

Among the individuals, institutions, and events that are identified in the New Testament as fulfilled in Christ through explicit quotation of and commentary on Old Testament passages are the creation of Adam (1 Cor. 15:45, quoting Gen. 2:7), the union of Adam and Eve in marriage (Eph. 5:31, quoting Gen. 2:24), the Passover lamb (John 19:36, quoting Ex. 12:46), David's betrayal by a close friend (John 13:18, quoting Ps. 41:9; cf. Acts 1:20), the groundless hatred of David's enemies (John 15:25, quoting Ps. 35:19), opponents gambling over David's garments (John 19:24, quoting Ps. 22:18), the transmission of proverbial wisdom by Israel's sages (Matt. 13:35, quoting Ps. 78:2), Israel's deafness to the prophets' words (Matt. 13:14–15, quoting Isa. 6:9–10), and the grief of Judah's exile (Matt. 2:18, quoting Jer. 31:15). Even this brief sampling gives us a glimpse of the complex texture of interconnections that link Israel's history to Jesus as the fulfillment of that history.

Even when they don't directly quote and comment on an Old Testament passage that describes an ancient individual, event, or institution, the New Testament authors signal how such patterns preview Jesus, his saving mission, and his church through unmistakable allusions, sometimes even collecting a cluster of echoes of earlier historical realities. For example, in the Gospel according to Luke, we hear echoes of the prophetic ministries of Elijah and Elisha again and again. In chapter 1, we learn that John the Baptist will prepare for Christ's appearance by going before the Lord "in the spirit and power of Elijah, to turn the hearts of the fathers to the children" (Luke 1:17). This description of John's mission not only recalls Elijah's ministry in the days of King Ahab (1 Kings 17–2 Kings 2) but also includes the words of the prophet Malachi, which held out the hope of a herald like Elijah to come (Mal. 4:5–6). Jesus reminded his neighbors in Nazareth that God had sent Elijah and Elisha to serve Gentiles, a widow in Sidon and a commander from Syria (Luke 4:25–27). Later, Jesus raised a widow's son at Nain. The account climaxes in the simple sentence, "Jesus gave him to his mother" (7:15), an echo of the account of the resurrection of the widow's son at Zarephath through Elijah (1 Kings 17:23). In the transfiguration, Elijah appeared with Moses to talk with Jesus (Luke 9:30–31). James and John asked Jesus' permission to call fire down from heaven on an inhospitable Samaritan town, no doubt remembering the fire that had fallen at Elijah's word to destroy troops sent to take the prophet into custody (Luke 9:51–56; 2 Kings 1:9–12). They saw the parallel between the honor due to God's ancient messenger, Elijah, and God's ultimate Messenger, Jesus; but Jesus' rebuke of their eagerness for instant justice revealed that they did not yet grasp the difference between the type and its Fulfiller. That contrast is seen again when Jesus demands instant and total commitment from a would-be disciple, refusing to let him say goodbye to his family—the same expression of filial respect that Elijah did permit Elisha to perform, when he called him from the plow (Luke 9:61–62; 1 Kings 19:19–21).

John's Gospel is also full of signposts that point the way from Old Testament institutions and events to Jesus, by way of clear allusions. Jesus' body was the "temple" that the son of David would rebuild after its destruction (John 2:18–22; 2 Sam. 7:13; cf. Zech. 4:6–14). As Israel was about to observe the Passover, recalling the exodus from slavery and the start of wilderness wanderings, Jesus identified himself as the God-given, heaven-sent bread to which manna pointed (John 6). At the Feast of Booths, commemorating Israel's forty years in the desert, Jesus announced that he was the fulfillment both of the rock that gave living water and of the fiery cloud that gave light to the camp (John 7:38; 8:12; Ex. 13:21–22; 17:1–7). David had gone from tending sheep to shepherding God's people (2 Sam. 7:8), and his royal successors inherited the shepherd's obligations. But they failed miserably (Jer. 23:1–8; Ezek. 34:1–24). Unlike his predecessors—thieves, hired hands, and predatory beasts—Jesus was the Good Shepherd who would protect his sheep at the price of his life (John 10:1–18; see Luke 15:1–7).

One more example illustrates the pattern interwoven into the fabric of the Old Testament Scriptures, which the inspired authors of the New Testament trace for our comfort and instruction. Consider the patriarch Joseph, Jacob's eleventh son. As we read the account of Joseph's life in Genesis 37–50, many details suggest similarities to the ministry of Jesus. Joseph was rejected by his brothers, almost murdered but then handed over to Gentiles, falsely accused, imprisoned, and abused. But then he was exalted to be Egypt's second-in-command, ruling that great kingdom on behalf of its pharaoh. From his high position of authority and power, he saved the lives of the very men who had tried to get rid of him years before. Joseph seems to foreshadow Jesus' rejection and suffering, his resurrection and exaltation to God's right hand, and the salvation that flows from his descent and ascent. Is he a type of Jesus?

Well, the New Testament never says point-blank that Joseph was a type of Jesus. But before he became the first recorded Christian martyr, Stephen, a man "full of faith and of the Holy Spirit" (Acts 6:5) and "full of grace and power" (v. 8), eloquently outlined a repeated pattern in the history of Israel. His forceful speech showed that the Israelites, over and over, rejected and abused leaders whom God had raised up to rescue them from slavery and death. It happened with Joseph and his brothers (7:9–14), with Moses whom God chose to rescue his kinfolk from Egyptian slavery (vv. 23–29, 35), with the prophets who foretold the coming of "the righteous one" (a title of the Suffering Servant in Isaiah 53:11–12), and finally with the Sanhedrin's condemnation of Jesus to be killed by Gentiles (Acts 7:52). Without using the term *pattern* (that is, *typos*) or issuing a signal formula such as "it is written" or "this was to fulfill," Stephen traces the repeating pattern in the fabric of Israel's history—the interplay of the people's rebellion and God's patient and saving grace—leading his hostile hearers and Luke's believing readers (including us) to the rejected and righteous Servant of the Lord, whose wounds bring us healing. As we watch the New Testament authors tracing the threads and designs in the fabric of earlier Scripture, our eyes, too, will be sharpened to see the shape of the Savior throughout the tapestry.

The New Testament overflows with echoes of imagery from Israel's history and Israel's Scriptures, showing how past events and practices have finally found their meaning focused to crystal-clarity through the lens of Jesus. Not only is Jesus himself our temple, but also his indwelling Spirit makes us, his church, a temple under construction and the residence of God on earth (1 Cor. 3:16–17; 6:19; Eph. 2:20–22; 1 Peter 2:4–5). Jesus is our Passover Lamb (1 Cor. 5:7). Jesus is the prophet like Moses, promised in Deuteronomy 18 (Acts 3:22–24). These echoes and allusions that link the Old Testament to Christ sometimes stand so "thick" and seem so familiar that those who have known the Bible for years might drive past these road signs without noticing how richly God has mapped out and marked for us the routes that bring us to his Son.

How Do Types Connect to Christ?

As we would expect from some of the uses of *typos* in ancient Greek (the pattern of nails in Jesus' hands) and the analogies already cited (a seal's imprint in wax, a typewriter), one aspect of the relationship between an Old Testament type and its fulfillment in Christ is *similarity* or *resemblance*. Christ is always *like* the Old Testament pattern that foreshadowed him in significant ways. Adam made a life-or-death decision that affected many others; so did Christ. In the tabernacle and the temple, God dwelt in the midst of his people Israel; in Jesus' coming to earth, God dwelt in the midst of his people; and by the Spirit's presence, his church is now the sanctuary in which God resides on earth. Aaron and his sons served as priests, offering sacrifice and prayers for others in God's sanctuary; Jesus is the Great High Priest who offered himself once for all to atone for sins and lives forever to pray for his people in heaven itself.

Yet the second feature of the relationship between Old Testament previews and Jesus, the reality whom they anticipated, is *contrast*. The fulfillment in Christ is also *unlike* and *better than* the Old Testament event, person, institution, or office. Jesus brings a deeper, fuller, more lasting blessing. The contrast between the types and their Fulfiller may take a

64

couple of forms. On the one hand, the contrast may be sharp: whereas his Old Testament counterpart failed miserably, Jesus succeeded gloriously! This is what we saw in Paul's comparison and contrast between Adam and Christ in Romans 5: Adam's one transgression brought condemnation and death to many, but Christ's one act of obedience brought justification and life to many. This diametrical opposition is also in view in Paul's discussion of Adam and Christ in 1 Corinthians 15, especially in verses 21–22: "For as by a man came death, by a man has come also the resurrection of the dead. For as in Adam all die, so also in Christ shall all be made alive."

On the other hand, sometimes the contrast between the type or shadow and Jesus the Fulfiller is the *relative or comparative* difference between what is *good* and what is *best*. In a sense, Paul sees this milder contrast between Adam and Christ, as well as the sharper opposition. So in 1 Corinthians 15 he presents Adam's original creation as an anticipation of Christ's resurrection, which launches the new creation: "Thus it is written, 'The first man Adam became a living being'; the last Adam became a life-giving spirit" (v. 45). Similarly, the author to the Hebrews recognizes that the animal sacrifices offered in the Old Testament sanctuary accomplished a certain type of ceremonial cleansing that qualified people to participate in worship. They produced "the purification of the flesh," although they could not perfect the conscience of the worshiper (Heb. 9:9–10, 13). Christ's once-for-all sacrifice of himself, on the other hand, effects a far better, far deeper cleansing: "how much more will the blood of Christ, who through the eternal Spirit offered himself without blemish to God, purify our conscience from dead works to serve the living God" (v. 14).

Hebrews 4:8 provides another illustration of the way in which the move from Old Testament type to Christ-focused fulfillment involves a contrast between what is *good* and what is *best*. The author is commenting on Psalm 95, in which Israelites of David's time are cautioned against imitating the hard hearts of their ancestors, who through unbelief died in the desert in Moses' day. That earlier generation failed to enter God's Promised Land, which the psalmist identifies with God's "rest" (Ps. 95:11, quoted in Heb. 4:5–6). But the author to the Hebrews notices that in this psalm, written "so long afterward"—after Israel's wilderness wanderings— God invites David's contemporaries to enter his rest "today" by believing the Lord as they "hear his voice." The psalm is not merely a record of the tragedy of a bygone generation; it is a warning and invitation to David's generation—and to the first-century followers of Jesus who first received this epistle. This implies, therefore, that the promise of entering God's rest offers a much bigger blessing than the conquest of the Promised Land that was accomplished under Joshua's leadership. So the author reasons, "For if Joshua had given them rest, God would not have spoken of another day later on" (Heb. 4:8). In other words, our New Testament author concludes from the offer of entering God's rest in Psalm 95 that *Joshua did not give Israel rest.* Now, that is a surprising conclusion to draw, since toward the end of the book of Joshua, after the narrative of the conquest of Canaan, we read:

> Thus the LORD gave to Israel all the land that he swore to give to their fathers. And they took possession of it, and they settled there. *And the LORD gave them rest on every side* just as he had sworn to their fathers. Not one of all their enemies had withstood them, for the LORD had given all their enemies into their hands. Not one word of all the good promises that the LORD had made to the house of Israel had failed; all came to pass. (Josh. 21:43–45)

In some sense, the Lord gave Israel rest through Joshua. But between the successful completion of the conquest and the writing of Psalm 95 lay several restless centuries, in which Israel's judges had to fight off enemies again and again. Israel's grasp on the Promised Land was anything but restful. Even when the Lord gave David "rest from all his surrounding enemies" (2 Sam. 7:1, echoing Josh. 21:44), the peace lasted little more than a generation: when David's grandson came to the throne, the kingdom was ripped in two. So even though Joshua's conquest was good, it was not the ultimate good. Joshua did not confer on his countrymen *all* that "God's rest" entails. We need a better, more secure rest than Joshua could provide, in a better, more lasting homeland than Canaan. What Hebrews 4:8 implies, the author makes explicit later in his epistle, when he asserts that the homeland for which the patriarchs, Abraham, Isaac, and Jacob, hoped was not a piece of territory on this enemy-infested earth at all: "But as it is, they desire *a better country,* that is, *a heavenly one.* Therefore God is not ashamed to be called their God, for he has prepared for them a city" (Heb. 11:13–16). In response to God's promise, Abraham "was looking forward to the city that has foundations, whose designer and builder is God" (v. 10). This is the same city that Christian believers eagerly anticipate: "For here we have no lasting city, but we seek the city that is to come" (13:14). Joshua's rest—that is, Israel's conquest of Canaan—was good, to be sure, a demonstration that the Lord had kept his promises. But that earthly land was a preview—a fore-shadowing or type—of a far better rest that lasts forever in a country that is completely immune to enemy invasion and a city whose divine Designer guarantees its eternal security.

Typology's Roots in the Old Testament Prophets

The typological way of understanding God's past acts in history as sneak previews of coming events was not invented by Jesus during his earthly ministry, or by his apostles and the other New Testament authors. Nor did it originate with Jewish rabbis in the centuries between the completion of the Old Testament and the arrival of Christ. Through the writings of the Major and Minor Prophets, God had already been teaching Israel to conceive of the promised salvation to come in the shape of what he had done in the past—yet much more magnificent! Using our travel metaphor, we might say that the Lord placed these road signs in the terrain of the Old Testament itself, to point the way forward to Christ by pointing backward to God's mighty deeds in the past. Three samples will show that the Old Testament Scriptures themselves viewed God's past acts as previews and patterns for his climactic redemptive intervention in the future. Through his prophets, God promised to bring about a *new creation* and a *new covenant*, and to raise up a *new David* to shepherd his flock.

New Creation

Toward the end of Isaiah's prophecies, after predictions of judgments to come for Israel's rebellion and of Israel's redemption through a faithful, Suffering Servant of the Lord, the Lord promises to start again, from the beginning:

> "For behold, I create new heavens
>   and a new earth,
> and the former things shall not be remembered
>   or come into mind.
> But be glad and rejoice forever
>   in that which I create;
> for behold, I create Jerusalem to be a joy,
>   and her people to be a gladness.
>
> . . . .

67

No more shall be heard in it the sound of weeping
    and the cry of distress.
. . . .
They shall not labor in vain
    or bear children for calamity,
for they shall be the offspring of the blessed of the LORD,
    and their descendants with them.
. . . .
The wolf and the lamb shall graze together;
    the lion shall eat straw like the ox,
    and dust shall be the serpent's food.
They shall not hurt or destroy
    in all my holy mountain,"
          says the LORD. (Isa. 65:17–25)

We hear the echo of Genesis 1:1 in "I create . . . heavens and . . . earth." The Lord's sovereign creation of the universe in the beginning is a preview of a cosmic re-creation to come. Other echoes of Genesis show that God's new creation will reverse the damage wreaked by human sin at the fall: there will be no more sounds of grief and distress, no more frustrating toil in work and sorrow in childbearing (see Gen. 3:16–19). Peace will prevail between predator and prey, the wolf and the lamb. Yet "dust shall be the serpent's food," for through its mouth Satan hissed the lies that lured Adam and Eve to doubt and defy the Creator, unleashing guilt and misery on human history (see Gen. 3:14).

Isaiah's interpretation of the original creation as a pattern—a type— of God's final work of salvation, the creation of a new heavens and a new, curse-free earth, would subsequently be elaborated by the Holy Spirit in the New Testament. Peter informs believers that "according to [God's] promise we are waiting for new heavens and a new earth in which righteousness dwells" (2 Peter 3:13). John's visions on Patmos give a preview of "a new heaven and a new earth, for the first heaven and the first earth had passed away" (Rev. 21:1). In this new universe, God "will wipe away every tear from their eyes, and death shall be no more, neither shall there be mourning, nor crying, nor pain anymore, for the former things have passed away" (v. 4).

Not only will the new creation be consummated one day in a universe set free from its present stains and sorrows, but it also has already begun through the coming of Jesus Christ. Even before the new heavens and earth replace the old, new creation is happening whenever God's Spirit brings people into union with Jesus by faith: "Therefore, if anyone is in Christ, he is a new creation. The old has passed away; behold, the new has come" (2 Cor. 5:17). Those who have been dead in sins are now made alive, raised from the dead, and enthroned with Christ by God's almighty grace, and their affections, values, desires, and behavior bear the marks of the new creation: "For we are his workmanship, created in Christ Jesus for good works, which God prepared beforehand, that we should walk in them" (Eph. 2:10). This new creation dismantles walls of demographic and religious division that fractured Adam's fallen family, for Christ's purpose in shedding his blood was that "he might create in himself one new man in place of the two [Jew and Gentile], so making peace, and might reconcile us both to God in one body through the cross" (vv. 15–16). Paul echoes God's utterance on the first day of the first creation, "Let there be light" (Gen. 1:3), in order to show believers that we have experienced a radiance that far outshines the light that is merely visible: "For God, who said, 'Let light shine out of darkness,' has shone in our hearts to give the light of the knowledge of the glory of God in the face of Jesus Christ" (2 Cor. 4:6).

New Covenant

For the people of Israel, creation took place not only at the dawn of history but also in the covenant that God made with Israel at Mount Sinai, after liberating the people from slavery in Egypt. That is, the divine words that summoned heaven and earth into existence in the beginning foreshadowed not only the future creation of a new heaven and earth, but also the formation of God's covenant people through the covenant words delivered to Moses. As the Spirit of God was hovering over the face of the waters at the first creation, so Moses compared the Lord's protection of Israel in the wilderness to an eagle "that flutters over its young, spreading out its wings, catching them, bearing them on its pinions" (Deut. 32:11). Later prophets anticipated that the Lord would begin his merciful restoration of his wayward people by leading them out into the wilderness, as he had done in the exodus from Egypt:

> A voice cries:
> "In the wilderness prepare the way of the LORD;
>   make straight in the desert a highway for our God.
> . . . .

And the glory of the LORD shall be revealed,
    and all flesh shall see it together,
      for the mouth of the LORD has spoken." (Isa. 40:3–5)

Through the prophet Jeremiah, God signaled even more overtly the typological significance of the covenant that he had contracted at Sinai with the people he had redeemed from Egypt. They had violated their covenant commitments promptly, repeatedly, and flagrantly; but in the future, the Lord would inaugurate a new covenant, one that could not be shattered by the covenant servants' acts of treason:

> Behold, the days are coming, declares the LORD, when I will make a new covenant with the house of Israel and the house of Judah, not like the covenant that I made with their fathers on the day when I took them by the hand to bring them out of the land of Egypt, my covenant that they broke, though I was their husband, declares the LORD. But this is the covenant that I will make with the house of Israel after those days, declares the LORD: I will put my law within them, and I will write it on their hearts. And I will be their God, and they shall be my people. And no longer shall each one teach his neighbor and each his brother, saying, "Know the LORD," for they shall all know me, from the least of them to the greatest, declares the LORD. For I will forgive their iniquity, and I will remember their sin no more. (Jer. 31:31–34)

We will return to this promise in later chapters, where I will suggest that the covenant relationship between the Lord and humans made in his image constitutes the lay of the land that helps us to traverse the Bible's vast terrain toward God's intended destination for our journey: our glad submission to our Creator. Sometimes the covenants by which the Lord structures his relationship with his people loom like mountain peaks, visible landmarks to show the route of our pilgrimage; elsewhere, the covenant motif quietly undergirds other themes that seize our attention. Whether obvious or subtle, God's covenant bond always leads us toward the One who not only mediates the new covenant but also guarantees its better benefits (Heb. 7:22; 8:6; 12:24).

At this point, we pause at Jeremiah 31 simply to notice that God's promise had already set the precedent for looking back to Sinai's covenant as a pattern awaiting future fulfillment in a new and better bond, long before Jesus spoke of "the new covenant in my blood" (Luke 22:20) and long before Paul served as a minister of the new covenant whose role, unlike that of Moses, brings life (not death) by writing God's message on hearts (not stone) and gives all of God's people (not one man only) unveiled access to see the growing (not fading) glory of God in Jesus' face (2 Cor. 3). Through his ancient prophets, the Lord taught Israel to see in the exodus and the Sinai covenant—the momentous events that made her a nation, God's people—forecasts of a mightier rescue and a more lasting union to come.

New David

The account of David's life and career recorded in the books of Samuel bluntly exposes the grave flaws in his character. His adultery with Bathsheba and murderous conspiracy to eliminate her husband are the most glaring acts by which, as God's prophet said, he had "despised the word of the LORD, to do what is evil in his sight" (2 Sam. 12:9–14); but they were not his only failings (see 2 Sam. 24). Nonetheless, David (unlike King Saul, his predecessor) is called a man after the Lord's heart (1 Sam. 13:14; Acts 13:22); and David became the yardstick of wholehearted loyalty to the Lord against which his successors were measured (1 Kings 9:4–5; 11:4–6, 34, 38; 14:8; 15:3; etc.). Moreover, the Lord made a special covenant with him, promising to maintain David's descendants on the throne of Israel through endless generations (2 Sam. 7:11–17). Therefore, despite David's personal shortcomings, God's later prophets invoked the pattern of David as they foresaw and foretold the future rise of a Great King, descended from David's dynasty, who would both defeat Israel's enemies and rule Israel in righteousness.

In Ezekiel 34, the Lord uses the metaphor of shepherding (drawn from David's occupation before his royal anointing) as he accuses Israel's rulers of selfishly exploiting and neglecting his sheep, his people. For their failures the Lord will banish all human "shepherds," and he will come in person to find, rescue, feed, and heal his sheep:

> For thus says the Lord GOD: Behold, I, I myself will search for my sheep and will seek them out. As a shepherd seeks out his flock when he is among his sheep that have been scattered, so will I seek out my sheep, and I will rescue them from all places where they have been scattered on a day of clouds and thick darkness. . . . I will feed them with good pasture . . . . I myself will be the shepherd of my sheep . . . . I will seek the lost, and I will bring back the strayed, and I will bind up the injured, and I will strengthen the weak. (Ezek. 34:11–16)

It would appear that Israel's human shepherds, even those descended from David's royal house, have so miserably failed in their duties that the Lord plans to simply dispense with them altogether and take direct charge of his sheep and their welfare. Yet in this same text, Israel's divine shepherd goes on to promise:

> And I will set up over them one shepherd, my servant David, and he shall feed them: he shall feed them and be their shepherd. And I, the LORD, will be their God, and my servant David shall be prince among them. I am the LORD; I have spoken. (Ezek. 34:23–24)

This is not speaking of a reincarnation or revivification of the historical David from centuries earlier. Rather, this is a vivid way of promising a coming human King whose wholehearted devotion to the Lord was patterned, though imperfectly, in David long ago. David's heart for God and readiness to defend God's people "in the name of the LORD of hosts, the God of the armies of Israel" (1 Sam. 17:45), made him a preview, a template, a type of the future descendant of David whom God would send one day as Warrior-King, Savior, and wise Judge. David himself described such an ideal Ruler in his "last words," recorded in 2 Samuel 23:1–7. Yet the preceding narrative in the books of Samuel and the following narrative in the books of Kings show, sadly, that neither David nor those who occupied Israel's and Judah's thrones after him could match up to the benchmark. God's people stood in need of a shepherd who would be both the Lord, Israel's shepherd (Pss. 23:1; 80:1), and the fulfillment of the Lord's promise to establish David's royal house forever (2 Sam. 7). The complex of promises in Ezekiel 34 mysteriously anticipates the arrival of a divine and human shepherd at last.

Ezekiel's contemporary Jeremiah received the same promise from the Lord, in a form that made clear the distinction between King David and his royal Son, the eschatological King who would fulfill to perfection the pattern of just, wise, and utterly devoted leadership, which David himself exemplified only inconsistently:

> Behold, the days are coming, declares the LORD, when I will raise up for David a righteous Branch, and he shall reign as king and deal wisely, and shall execute justice and righteousness in the land. In his days Judah will be saved, and Israel will dwell securely. And this is the name by which he will be called: "The LORD is our righteousness." (Jer. 23:5–6)

The title "branch" appears in various Old Testament prophecies as a name for the promised Messiah and Servant of the Lord. In Isaiah's prophecies, long before the exile during which Ezekiel and Jeremiah preached, the Lord foretold that severe judgment on David's house—the great "tree" of Jesse, David's father, cut down to a "stump"—would be followed by the sprouting of "a branch from his roots" that would bear fruit (Isa. 11:1). Later, Zechariah would see a vision portraying the future cleansing of Israel from iniquity when, the Lord promises, "I will bring my servant the Branch" (Zech. 3:8).

In such prophetic texts as these, given centuries before the coming of Jesus, "the son of David" (Matt. 1:1) and Anointed King (16:16), God had already set the precedent for viewing David personally (and, we will see, the kingly office generally) as a preview, a type, of the mission that his eternal and incarnate Son would accomplish as the Good Shepherd who finds, feeds, protects, and leads his sheep (Luke 15:3–7; John 10:1–30). Again we see that viewing earlier figures in Israel's history as foreshadowings of the coming Redeemer is a way of interpreting the Bible that was already embedded in God's Word when Jesus the Fulfiller arrived and showed his friends "in all the Scriptures the things concerning himself" (Luke 24:27).

Typology's Foundation: The Sovereign of History and Speaker of Scripture

By this point, it is obvious that biblical typology would not "work" unless the God who speaks in the Bible were also the Sovereign Lord who controls history. Unless God were able to design real events involving real people in real history according to his plan, when we find striking parallels between earlier Old Testament texts and later New Testament texts, we would have to attribute the similarities either to sheer coincidence or to later authors' inventive reinterpretations of older passages and events. If the Bible were simply a collection of human documents produced over a millennium and a half, we might find it interesting to trace the sacrificial-lamb motif from the Passover in Moses' day, through Isaiah 53, to John the Baptist's declaration that Jesus is the Lamb of God, and then to Peter's description of "the precious blood of Christ, like that of a lamb without blemish or spot" (1 Peter 1:19). But unless the God who spoke through Moses and through Peter actually spared Israel's firstborn sons (safe behind blood-marked doorways) and unless he did so deliberately to provide a preview of the death that his Son would die centuries later, those intriguing connections stay "on the surface," at the superficial level of literary influence or the trajectory of tradition, not woven into the tapestry of Israel's historical experience.

The biblical authors are making a more daring claim in their typological interpretations of earlier Scriptures and events in redemptive history. They announce that those former historical realities were actually orchestrated by God himself to set patterns and provide foretastes of his wider agenda, which would come to its climax centuries later in Jesus the Messiah. In other words, the credibility of biblical typology depends on your view of God himself. The road signs erected in the writings of the Old Testament prophets and the New Testament apostles will persuade you and set your heart afire only if you share the biblical authors' view of and faith in the living God. Because God is sovereign, New Testament authors are not just claiming, "*I see* an interesting analogy between Israel's exodus and Jesus' setting us free from Satan's dominion. Do you?" Rather, they claim, "*God designed and accomplished* Israel's exodus to provide a flesh-and-blood preview of the greater rescue that he would achieve at Christ's cross and resurrection."

Both *types*, which are previews embedded in historical realities and experiences, and *prophecies*, which are previews expressed in words, rest on the foundation of trust in and awe before the infinite, personal, all-wise, and almighty Creator-Ruler who really is in control of his created universe and of every detail of human history, human life, and human choice. In Isaiah 43–46, the Lord asserts that he alone, in contrast to the dead idols worshiped by pagans, can foretell future events because he alone controls history from start to finish, from first to last. When he speaks *prophecy in words* (for example, the prediction—by name!—that Cyrus will give the order for the temple to be rebuilt, Isa. 45:1ff; or that a Suffering Servant will come to bear the sins of others, Isa. 53), he alone can make the words that he has spoken come true. When he enacts *prophecy in events* (an original creation to forecast a new creation, Isa. 65:17; or a past exodus pointing forward to a new one, Isa. 40:3ff.), his sovereign action in past history and future history secures their connection and their certainty. Both prophetic words and typological individuals and events rest on the reality that the God who speaks Scripture rules history, and that he is directing every detail of what happens in his universe toward the goal of his redemptive agenda.

Conclusion

The infinite personal God who speaks in the Bible stands sovereign over every detail of cosmic history—every atom, every force, every event, every person. He has an inconceivably complex and marvelously unified agenda for history: to magnify his own glory by redeeming a people for himself and ultimately renewing his whole created order. As he has executed that plan, he has also increasingly revealed its plotline and central Protagonist, Christ the Redeemer, both in Scripture's words and in a vast supporting cast of real flesh-and-blood individuals whose experiences and actions Scripture has recorded. As only a supremely sovereign Creator-Redeemer could, the Father of our Lord Jesus Christ has perfectly orchestrated the events of history—from creation through humanity's fall into sin to God's promise and fulfillment of the remedy for our sin—in such a way that ancient persons and events and institutions serve as previews and patterns of the redemptive, re-creative mission that Jesus would accomplish in the fullness of time. Even through the Old Testament prophets, the Lord was directing his people Israel to look back to earlier historical events as samples of his ways of working, so that they could use those categories to look into the future in anticipation of his coming triumph over all evil in a new creation, a new liberation, and a new covenant.

Some of those previews and patterns are shown to us overtly by New Testament texts that call them *types* or affirm that Christ, his saving work, and its benefits for the Lord's people have "fulfilled" ancient Scriptures, whether those passages explicitly promise God's future deliverance or testify to his past and present intervention in the life of Israel. Other ancient patterns become visible more subtly as we traverse the distance from Old Testament promise to New Testament fulfillment. Rather than bearing the obvious label *types* or being identified explicitly as events now "fulfilled" in Christ, these links are often hinted at through verbal allusions and parallels in circumstances. Whether obvious or subtle, biblical types function like street signs to point travelers forward toward the desired destination, to Jesus the Christ.

Of course, none of the previews can match the Protagonist to whom they point. Each is like Christ in some way, so each serves as a faithful template for his unique person or his redemptive achievement. Yet each falls short of the perfect Rescuer, Reconciler, Revealer, and Ruler who alone can repair the damage done by Adam and restore us to communion with our

Creator. So whenever and wherever God's Word points out a type of Christ, we ask the Lord to show us both how it resembles the Savior and how he transcends it. Through biblical typology, God kept whetting Israel's appetite for the Messiah to come; and through biblical typology, God prepared experiential and conceptual categories to help both ancient Israelites and us today grasp more fully the dimensions of Christ's heroic achievement for his people.

Putting It into Practice: The Serpent in the Desert (Numbers 21:4–9; John 3:14–15)

In conversation with Nicodemus, a representative of the council of Judaism's leaders (John 3:1; 7:50), Jesus suddenly turned the topic from Nicodemus's need of birth from above, by God's Spirit, to his own coming death as fitting the pattern of an incident in Israel's past: "And as Moses lifted up the serpent in the wilderness, so must the Son of Man be lifted up, that whoever believes in him may have eternal life" (3:14–15).

The incident, no doubt well known to Nicodemus as "the teacher of Israel," is recorded in Numbers 21:4–9. When the Israelites complained (yet again!) about the Lord's provision of food and water, God judged their toxic unbelief and discontent by sending poisonous serpents into their camp. Many Israelites died of snakebite, moving the survivors to repent and beg for rescue from the serpents' venom. Perhaps surprisingly, the Lord commanded Moses to fashion the image of his holy judgment into a means of his salvation:

> And the LORD said to Moses, "Make a fiery serpent and set it on a pole, and everyone who is bitten, when he sees it, shall live." So Moses made a bronze serpent and set it on a pole. And if a serpent bit anyone, he would look at the bronze serpent and live. (Num. 21:8–9)

In order to be saved from death, the people had to look at the symbol of the curse they deserved; and they had to believe God's promise that by looking, they would live. In its Old Testament context, to seek life by looking in faith on the emblem of God's judgment was to confront, honestly and humbly, the poisonous consequence of their rebellious discontent. This is not primitive magic, not primitive superstitious homeopathy in which fixation on venomous snakes cures venomous snakebites. Later in Israel's history, in fact, when the bronze serpent cast by Moses was misused as an object of worship, the faithful King Hezekiah smashed it into pieces (2 Kings 18:4). So there remains something shocking about the Lord's instruction to cast an image of the thing that was causing death and to summon sufferers to look at it in order to escape that death. In the frame of reference of the Israelites' wilderness generation and their children, Moses' readers, the bronze serpent posed a puzzling question: how could a cursed thing set people free from its curse?

The answer to that dilemma would be seen centuries later, when the Son of Man was lifted up on a Roman cross in a form of execution that, as Jews had learned from the ancient Scriptures, emblemized God's curse. To Nicodemus, Jesus simply pointed out the pattern that linked the bronze serpent in Moses' day to his own upcoming "lifting up" on the cross (John 8:28; 12:32–33). The apostle Paul would write that in order to redeem us from the curse that the law pronounces on its violators, "Christ . . . [became] a curse for us," even as Moses had written in Deuteronomy 21:23, "Cursed is everyone who is hanged on a tree" (Gal. 3:10, 13). Between Moses and Paul in God's unfolding revelation, Isaiah described a Suffering Servant who was so wounded and disfigured that others turned away from him, rejecting him as "stricken, smitten by God, and afflicted," although his grief was caused by their iniquities and his wounds brought them healing (Isa. 53:2–6).

In that nighttime conversation, Jesus pointed Nicodemus, one of Judaism's premier biblical scholars, to a road sign planted centuries earlier in the Sinai desert and the fourth book of Moses, in the historical experience of God's unruly but beloved people. The term *type* does not appear in Jesus' conversation with Nicodemus. Yet the substance of typology—patterns woven into the fabric of Israel's history, drawing hope forward toward God's great rescue through the promised Rescuer—is expressed in Jesus' simple analogy: "as Moses lifted up . . . , so must the Son of Man be lifted up" (John 3:14).

When we hear Jesus drawing parallels between ancient events and himself, it's as though we are eavesdropping on those Bible studies with his apostles in the forty days between his resurrection and his ascension. As we hear Christ providing Christ-centered explanations of biblical passages, we can learn how to pick up the clues in our own Bible reading, how to find and follow the paths that will lead us from all sorts of texts to Christ, the destination to which every trail in God's Word eventually leads. Paying attention to the road signs will sharpen our minds' eyesight and sensitize our hearts to discern the complex and coherent pattern of the Bible's single, central message.

Questions for Reflection and Discussion

1. Is there a problem with Augustine's explanation of the three floors of Noah's ark? If so, what is the problem?

2. When a New Testament author interprets an Old Testament individual, event, institution, or office as a *type* of Christ, how does this approach differ from what Augustine was doing?

3. What should we learn about biblical typology from Paul's use of *typos* terms in Romans 5 and 1 Corinthians 10 to interpret Old Testament passages?

4. What do the parallels between Romans 5 and 1 Corinthians 15 show us about the New Testament authors' reading of the Old Testament through typology, even where they do not use *typos* terms?

5. List and explain the different ways in which New Testament authors clearly identify Old Testament events, individuals, institutions, and offices as *types*—previews designed by God and embedded in ancient history and Scripture—pointing to Christ and his redemptive mission. Give example New Testament passages to illustrate the various ways.

6. To show that the New Testament writers learned to read the Old Testament "typologically" not only from Jesus himself but also from the ancient prophets, this chapter gives three examples of prior historical events and figures (creation, exodus/covenant, David) that *the Old Testament prophets evoked* as patterns (types!) to forecast great works of God to come in the future. Can you find other features in Israel's ancient history that *the prophets saw* as foreshadowing coming events? (Hint: Start with Matthew 2:17–18, and trace it back through Jeremiah 31:15 to Genesis 35:16–20. Notice places as well as people.)

7. How should we understand the Bible's use of language in such statements as the prediction that "I will set up over them one shepherd, my servant David" (Ezek. 34:23), or Paul's comment that "the Rock was Christ" (1 Cor. 10:4)? What misunderstandings of such statements should we avoid?

8. Why is the Lord's complete sovereignty over history absolutely indispensable in order for the Bible's typology to "work"—that is, so that the parallels that the New Testament draws between ancient events and individuals, on the one hand, and Christ, on the other, are not just the fruit of creative human imagination but the disclosure of God's own plan of redemption, worked out in time and space?

9. What does the account of the bronze serpent raised by Moses in the wilderness (Num. 21:4–9) reveal about the seriousness of sinful unbelief and discontent with God's provision? About the means that God would graciously provide, the price he would pay, to rescue us from his own judgment?

10. Can you think of other portions of the Bible, earlier and later, that show how fitting it was that God used *serpents* to judge his people in Numbers 21?

PART 4

Getting the Lay of the Land

4

The Covenant Fabric of the Bible: The Book of Divine-Human Bonding

WHEN WE TRAVEL well-labeled highways, marked by visible and clear road signs, we usually find it easy to reach our desired destination. When we come to intersections and crossroads and we see directional signs, we proceed without confusion or hesitation, confident that those placards will not send us off on wrong turns. Likewise, when New Testament texts explicitly identify Old Testament individuals (such as Adam, Rom. 5:14) or events (such as Israel's desert pilgrimage, 1 Cor. 10:11) or institutions (such as the tabernacle and its sacrifices, Heb. 10:1) as *types* or *shadows*, we can follow the route they mark for us easily and confidently, making our way from ancient events and institutions and individuals to the Bible's final destination, Jesus Christ. Even when special terms such as *type* are absent, when a New Testament author quotes an Old Testament text and comments that it has been "fulfilled" in Christ (e.g., God's son called out of Egypt, Matt. 2:15) or connects an Old Testament theme to Jesus by allusion or analogy ("Christ, our Passover lamb," 1 Cor. 5:7), we can still move confidently from Old Testament previews toward Jesus, who has brought into sharpest focus the whole array of God's gracious promises and his people's hopeful longings for rescue and renewal.

But what if you find yourself in a trackless forest? You see no road signs or trail markers. What seemed, when you set out on it, to be a well-worn path has disappeared into an impassable thicket, or has forked in two different directions. How do you find your way in that situation? It is one thing to read how the Lord provided water from the rock for grumbling Israelites (Ex. 17:1–7), and then to have Paul tell us that the rock represented Christ (1 Cor. 10:4). It is a very different thing to read Numbers 33, which lists the sites in the wilderness in which the Israelites pitched their camp over the four decades between their exodus from Egypt and their entrance into Canaan. Without guidance from the New Testament to point the way, how can we travel from Israel's wilderness itinerary to Christ? Must we (as Spurgeon's Welsh preacher said) find some way or other to climb over hedges and through ditches, or to chop our own path through unrelenting underbrush?

Suppose, however, that you are an experienced hiker. Though no trail can be seen, you have come upon a gently flowing creek. You know that every stream in those rolling hills eventually wends its way down to the lake in the valley and that beside the lake is a town that offers shelter from the coming storm. Which direction will you head? Will you wade upstream, pushing against the current? Will you splash across the stream and continue your trek at a ninety-degree angle from its bed? No. If you know your trailblazing craft, you will head downstream, following the flow of the water. Although you cannot foresee the creek's every twist and turn, you know that gravity is pulling its waters down to the lake. Its flow shows the lay of the land, and you know that you want to end up where that water is heading—down to the lake and the town.

This scenario illustrates the importance of paying attention to how a specific passage fits into the overall terrain, the big landscape, of the Bible. For all of the Bible's diversity of speakers and actors, people and places, prose and poetry, descriptions and demands, at its heart Holy Scripture is about the *relationship* of God the Creator to his human creatures. The books of the Bible trace the unfolding history of that relationship from (1) its pristine joy at creation, through (2) its disruption by our fall into sin, to (3) its restoration through God's merciful rescue, which is first (a) *anticipated* in the promises and previews in the Old Testament, then (b) *accomplished* by Jesus (in his obedient life, sacrificial death, and triumphant resurrection), now being (c) *applied* to our lives by the Holy Spirit, and finally to be (d) *consummated* in the new heavens and earth. Through all of the Bible's mountains and valleys, flatlands and rolling meadows and dense woods, "the lay of the land" is always this relationship between the personal Creator and his personal, human creatures, made in his own image.

The biblical way to say that the Bible is about the *relationship* of God and human beings is to say that it is about *covenant.* To get the lay of the land that shows how all roads (and even faint footpaths) lead to Scripture's metropolis—or, to shift the image slightly, to follow the current of each biblical stream as it flows toward the lake—we need to view the whole Bible as the book of the covenant, the book about the bond between our Creator-Lord and us, his creature-servants.

In this chapter and the next two, we will explore how seeing the "covenant thread" in the fabric of Scripture helps us to discover its Christ-centered unity. First we will see how the Bible itself reveals the importance of the theme of covenant, and we will survey the main features of that special relationship that the biblical writers call *covenant.* Then, in chapters 5 and 6, respectively, we will look more specifically at each party to the covenant relationship—the Lord and his human servant. We will survey the commitments of each to the other, and we will discover how Jesus fulfills these covenant commitments from both sides, as Lord and as Servant. Because Jesus is both the divine Son who keeps God's commitments to us and our human brother who keeps our commitments to God, he is the Mediator *and Guarantor* of the new and better covenant (Heb. 7:22; 8:6; 12:24). In fact, in an ultimate sense he is the *only* Mediator between God and man (1 Tim. 2:5).

Covenant as the Golden Thread Woven through the Fabric of Scripture

Open your Bible to the page just before Genesis 1, and then to the page just before Matthew 1. I am almost certain that on those two pages you will read the words *Old Testament* and *New Testament.*[1] Christian readers of the Bible are so accustomed to these terms that we might skip past those "title pages" for the two sections of Scripture without much thought; but we need to consider where these titles came from, and what they tell us about the structure and content of God's written Word.

---

1. If you are reading a study Bible, you will find an article introducing the book of Genesis between the page bearing the words *Old Testament* and the first page of Genesis itself, and an introductory article on Matthew between the page announcing the *New Testament* and the first chapter of the Gospel according to Matthew. But the fact remains: the two major sections of the Christian Bible are designated *Old Testament* and *New Testament*, and these terms go back many centuries, as we will see.

Consider, first, the implications of the words *Old* and *New*. They draw a distinction in time, between what came earlier and what has come later. In other words, they signal that the Bible's lay of the land is historical. Although the Bible displays a deep and amazing unity, it is not a single document written over a few years or even in a single generation. It is a whole library, penned by many different authors, and it is a library that grew for over a thousand years. That growth was integrally related to the history of the people to whom the Lord was speaking his Word.

Consider this comparison and contrast: The Bible shares some characteristics with the typical encyclopedia. Each is, in a sense, a library of information assembled on many topics by many authors over an extended period. But in its relation to time and history, the Bible is very different from an encyclopedia. Although Zoroaster lived long before Bach (and the article on Zoroaster might have been drafted before the same set's essay on Bach), in an encyclopedia you can expect to meet Bach in volume 2 and not come to Zoroaster until volume 26. In the library that we call the Bible, on the other hand, not only does its structure (in general) reflect the order in which its documents were composed, but also its content (in general) is anchored in the historical events that were happening as God was unfolding his written Word, chapter by chapter and book by book. The Bible is the self-disclosure of the God who does things in history, who does not "keep his place" as an aloof, safe, super-spiritual abstraction that we can admire or discuss from afar (as the deists of the eighteenth century thought). No, this is a God who "meddles" in the affairs of individuals and nations, who creates and calls and intervenes to rescue and to judge. The God who speaks in the Bible has an agenda for history, and he is on the move to direct history toward his good goal for his creation.

Because this God is on the move, history is moving in a specific direction, toward the future, from Old to New. The eons of human life on earth do not merely travel round and round in recurrent circles or cycles, as some Greek philosophers theorized—centuries of order and cool reason, followed by centuries of random chaos and wild sensuality, then back around again to good sense and restraint. No, the God who speaks and acts in the Scriptures of the Old and New Testaments, rather than running history around in circles, persistently drives it forward toward the goal for which he designed it—from an old paradise lost, through a costly mission to recapture the kingdom that is rightly his and to rescue and restore his subjects, and eventually on into a new heavens and a new earth, to a paradise regained by Christ, the last Adam, and regranted to his flawed and fallen people by God's atoning grace and his life-giving Spirit. So those simple words *Old* and *New* stand at the momentous boundary that lies between Malachi and Matthew, showing that the Bible's lay of the land is *historical*, tracing the unfolding story of the God who works out his victory plan in time and space.

Second, consider the word *Testament*. In our day, *testament* has legal overtones. It often appears in the term *last will and testament*, denoting the document by which an individual directs how his or her property is to be distributed to heirs when he or she has died. This contemporary usage provides valuable clues to the significance of *testament* as a term designating the two subdivisions of the Bible. We are on the right track when we hear *testament* and think of a *legal document*, and specifically when we think of a document in which *one individual unilaterally issues directives* that affect others, though they had no "input" into the decisions expressed in the document. To discover the full significance of this term as it appears in our Bibles, however, we need to trace its roots back through the history of Bible translation.

Our English word *testament* comes from the Latin word *testamentum*. Early Christian translators (most influentially the church father Jerome), as they brought the Bible from Hebrew, Aramaic, and Greek into Latin, used *testamentum* to try to convey the sense of the New Testament Greek term *diathēkē*. Like *testament* in English, *testamentum* in Latin and *diathēkē* in Greek typically referred to the document by which a wealthy nobleman would direct how his estate would be distributed after his death. The New Testament authors used *diathēkē* in such passages as Luke 22:20, 2 Corinthians 3, and Hebrews 7–10—passages that, as we will soon see, refer to God's promise in Jeremiah 31:31–34 to institute a "new covenant" to succeed the broken covenant of Mount Sinai. They used this term primarily because in the second century B.C., the Jewish scholars who produced the Septuagint (the Greek translation of the Old Testament that was used by both Jews and Christians by the time of the apostles) had most often used the Greek word *diathēkē* to translate the Hebrew word *berith*.

The translators of the Septuagint seem to have faced a dilemma when they came to *berith*. From the way in which *berith* was used in the Hebrew Scriptures, they could probably tell that *diathēkē* was not exactly equivalent to that Hebrew term. (Translators often face that challenge, since words in different languages don't exactly "overlap" each other in meaning.) In Hebrew, a *berith* is a solemn, legal bond in which one person sets the terms of the relationship and others are affected by the *berith*-initiator's decisions—often expressed in a written document. In these ways, a *berith* resembled a last will and testament in Greek and Roman law. But there was one crucial difference: in the Hebrew Scriptures, a *berith* was a solemn, legal commitment between *living persons*—a dominant king and a weaker king (2 Chron. 16:1–4), a husband and a wife (Mal. 2:14), a father-in-law and a son-in-law (in the case of Laban and Jacob, Gen. 31:44–54), and, of course, the Lord and Israel (Ex. 24:7–8). The *berith*-maker did not have to die in order for the requirements of the *berith* to be implemented. In that sense, it was more like a political treaty between nations or a commercial contract in business: it obligated the parties to keep their respective "ends of the bargain" as soon as it was ratified. Ancient Greek had another word that described legal commitments with obligations between living persons. It was *synthēkē*. But *synthēkē* usually referred to negotiated agreements worked out between equals through quid pro quo trade-offs and compromises. Obviously, the Lord's committed relationships with his creatures—the *berith* with Noah (and every other living creature, Gen. 9:8–17), and with Abraham (Gen. 15:18), and with Israel at Mount Sinai (Ex. 24:7–8), and with David (Ps. 89:3–4)—were *not* contracts negotiated between equal parties! The Lord set the terms through his promises and commands, and he announced the consequences for "breach of contract." His servants' role in the establishing of these *beriths*—these covenants—was simply to say, "Yes, sir!" and "Thank you!" to God's promises, and "We will!" and "Your wish is our command!" to God's requirements . . . and then, from that point on, to trust and obey.

So the Septuagint translators, to try to convey the significance of the Hebrew *berith* to their Greek-speaking readers, bypassed *synthēkē* and chose *diathēkē*, to capture the combination of legal commitment and God's sovereign authority in initiating that committed relationship between God and his people. Following their lead, Jerome chose *testamentum* in his translation of the New Testament.[2] Following Jerome's lead, the translators of many

2. Interestingly, in the Old Testament, which Jerome translated directly from Hebrew, he often translated the Hebrew *berith* with other Latin terms (*pactum* and *foedus*), which refer to treaties or compacts between living parties. But that's another story.

of our early English versions (including the Geneva Bible in the sixteenth century) chose *testament* for New Testament passages containing *diathēkē*. They also carried on the practice of designating the two parts of the Bible as *Old Testament* and *New Testament*.

English has another word that captures the concept that we are talking about (namely, a one-sided relationship in which the dominant party sets the rules), without the implication that the document goes into effect only after the dominant party dies. That word is *covenant*. The King James Version (1611), produced only a few decades after the Geneva Bible, used both *testament* (thirteen times) and *covenant* (twenty times) in New Testament texts where *diathēkē* appears in the Greek. More recent English versions (NASB, NIV, ESV), benefiting from further study in Scripture's covenant motif, consistently use *covenant* to represent *diathēkē* throughout the New Testament. So as we come to those pages just before Genesis 1 and Matthew 1, there is good reason to invest *Testament* with the fuller biblical significance that is expressed in the word *covenant*. In fact, the source of the old/new distinction in key biblical texts actually *requires* us to see the structure of Scripture as a whole as marked by the historical transition from an old *covenant* to a new *covenant*.

Jeremiah 31 and the Structure of the Scriptures

The basis for the age-old description of the Bible's two sections goes back to God's promise in Jeremiah 31:31–34. God spoke to his people in exile of a coming day of new beginnings—a "new covenant" that would not be like the bond he had made with their ancestors at Mount Sinai. Israel had violated that earlier covenant, and the people were suffering the consequences. But under the new covenant, God would write his law on the hearts of his people and forgive their sins once and for all, so that their disobedience and guilt could no longer disrupt their relationship with their covenant Lord.

What Jeremiah implied by calling the coming covenant "new" is spelled out in the New Testament: the bond that God made with the Israelites through Moses after rescuing them from Egypt was the "old covenant." Quoting Jeremiah 31:31–34, the epistle to the Hebrews comments: "In speaking of a new covenant, [God] makes the first one obsolete" (Heb. 8:13). The apostle Paul makes the same point in 2 Corinthians 3, where he says that he and other preachers of the gospel have now been appointed and qualified by God to be "ministers of a new covenant" (2 Cor. 3:3, 6). Then Paul goes on to describe the weekly reading of the law of Moses in Jewish synagogues as the reading of "the old covenant" (vv. 14–15). Paul and the author to the Hebrews are unfolding the implications of the fact that the Lord Jesus himself connected his death on the cross directly to God's "new covenant" promise in Jeremiah 31. In instituting the Lord's Supper the evening before his sacrifice, Jesus spoke of the wine: "This cup that is poured out for you is the new covenant in my blood" (Luke 22:20; see the similar wording of 1 Cor. 11:25). In the record of Matthew 26:28 and Mark 14:24, Jesus does not use the word *new*. Instead, he implies in other words that his death is about to establish a bond that replaces the covenant made at Sinai, alluding to Exodus 24:8 when he says that the cup of the Lord's Supper symbolizes "my blood of the covenant."

So the very structure of your Bible, with its two sections labeled *Old Testament* and *New Testament*, bears witness to the significance of the concept of *covenant*. This terminology comes from Jeremiah 31:31–34, in which God promises a "new covenant," and from the New Testament passages that show that Jesus has initiated this new covenant through his blood, shed in death for the forgiveness of sins.

The Components of Biblical Covenants

What does the Bible mean when it uses *covenant* to characterize the relationship of the Creator with his creatures, and specifically with human beings? We have seen that the Bible is about the *interpersonal* relationship of the *personal* Creator with his human creatures, the *persons* he made in his own image. And it is about the unfolding history of that relationship, from old to new. But of course, there are all sorts of relationships in the world: superficial acquaintances, business contracts, employment agreements, international treaties, friendship, casual dating, marriage, and more. The Bible applies the term *covenant* to some of these relationships, particularly those involving explicitly stated and structured obligations, such as marriage (Mal. 2:14) and the friendship covenant between Jonathan and David, which obligated David even after Jonathan's death (1 Sam. 18:3–4; 20:13–17; 23:16–18; 2 Sam. 9:1–13; 21:7). Covenants between the Lord and human beings are like some of these in some respects, and radically different from others in virtually every way. To pick up the clues to the lay of the land that the covenant focus of the Bible provides, we need a clear idea of the components that come together in the biblical covenants that bind God the covenant Lord to humans who are his covenant servants.[3]

The covenants in the Bible differ in various details, so a *definition* of *covenant* that comprehends all the divine-human covenants as we find them throughout Scripture could well turn out to be so general as to be unhelpful. Nevertheless, this working *description* helpfully captures, I believe, the main features that aid us in grasping the key components of the Lord's covenant bond with his human servants:

> The Lord's covenant with his human servants is a bond of interpersonal commitment involving exclusive loyalty, sovereignly instituted by the Lord, expressed through their mutual obligations, and enforced by life-or-death consequences.[4]

Let's examine these components one by one.

In the Bible, a covenant is, first, a *committed* relationship, a relationship of *exclusive loyalty*. Between the Lord and his people the bond is intimate and affectionate, so it is compared to marriage. As a husband who loves his wife passionately and expects her affection and fidelity in return, so the Lord is jealous for his people to love and trust him alone, not wandering after any other god. This bond is also legal and structured, so some biblical covenants have formal features that make them resemble international treaties among ancient Near Eastern monarchs. At the core of God's covenant with us is his demand for exclusive love, loyalty, and trust. He pledges his allegiance—he "plights his troth," as wedding services once said—to his people, and in return he expects them to love and obey him—and him alone—as their Lord and Protector.

Second, these bonds are *sovereignly instituted* by the Lord. They are not negotiated contracts between equals, but bonds between unequals (Lord

---

3. Theologians also speak, rightly I believe, of a "covenant of redemption" or "pact of salvation" that was entered into by God the Father and God the Son before the creation of the universe, in which each willingly committed himself to fulfill a distinctive role in the rescue and re-creation of the (to-be-created) people through whom the glory of God's grace would be displayed throughout the whole (to-be-created) heavens and earth. The Bible gives us brief glimpses of this compact (e.g., John 17:4–6); but the relationship of its Parties and its features differ so significantly from God's covenants with his creatures that we will exclude it from our discussion of how the covenant theme shows us the scriptural lay of the land that leads us to Jesus.

4. Expanded from O. Palmer Robertson, *The Christ of the Covenants* (Phillipsburg, NJ: P&R Publishing, 1980), 3–15. Robertson states concisely: "A covenant is *a bond in blood sovereignly administered.*" Ibid., 4 (emphasis in original).

and servant, Creator and creature, Sovereign and subordinate). Covenants are imposed by the Lord, whose powerful prior actions have made the covenant bond possible and create its context. He exercises his right to set covenantal terms. Covenants begin with what God has done (creation, exodus, cross); and from God's action flow the motive, rationale, and form for our response as his servants.

Third, the covenant loyalty between the Lord and his servants is more than emotional attachment. It is a costly commitment, to be lived out in action, in the keeping of *mutual obligations*. Words—or symbolic actions, which function as visible words—are crucial to God's covenants, for through his words and signs God binds himself to his people and binds his people to himself. God freely chooses to obligate himself through his promises, committing himself to rescue and protect his people. God obligates us through his commands. These obligations of the Lord and the servant in this covenant bond are not strictly parallel, of course. God is the Lord and we are the servant. He obligates us whether we want to be obligated or not, whether we "vote" to adopt his treaty or not! On the other hand, God freely and voluntarily obligates himself. Even in the beginning, when they were innocent and had not sinned, God did not *owe* it to his human creatures to engage them in covenant or to promise to bless them for the obedience that they owed him anyway.

Finally, there are *consequences* that will result, depending on the parties' performance of their respective obligations. In the Lord's covenants with his people, of course there can be no question about the Lord's faithfulness to fulfill his commitments (although his people sometimes have their doubts, Ps. 89:38–51). The Lord's very identity sets the norm for truth and trustworthiness, and his power and wisdom are boundless, so it is impossible for him to lie (Heb. 6:18) or to fail to deliver on what he has promised. On the other hand, the Bible is realistic about the possibility that the covenant servants will fail to keep their obligations, and thereby incur disastrously negative consequences. To be sure, from the outset of their covenant relationship, the Lord announced positive consequences that would follow if his servants stayed loyal and lived out their loyalty in obedient behavior: long life, thriving families and flocks, joy in his presence, and more. But the sober reality is that only one covenant Servant in all of human history actually kept his commitment flawlessly—and he, Jesus, was the Lord who became Servant both to obey and to suffer the consequences that his people deserved. Jesus came to keep the servant's obligation of loving, obedient loyalty on our beh..'f, and so to share with us the reward of eternal life in God's favor that his sinless perfection deserves. He also came to endure, on our behalf, the death that our own disloyal rebellion deserves, setting us free from that cursed consequence. Jesus' mission as covenant-keeper and curse-bearer in our place is the amazing grace that lies at the foundation of the covenant of grace.

These components can be seen often in the covenantal arrangements throughout the Bible. When you look carefully, the whole book of Deuteronomy has a structure that reflects these components: the commitment of exclusive loyalty (Deut. 6:4–5), its sovereign inauguration through the Lord's rescue in the exodus, preservation in the wilderness, and lawgiving on Sinai (chaps. 1–5), its implementation in concrete commands (chaps. 6–26), and its consequences (chaps. 27–30).

For simplicity, we can see them all in the Ten Commandments given to Moses in Exodus 20. Like the treaties that the kings of Israel's neighbors in the ancient Near East made with other kings in the region, God's covenant treaty with Israel begins with a little history of what the Lord has done to *show his commitment* to his covenant servant people by rescuing and protecting them from their enemies. In the books of Moses as a whole, the entire book of Genesis and the first nineteen chapters of Exodus fulfill this "prologue" function, but in the Ten Commandments it appears in brief as "I am the LORD your God, who brought you out of the land of Egypt, out of the house of slavery" (Ex. 20:2).

Unquestionably, this relationship has been *sovereignly initiated* by God's great acts of creation and liberation, and it is now being *sovereignly imposed* on the Israelites, whom he has redeemed from both slavery and death. These ten words are not the Lord's starting point for negotiations to which his people were free to make a counteroffer. In view of who he is and what he has done for them and in view of who they are and what they have received from him, the Lord's word will define their relationship from now on. Even when, having heard God's commands, they respond (as they should), "All the words that the LORD has spoken we will do" (Ex. 24:3), it is not as though they had other options: "No, thank you," or "These rules we accept, but not those."

Because the Lord has shown his own commitment in so faithful and merciful and powerful a way, Israel is obligated to respond with *commitment*—absolute, exclusive loyalty to the Lord. That is the point of the first commandment, which functions like an umbrella under which are gathered all the directives that follow it: "You shall have no other gods before me" (Ex. 20:3). In other words, "No rival, no competitor for your devotion, your affection, your trust and obedience is permitted in my presence!" A picture of this wholehearted, whole-person, exclusive commitment is seen in a good marriage, in which bride and groom keep their vows to be faithful, each to the other and to each other only. Later in the Old Testament, in fact, the Lord compares the covenant ceremony of Sinai to a wedding celebration and Israel's honeymoon period, when she and the Lord were head over heels in love with each other (Jer. 2:1–2).

The *mutual obligations* between the Lord and his servant people come to expression in the Ten Commandments, both in God's promises and, obviously, in his commands. Notice the promises that God freely chooses to embed in the Ten Commandments as reasons to motivate his servants' trusting obedience. Although treachery against the Lord by the worship of idols will bring disaster on rebels' grandchildren and great-grandchildren (a dire negative consequence!), our jealous God also shows "steadfast love to thousands [probably 'thousands of generations'] of those who love me and keep my commandments" (Ex. 20:6). Similarly, those who exhibit their honor for the Lord by honoring their parents will live "long in the land that the LORD your God is giving you" (v. 12)—a twofold promise both of life and of homeland!

Meanwhile, he also says in effect, in the commands themselves: "Not only must you be loyal to me, but your loyalty needs to show in *concrete actions*—not just warm, fuzzy feelings in your heart. Do not make images of me—as if anything you imagine could do justice to my glory (Ex. 20:4–6). Do not use my name lightly, calling me to witness and enforce oaths that you have no intention of keeping (v. 7). Do not defile the day that I have set apart for holy rest by my own example of resting in delight after I created the universe (vv. 8–11). Honor your parents, for they represent and administer my authority over you (v. 12). Do not murder: that is, hold human life in honor, for people are created in my image (v. 13). Do not commit adultery: that is, hold your marital vows as sacred and unbreakable, because your marriages are to be little replicas of my covenant bond with you, my people (v. 14). Do not steal: that is, respect my providence in giving things to others that I have not given to you (v. 15). Do not bear false witness: that is, speak truth, because I am truth (v. 16). Do not covet: that is, guard your heart from the lie that your happiness depends on getting what you do not have, rather than on discovering what you have in me (v. 17)."

The third component of covenants is *consequences*. Faithfulness brings blessing, but treason brings cursing. The Lord's promises, which he issued in support of the second and fifth commandments, predicted the favored and long life that would ensue if the Israelites loved the Lord and kept his commandments. On the other hand, two of the commandments mention the negative consequences that will fall on those who violate the Lord's commandments: Israel, the servant, must not serve images because her Lord is "a jealous God, visiting the iniquity of the fathers on the children to the third and the fourth generation of those who hate me" (Ex. 20:5). The adverse consequences of such covenant treason would harm multiple generations to come. Dire and dreadful consequences are implied, though not spelled out in detail, in the rationale for the third commandment: "You shall not take the name of the LORD your God in vain, for the LORD will not hold him guiltless who takes his name in vain" (v. 7). Later, when Israel was on the verge of entering the land that the Lord had promised to Abraham, Moses delivered an extended list of the consequences that would ensue if, on the one hand, Israel were to stay true to the Lord in the generations to come (Deut. 28:1–14) or if, on the other, Israel were to prove treacherous and unfaithful (as the Lord predicted she would): terrible, unspeakable torments that would fall on the Israelites and their descendants, as they would rightly deserve (vv. 15–68).

Having surveyed the components of biblical covenants, we now need to answer two more questions. Our first question concerns the extent to which the covenant thread runs through the entire fabric of God's Word. The second deals with the ways in which noticing covenant themes helps us to discern the paths in Scripture that lead us to Jesus.

Does the Covenant Theme Appear before Sinai?

Jeremiah 31 refers to God's covenant with the Israelites inaugurated at Mount Sinai and delivered through Moses "on the day when I took them by the hand to bring them out of the land of Egypt" (Jer. 31:32). Since this covenant at Sinai is contrasted with a promised "new covenant," New Testament authors call it "the old covenant" (2 Cor. 3:14; see Heb. 8:13). But some momentous events in God's relationship with his creation, and humanity in particular, occurred long before Israel arrived at that mountain: creation itself, our fall into sin, the flood of Noah's day, and God's call to Abraham, among others. If *covenant* is the biblical way to characterize God's relationship with his human image-bearers, do we see the covenant theme expressed in Scripture and in the early history of God's redemptive plan before Sinai? Indeed we do!

Let's work our way back in time toward the beginning. The exodus that set the Israelites free from centuries of slavery in Egypt and brought them to God's mountain in the wilderness was the result of the Lord's "remembering" and keeping his promises to their ancestors, the patriarchs Abraham, Isaac, and Jacob. "And God heard their groaning, and God remembered his covenant with Abraham, with Isaac, and with Jacob" (Ex. 2:24). As we trace this thread back into the life of Abraham, we learn that God made a covenant with Abraham, promising the aged, childless nomad that one day his children would be as countless as the stars in the sky, and that they would eventually enjoy a land to call "home" (Gen. 15:18). (At the end of this chapter, as we put into practice this "lay of the land" perspective, we will examine the bizarre ratification ceremony by which God sealed his covenant commitment to Abraham.) The Lord also established a covenant sign, circumcision, which was to be applied to each male in Abraham's household, both sons and slaves (Gen. 17). In fact, those not circumcised were to be excluded from the community of the Lord's covenant with Abraham. So God's covenant with Abraham exhibited the covenant components that we have discussed—God's sovereign initiation, exclusive interpersonal commitment, mutual obligations (the Lord's promises primarily, but also Abraham's response of trust, displayed in action), and ultimate consequences. Established more than four centuries before Moses, the Lord's covenant commitment to Abraham set the context for Israel's release from Egypt and consecration as the Lord's treasured people at Sinai.

Even earlier, after God's floodwaters purged the ancient world of human evil run rampant, the Lord made a covenant with Noah and his family and all other living things, designating his rainbow in the clouds as a sign of his promise not to use water to wash the world clean of human filth ever again (Gen. 9:9–17). In this covenant, the Creator's commitment embraced more than a particular individual or family or national group. As supreme Judge, he promised to withhold his final judgment for a time, to sustain the orderly succession of seasons; and he made that promise to the whole order of living beings, human and subhuman, on earth. This blessing of the orderly variation of sunshine and rain, warmth and cold, would not be a "consequence" dependent on creatures' fulfilling their covenant obligations. Rather, the Lord of the covenant secured it by his unilateral promise. His covenant commitment to all creaturely life on earth established an ongoing, stable global context in which he would pursue his special, redemptive covenant agenda for his special people, set apart by his sovereign grace, as we see in Abraham's life.

The earliest appearances of the word *covenant* are in the narrative about Noah (Gen. 6:18 and repeatedly in Gen. 9). But it would be premature to conclude from the absence of the word that God had no covenant relationship with human beings before the flood. For one thing, God's authorization to Noah when the floodwaters receded, which is an extension of the covenant commitment signified in the rainbow, echoes God's words to the first man and woman at the very dawn of history: "Be fruitful and multiply and fill the earth. The fear of you and the dread of you shall be upon every beast of the earth and upon every bird of the heavens, upon everything that creeps on the ground and all the fish of the sea. . . . Every moving thing that lives shall be food for you. And as I gave you the green plants, I give you everything" (9:1–3). This echo raises the intriguing possibility that God's original relationship with the first man and woman, Adam and Eve, was in fact a covenant without the label.

As tantalizingly brief as the account of the creation and commissioning of the first human beings is in Genesis 1–2, do we see indications that their relationship with their Creator exhibited the components that we have seen converging to define biblical covenants? Was their relationship with their Creator sovereignly initiated by him? Absolutely! He not only made them, but also engaged them through words by which he both empowered and obligated them:

> And God blessed them. And God said to them, "Be fruitful and multiply and fill the earth and subdue it and have dominion over the fish of the sea and over the birds of the heavens and over every living thing that moves on the earth." And God said, "Behold, I have given you every plant yielding seed that is on the face of all the earth, and every tree with seed in its fruit. You shall have them for food." (Gen. 1:28–29).

Was their relationship to be a commitment of exclusive loyalty? Indeed, they were to believe his words implicitly and to base their decisions on those words, even when Satan, speaking through a serpent, invited them to doubt both their generous Lord's motives and his veracity (Gen. 2:15–17; 3:1–5). Were there mutual obligations? The presence of the tree of life in God's garden symbolized his freely made promise of abundant life in his favor and presence forever (2:9; 3:22). As his servants, Adam and Eve were certainly obligated to obey both his positive commands to work the earth and rule other creatures and his negative prohibition against eating from the tree of the knowledge of good and evil. Were there consequences? Disastrously, yes. God had announced beforehand that death would ensue if the man and woman disregarded his word: "in the day that you eat of [the tree of the knowledge of good and evil] you shall surely die" (2:17). So our first parents' unbelief and rebellion brought disruption and shame to their relationship with their Creator, death to themselves and all their children, disorder to their relation to each other, and frustration to their tasks (3:8–12, 16–19).

All the covenant components were there, so it seems that at the very beginning God created Adam and Eve to be in covenant with him. That, in fact, is what is implied in a striking comparison drawn by the later prophet Hosea, who compared Israel's rebellion and violation of the covenant at Sinai with Adam's first sin in eating the forbidden fruit: "But like Adam they transgressed the covenant; there they dealt faithlessly with me" (Hos. 6:7). Of course, this earliest covenant does not include all the detailed rituals and documents that would be associated with later covenants. In later covenants, for instance, animal sacrifices and blood symbolized the dreadful consequences that would ensue if the covenant servant were to break faith with his Lord (Ex. 24:4–8; Jer. 34:18–20). (We will revisit the significance of these rituals at the end of this chapter, using the covenant theme to understand a specific Old Testament passage, Genesis 15.) Nevertheless, as Hosea looks all the way back to the beginning and then to Sinai in the less-distant past, he sees that his Israelite kinfolk are fallen, traitorous children of Adam, and that like their father they have broken the Lord's covenant. That bad news implies that when God made the man and woman in his own image, the committed relationship that he established with them was a covenant. The Protestant pastors who gathered in Westminster Abbey in London in the 1640s to formulate a fresh summary of the Bible's teaching came to the same conclusion that we have reached: "The first covenant made with man was a covenant of works, wherein life was promised to Adam; and in him to his posterity, upon condition of perfect and personal obedience" (Westminster Confession of Faith [WCF] 7.2).

Now, physical death did not befall Adam and Eve at the very moment of their rebellion, although the seeds of guilt and shame had been sown and would in time produce their bitter harvest of pain and destruction. Why not? Clearly, Adam and Eve's original relationship with God—their covenant of complete commitment and communion with their Creator—had been shattered. Would it be replaced by a hopeless stretch of ongoing existence, altogether disconnected from the Lord who had given them life, until they finally succumbed to death and decay in the dust? Surprisingly, no. (Well, perhaps not so surprising for Moses' first Israelite readers or for us, since we like they have experienced mercy despite what we deserve from the Creator, whose lavish love will not let us go off so easily into our self-chosen, self-made destruction. But still, what comes next should fill us with wonder!) Immediately after Adam and Eve's fall into sin, Genesis describes God's establishing of a new and different kind of relationship, a "covenant of grace," as the pastors at Westminster called it:

> Man, by his fall, having made himself incapable of life by that covenant, the Lord was pleased to make a second, commonly called the covenant of grace; wherein he freely offereth unto sinners life and salvation by Jesus Christ; requiring of them faith in him, that they may be saved, and promising to give unto all those that are ordained unto eternal life his Holy Spirit, to make them willing, and able to believe. (WCF 7.3)

This time, the promise of eternal life in joyful communion with the Creator would not depend on the first Adam's performance of "perfect and personal obedience" (WCF 7.2). Instead, it would depend on the perfect, personal obedience of a second Adam, Jesus Christ, which would then be bestowed as a free gift, unearned and undeserved, on guilty sinners who simply have faith in Christ. In this covenant the Lord binds himself to bless his guilty but trusting servants despite their infidelity, on the basis of a Substitute's covenant-keeping, graciously credited to those who would, left to themselves, be liable only to covenant curse. Was the Assembly at Westminster right to hear, amid the wreckage of Genesis 3, hints of a restored relationship, sovereignly initiated and defined by God, entailing exclusive loyalty and commitments spelled out in mutual obligations, with consequences to follow?

Even though we do not see in Genesis 3 all the details that appear in later covenant-making rituals, we do hear God committing himself by a promise to separate Eve from her lethal alliance with the enemy, Satan, and ultimately to destroy that enemy (3:15). And we see God covering Adam and Eve's shame through bloodshed, the death of animals with whose skins God clothed them (v. 21). This different type of covenant appears in seed form in Genesis 3:15, which students of Scripture have often called the *protoevangelium*, the "first gospel":

> I will put enmity between you and the woman,
>   and between your offspring and her offspring;
> he shall bruise your head,
>   and you shall bruise his heel. (Gen. 3:15)

God addresses these words to Satan, the archliar and archmurderer, who spoke through the serpent and lured Eve (and her husband with her) into his lie and so into guilt and death. In cursing the evil tempter, God implicitly promised rescue to those who had let themselves be duped by the devil's lies.

In fact, this first postfall covenant, brief as it is, brings into view the participation of both parties to the covenant, Lord and servant, in undoing the damage done through Adam's failure. At this early stage, the wording is very general: "*I* will put enmity between you [Satan/the serpent] and the woman, and between your offspring [the enemy's allies down through the generations] and her offspring [Eve's descendants, ultimately focused in a single Descendant]; *he* [that singular Descendant] shall bruise your head, and you shall bruise his heel." Entailed in this terse curse on the evil one is the announcement that the bringing of redemption to mankind is both God's gift and man's accomplishment. We see God's initiative in his promise, "I will put enmity between [the serpent] and the woman." The Lord will not leave Eve a guilt-ridden and helpless captive in thrall to her deceiver and destroyer. But we also see a crucial role for the woman's offspring, a human being who will be a faithful covenant Servant, who through his own suffering (his heel bruised) will crush the evil one's power (bruise Satan's head).

Now we can connect the clues in Genesis 3, which signal God's commitment to rescue and restore sin-stained people to covenant communion with himself, to the "road signs" that we observed in the previous chapter, the comparison and contrast between Adam and Christ that Paul drew in Romans 5 and 1 Corinthians 15. Genesis 3:15 is God's hint that, though

Jesus the second Adam (the covenant-keeping Adam) would not appear in history for many centuries, his eventual arrival was sure and his victory over Satan secure. The first Adam, choosing and acting on behalf of all his natural children as our covenant representative, plunged us all into condemnation and the sentence of death. The last Adam, already promised in that tiny seed of hope implied in God's sentence of doom on the devil, would arise in due time not only to endure the poisonous curse that our breach deserved (his heel "bruised") but also to keep the covenant commitments that neither our father Adam nor we could keep. The pastors gathered at Westminster were right to see the whole history of humanity's relationship with our Maker—the whole sweep of the Bible's narrative—as fabric interwoven and held together by the golden thread of covenant—first, the covenant of works that Adam broke, and then the covenant of grace that Jesus kept on believers' behalf.

Conclusion

How does the golden covenant thread inform our grasp of God's Word? A more complete answer to this question will come in the next two chapters, as we examine in turn the role of the two parties to the divine covenants, God the covenant Lord and his human servants. Here, by way of anticipation, consider how our reading of every portion of the Bible is enriched as we recall that its very fabric is permeated with the theme of the relationship between the Creator and his human creatures—a relationship that is sovereignly initiated and defined by the Lord, that entails exclusive interpersonal loyalty and commitment, that is given texture by mutual obligations (his free promises and his commands for our character and conduct), and that presents future trajectories of consequences, either of unimaginable joy or of unbearable torment.

In chapters 7 through 9, we will notice ways that, by virtue of their distinctive roles and responsibilities, Israel's official leaders—prophets, priests, kings, sages, judges—tended either to reproduce Adam's covenant failure or to preview, in finite and flawed ways, Christ's complete and flawless covenant faithfulness. Here we can observe that it is also true for every rank-and-file Israelite (or foreigner) who appears on the pages of Scripture that he or she (like each of us) stands related to God by way of covenant. The *New England Primer* taught children in the American colonies not only the alphabet but also sound biblical truth when it introduced the letter *A* with the couplet: "In Adam's fall / We sinned all." No person whom we meet in the Bible (or, for that matter, in our everyday lives) enjoys an independent life, utterly unrelated to the God who made him or her. Every natural child of Adam (and that is every one of us) is implicated in our ancestor's violation of that pristine covenant of works at history's dawn. Given the opportunity, every one of us consequently follows his lead in breaching, again and again, the bond that should have linked us to the Lord in the closest of interpersonal communion. The Bible's every record of human sin, whether "large" or "small" in our eyes, compounds the indictment of our ingrate race's defiance of the Lord whose friendship is life and our preference for the lie that breeds nothing but death. So every page of Scripture that speaks of human failure and faithlessness whets our hearts' appetite for the coming of the woman's offspring, who would love and serve the Lord with heart, soul, strength, and mind.

On the other hand, every figure in Scripture's pages who maintains loyalty and keeps commitments, however fleetingly, gives a glimpse of paradise lost, of the image of God that once reflected the Creator in untarnished radiance but has since suffered distortion and defilement. Every truthful word and trustworthy deed produced by Adam's morally mottled children also gives glimpses of two rays of hope: First, Eve's very flawed offspring down through the generations, distinguished from the serpent's offspring (Isaac vs. Ishmael, Jacob vs. Esau, David vs. Saul, etc.), point our hopes ahead to the final arrival of Eve's flawless offspring, Jesus. Second, the glimmers of covenant faithfulness that make their way to the surface in the lives of Old and New Testament believers, damaged though they still are, give evidence of a revitalization project that God's gracious Spirit has set in motion deep within them.

So when we see in Scripture scenes of other covenant relationships that function somewhat as they should—exclusive commitment expressed in promises and commands kept and yielding interpersonal delight—then every such scene should lift our minds and hearts to appreciate the redemptive bond that is the template for all such creaturely replicas. When a husband like Hosea loves and goes on loving a wife who scorns his love, he becomes a reflection of the heavenly husband who pursues his unfaithful bride and will not let her (us) go. When Israel celebrates a royal wedding (Ps. 45), the beauty and joy of both bride and groom offer glimpses of the consummation of God's covenant with his beloved people. The friendship of Jonathan, the royal prince who gladly risked his life and relinquished his throne to David, the man of God's choosing, displays the costliness of covenant commitment. Such selfless devotion whets our soul's longing for a friend who loves with such constancy and commitment. The golden covenant thread interwoven throughout the tapestry of Scripture leads us to Christ. The mountain stream of covenant motifs shows us the lay of the land, how everything in biblical history, law, wisdom, prophecy, and more slopes and flows toward Jesus, the reservoir of God's glory and grace.

Putting It into Practice: Fire between the Carcasses (Genesis 15:7–21)

Genesis 15 narrates a strange covenant-ratification ceremony. Although God had already made great promises to Abraham, here for the first time we read, "On that day the LORD made a *covenant* with Abram" (15:18). God had previously called Abraham to travel from Mesopotamia "to the land that I will show you" and promised to bless Abraham and to make him a means of blessing to "all the families of the earth" (12:1–3). Upon his arrival in the Promised Land, Abraham received God's promise that it would one day belong to "your offspring" (v. 7). Yet when God again spoke in Genesis 15:1, Abraham was still childless. In response to Abraham's complaint, God promised descendants as countless as the stars in the night sky. Abraham "believed the LORD," yet still he wondered, "O Lord GOD, how am I to know that I shall possess" the land (15:6, 8)?

To confirm his promises of offspring and land, the Lord instructed Abraham to make preparations for a solemn rite of covenant ratification. Abraham was to slay a heifer, a goat, a ram, and two birds, cut the carcasses of the larger animals in half, and arrange the bloody pieces in two rows on the ground, creating a gruesome corridor of death. This is the ancient ritual referred to centuries later by the weeping prophet, Jeremiah (Jer. 34:18–20). In Jeremiah's day, the leaders and people of Judah had entered a covenant with the Lord by dividing a slain calf in two and passing between the split halves of its carcass. (This could be why the Hebrew Scriptures speak of "cutting" a covenant in Genesis 15, Jeremiah 34, and elsewhere.) By doing so, they said, in effect, "We promise to free our Israelite slaves, as God's law requires; and if we fail to keep our covenant commitment, may we be ripped limb from limb like this calf and made carrion for birds of prey." In response to the Lord's command, they made a commitment with serious consequences. Those who passed between the carcasses were sealing their word with their blood, placing their lives on the line. In a similar rite at Sinai, the splashing of the blood of slain animals on the Lord's altar and on the Lord's people delivered the same graphic message: as the Lord sealed his promises with his very life, so his people also swore their allegiance and steadfast obedience on their very lives (Ex. 24:3–8). Woe be to either party, Lord or servant, should he prove false!

Now, in view of all that the Bible reveals about the utter faithfulness of God the covenant Lord and the instability of sinful covenant servants such as Abraham, we would anticipate that in Genesis 15, even though the issue is the reliability of God's promises, the next step would be the Lord's directive for *Abraham* to walk through those gruesome tokens of covenant curse. After all, it is Abraham who shaded the truth not once but twice, fearing human sheiks more than the Sovereign Lord who had called his name (Gen. 12:11–20; 20:1–18). Instead, however, we read that "a deep sleep fell on Abram," and that as he lay sedated, "a smoking fire pot and a flaming torch" (a preview of the pillar of cloud and fire in the desert) passed through the corpses of the sacrificed animals (15:12, 17). The Lord himself—the God of truth whose word sets the standard for truth, the ever-living God who cannot die—secured his word with his life to assure his servant of his boundless commitment to fulfill all that he had promised: countless descendants like the starry sky, and a land to call home.

Later, God would reaffirm his commitment to Abraham in the words of an oath: "By myself I have sworn . . . . I will surely bless you, and I will surely multiply your offspring as the stars of heaven and as the sand that is on the seashore" (Gen. 22:16–17). Among ancient pagans, to swear an oath was to invoke the gods as witnesses of a covenant and enforcers of its commitments. For Abraham, the Lord "swore by himself," summoning himself (since there is no deity as mighty as he) to inflict the curse on himself if he should fail to keep his commitments to Abraham. This is why Hebrews 6:13–18 says that God secured his promise to Abraham by two unchangeable things—first, his *word* of promise, and then the *oath* by which he bound his own life to the promise—to give Abraham strong encouragement to hold fast to God's word of commitment.

This is the meaning of the strange covenant-ratification ritual of Genesis 15: The Lord who has every right to demand unwavering trust and complete devotion binds himself in covenant to servants whose faith and faithfulness are flawed and fluctuating. His commitment to bestow blessing on those who deserve covenant curse is sealed not only by his ever-reliable word but also by his very life.

Now, notice the surprising way in which Jesus meets us in this bizarre event, in which the Lord's servant Abraham sleeps as the Lord puts his own life in jeopardy: In the fullness of time, this gracious and faithful covenant Lord would in fact endure his own curse, not because he had failed to keep his word but precisely *in order to* keep his covenant commitment to unfaithful people like us. Only by absorbing the curse that we had earned for ourselves by defying his majesty and denying his authority could he justly bestow blessing on all who, like Abraham, cling to him in dependent trust. Later in the books of Moses, we read that hanging an executed lawbreaker's body on a tree signaled his cursedness before God (Deut. 21:23). That is precisely the way that Jesus was executed; and the form of his exposure in death was not lost on Paul, who applied this Deuteronomy text to Christ's cross:

> Christ redeemed us from the curse of the law by becoming a curse for us—for it is written, "Cursed is everyone who is hanged on a tree"—so that in Christ Jesus the blessing of Abraham might come to the Gentiles, so that we might receive the promised Spirit through faith. (Gal. 3:13–14)

So the covenant that God cut with Abraham graphically foreshadows the ultimate price that the covenant Lord would pay in order to spare his curse-deserving servants and to keep his promise to bestow, in place of the wrath we deserve, the indescribable blessing of life in his friendship and favor forever.

Questions for Reflection and Discussion

1. What do the titles of the two divisions of our Bibles—*Old Testament* and *New Testament*—reveal about the lay of the land for the terrain of God's Word, from Genesis to Revelation (the "golden thread" woven through the tapestry of Scripture)? What do the words *Old* and *New* highlight? What reality lies behind *Testament*?

2. How is the Bible put together differently from an encyclopedia set? How should the Bible's principle of organization influence the way we read it?

3. When you approach the Bible as a book about God's *relationship* with us, his human image-bearers (not merely a handbook of doctrinal concepts or ethical instruction, though it reveals both inerrant truth

105

and authoritative norms), how should that influence your purposes and expectations in reading and studying it?

4. How are the Lord's covenants with his people like and unlike a last will and testament? How are they like and unlike a negotiated contract between equal partners?

5. What New Testament evidence supports the claim that the new covenant promise of Jeremiah 31:31–34 unveils the fundamental structure of the Bible and of God's redemptive purpose being worked out in human history?

6. What are the main components of God's covenants with his human servants in the Bible? How do the Ten Commandments (and their prologue) in Exodus 20:1–17 illustrate each of these components?

7. Jeremiah 31 refers to the giving of God's law to Israel through Moses at Sinai, and Paul calls the law delivered at this event "the old covenant" (2 Cor. 3:14). What evidence can be found in Scripture that God related to humanity through covenants *even before Sinai*, with Abraham and Noah and Adam? Why is this important to our understanding of the work of Jesus as Mediator of the new covenant?

8. How do God's words of judgment to the serpent (Satan) in Genesis 3:15 hint at features of a "covenant of grace" that God had prepared for fallen humans like Eve, like us?

9. How did the strange ritual of Genesis 15:9–21—the flaming torch that passed between pieces of slain animals, as Abraham was in a deep sleep—answer Abraham's question: "O Lord God, how am I to know that I shall possess [this land]?" What does this rite reveal about the Lord's commitment to keep his oath to those who trust him?

10. Here's a challenge: Read through Israel's pilgrimage itinerary in Numbers 33, trying to answer these questions: How does the Bible's covenantal lay of the land cast light on the significance of this list of campsites in the Sinai Peninsula? (Notice details in verses 3–4, 9, 38–39, 40, 48–49.) How does this travelogue fit into the bigger story of God's covenant promises to his people?

5

Jesus the Strong and Faithful Lord: Sovereign Protector of His People

THE PERVASIVE THEME that ties the whole Bible together is the relationship between God the personal Creator and his personal, human creatures, whom he made in his own image. The Bible is not just a collection of books about God or about other theological themes or doctrines. In it God certainly does reveal truth about himself, about the universe and planet Earth that we inhabit, about our identity as human beings, and about his agenda for his cosmos. But all the truths that we discover in God's Word are not merely pieces of accurate information, such as those that we might pick up by reading a set of encyclopedias. They are integrated in what the apostle Paul called "the pattern of . . . sound words" (2 Tim. 1:13), a systematic network of interrelated truths. In fact, the truth revealed in the Bible is not only orderly and interconnected, but also focused on the Creator's relationship with his personal creatures. He designed us to be miniature replicas of his infinite personality and, more than that, to collaborate in his realm and consciously to enjoy his communion.

We have seen that the Bible's name for this relationship is *covenant*. This covenant theme is like a golden thread running through the whole fabric of Scripture, unifying the tapestry of God's unfolding plan for history. Or, to invoke our traveling metaphor, we could say that encountering covenant themes in God's Word is like coming across a stream in a mountain forest that shows us "the lay of the land" and directs us to our desired destination—to Jesus, "the mediator of a new covenant" (Heb. 9:15; 12:24) and the "one mediator between God and men" (1 Tim. 2:5).

Our survey of Scripture's descriptions of the Lord's covenants with his servant people yielded this description:

> The Lord's covenant with his human servants is a bond of interpersonal commitment involving exclusive loyalty, sovereignly instituted by the Lord, expressed through their mutual obligations, and enforced by life-or-death consequences.

We have considered the various components of the covenant relationship—commitment, commands and promises, consequences. In this chapter and the next, we turn our attention to the parties in the covenant, the divine Lord and his human servants. What are their respective roles, and how do those roles find fulfillment in the person and redemptive mission of Jesus Christ to restore us to his Father's covenant favor?

In this chapter, we explore some of the main ways that Scripture speaks of God's role as the Lord of the covenant, and how Jesus the God-man fulfills those roles. In the next, our focus will be on the calling of human beings as servants bound in covenant to their Creator, and how the incarnate Christ answers that calling to perfection for our sake. As we consider the Bible's presentation of God as covenant Lord, we will touch on five themes:

(1) The *identity* of the Lord as triune—simultaneously one and interpersonal.
(2) The Lord's *preparation and initiation* of his covenant with humanity, in creation and redemption.
(3) The Lord as *Provider*, loving husband for his bride and faithful shepherd for his sheep.
(4) The Lord as *Commander*, directing the thoughts, words, and deeds of his servants.
(5) The Lord as *Judge* of his servants and his enemies.

The Triune Lord of the Covenant

The opening sentence of the Bible introduces the Lord of the covenant: "In the beginning, God created the heavens and the earth" (Gen. 1:1). In these first words of the first book of Moses, we are introduced to a single, Sovereign God—not a host of competing, combative, or even cooperative deities, but one incomparable Creator; not a primordial soup of impersonal matter, but the supremely personal Architect and Artisan whose spoken word gave existence to the cosmos and its contents. This Lord is not a part of the created universe that is limited in time (since it had a beginning) and in space. Rather, he created everything else that is: both what we see ("the earth") and what we do not see ("the heavens"), as the inversion in Paul's couplets commenting on Genesis 1:1 shows:

> For by him all things were created,
> In heaven and on earth,
> Visible and invisible. (Col. 1:16)

This sovereign, self-existent Creator is distinct from and independent of all things created.

Yet before "the beginning," before he produced the cosmos, this singular, supreme Creator was not solitary, and certainly not lonely. For Genesis' first audience (recently freed slaves in the Sinai desert, who traced their bloodlines back to Abraham), Moses' first book came bundled with four others—Exodus, Leviticus, Numbers, and Deuteronomy. The context of the entire Pentateuch offers tantalizing clues about the identity of this one God. In Genesis 1:1, we learn that God created everything. Then in verse 2, we glimpse "the Spirit of God" hovering over the face of the waters. This God has a Spirit who is distinguishable from himself. In Genesis 2, another name, rendered "Lord" in our English versions, appears alongside "God" (2:5–8). Israelites after the exodus would recognize this as the personal name of the covenant-keeping God who called Moses at a burning bush to lead them to freedom (Ex. 3:13–16). But something surprising comes to light in Moses' meeting with "the Lord, the God of [our] fathers," at that bush that burned without burning up. "The angel of the Lord" who appeared to Moses (v. 2), an august messenger sent by the Lord, was actually the Lord himself: "I am the God of your father, the God of Abraham, the God of Isaac, and the God of Jacob" (v. 6). So on the one hand, the Pentateuch declares with unmistakable clarity, "The Lord our God, the Lord is one" (Deut. 6:4). On the other, the books of Moses also hint that this singular covenant Lord is not solitary. His Spirit hovers over the deep, and the Lord's messenger is also the Lord himself.

These hints that the Creator who calls us into covenant is one and, mysteriously, more than one launch the Bible's progressive unveiling of the living God as Trinity—three persons who are one in divine essence, equal in power and glory, and eternally interrelating with one another in perfect love. Through the prophet Isaiah centuries after Moses, the Lord promised to send a child, a son descended from David, who would be called "Mighty God, Everlasting Father" (Isa. 9:6). Isaiah also declared that the glory of the Lord in Israel's wilderness camp (Ex. 33:8–11, 14) had been the splendor of "the angel of his presence" and "his Holy Spirit" (Isa. 63:9–11). When we turn from Old Testament to New, the truth that God is one is reaffirmed (Mark 12:29; Rom. 3:30; 1 Cor. 8:4–6). We also learn that the Son, sent by the Father, is no less than God himself (John 1:1, 14; 10:30–33; Rom. 9:5). The Spirit, too, is divine and personal, since lying to God's Holy Spirit is lying to God himself (Acts 5:3–5, 9), and the Spirit, like the Son, prays on believers' behalf (Rom. 8:26–27, 34).

Much more biblical support could be offered for the biblical teaching that God is triune. This small survey serves a specific purpose: to show how fitting it was for God the Father, God the Son, and God the Spirit, who eternally enjoy interpersonal delight in one another, to make personal creatures in the divine image designed to be introduced into interpersonal communion with this triune God. Here and there the Bible gives glimpses of a pretemporal compact among the Trinity's three persons, for the purpose of displaying the glory of their divine grace in a redemptive plan worked out in human history. In his High Priestly Prayer, Jesus said that "before the world existed" the Father gave him a not-yet-born people, whom the Son committed himself to redeem by fulfilling the mission assigned by the Father (John 17:4–6). To secure the success of that mission, when the Son took on our humanity, God's Spirit anointed him not only to proclaim God's good news in words and deeds (Luke 4:18–21) but also to sacrifice his life to establish the new, better, unbreakable covenant that would bind believers' hearts to their Lord forever and ever (Heb. 9:14–15). As we see God the Son, the covenant Lord, in action throughout the history of redemption, we are encountering the divine Father who sent him and the divine Spirit who empowered him for his redemptive, covenant-establishing mission.

The Lord Prepares and Initiates the Covenant

International treaties between ancient Near Eastern kings and chieftains typically opened with a historical prologue that summarized the events that led up to their alliance. Not surprisingly, these introductory narratives tended to highlight the ways that the dominant party had helped and rescued the dependent, subordinate party. The steadfast loyalty of the lesser ruler should be secured by this rehearsal of the debt of gratitude he owed to his powerful protector.

Biblical covenants between the Lord and his servant people employ the same logic. The miniature prologue that introduces the Ten Commandments—"I am the LORD your God, who brought you out of the land of Egypt, out of the house of slavery" (Ex. 20:2)—fulfills this function for the covenant commitment executed at Mount Sinai. In a larger sense, so do the narrative of Genesis (creation, fall, flood, God's call to Abraham) and the early chapters of Exodus (Moses' call, the ten plagues, and Israel's exit from Egypt). The Lord had made extensive preparations for his covenant relationship with his human servants. The care and generosity he had displayed were strong grounds for his servants' response of wholehearted devotion and exclusive loyalty. We will consider God's preparations first from the standpoint of his work as Creator and then in terms of his work as Redeemer.

As Creator, God Made the Universe as the Ideal Setting for His Covenant of Works with Adam and Eve

The descriptions in Genesis 1 and 2, which portray the order, beauty, and bounty of the home that God prepared for his human image-bearers, show that they had every conceivable reason to trust and obey as loyal subjects and allies of the Lord who had brought them into covenant with himself. As God spoke his cosmos into existence, he set it all in order by separating light from darkness, upper from lower waters, seas from dry land. Then he populated the realms with lights, birds and fish, and beasts domesticated and wild. He paused to observe how good his handiwork was (Gen. 1:4, 10, 12, 18, 21, 25). Finally he created the first human couple, male and female, giving them dominion over other earthbound creatures. With this capstone of creation completed, "behold, it was very good" (1:31). Genesis 2 details the goodness of the garden planted by God to be his covenant servants' special home, the sanctuary in which they might enjoy his presence. Its trees were pleasant to behold and its fruit good to eat (2:9), its waters plentiful and its other resources abundant (2:10–14). For the man whose design in God's likeness entailed capacity for covenant communion, God created the woman, a companion and helper who fit him perfectly (2:18–25).

111

The home (cosmos, earth, and garden) that the Lord so lavishly prepared for their enjoyment was far beyond anything that mere creatures (even good and godly creatures) had any right to demand from their Creator. His generous preparation underscored the obligation that was already theirs by virtue of their very existence, to maintain covenant loyalty by keeping the Lord's word in perfect, personal obedience to his directives and to his prohibition.

Scripture speaks often of God's role as Creator. Even after Adam's fall subjected the earth and its occupants to "futility" and "bondage to corruption" (Rom. 8:20–21), still the Creator's perfections are displayed through his cosmos (1:20) as the heavens declare his glory (Ps. 19:1). The starry host overhead announces "the everlasting God, the Creator of the ends of the earth" (Isa. 40:28). Standing before our Maker humbles us (Job 4:17) and moves us to worship (Ps. 95:6) with joy (149:2). Wherever we hear this theme in the Bible, it should direct our thoughts to the role of God the Son as Lord in creation. The Creator, who is one, is also triune—three divine persons united in one divine essence. Eons before God the Son became our human brother as Jesus of Nazareth, he carried out the Father's plan in the creation of the universe, as various New Testament authors confess:

> *From the apostle John*: "In the beginning [an echo of Gen. 1:1] was the Word, and the Word was with God, and the Word was God.... All things were made through him, and without him was not any thing made that was made.... And the Word became flesh and dwelt among us, and we have seen his glory, glory as of the only Son from the Father, full of grace and truth" (John 1:1–3, 14).

> *From the apostle Paul*: "His beloved Son . . . is the image of the invisible God, the firstborn [preeminent heir] of all creation. For by him all things were created, in heaven and on earth, visible and invisible, whether thrones or dominions or rulers or authorities—all things were created through him and for him. And he is before all things, and in him all things hold together" (Col. 1:13, 15–17).

> *From the Epistle to the Hebrews*: "In these last days [God] has spoken to us by his Son, whom he appointed the heir of all things, through whom also he created the world. He is the radiance of the glory of God and the exact imprint of his nature, and he upholds the universe by the word of his power" (Heb. 1:2–3).

Wherever in the Bible you read "Creator," think "Christ." This is not to exclude the Father and the Holy Spirit, of course! The Father spoke, the Word enacted the Father's creative purpose, and the Spirit hovered over the deep to impart life to creatures.

As Redeemer, God Rescued Israel from Death and Enslavement in Order to Bind His People to Himself in Covenant Love and Loyalty

In the ancient Near East, a small nation's security depended a great deal on how powerful its allies were. So ancient treaties between dominant kings and chieftains with fewer military resources often opened with preambles that recounted how the former had come to the latter's rescue in war. Those documents also involved the covenant lord's promise to protect his dependents and their obligation, in return, to send troops into the lord's army when a military draft was issued.

Certainly for the Israelites—first a nomadic family, then slaves in Egypt, then homeless wanderers in a wilderness—the commitment of their covenant Lord to protect them from their enemies was vital to their hope of survival. He had prepared for their covenant alliance by rescuing them from slavery to one of the ancient world's superpowers, Egypt, amid terrifying acts of power. Later, under Joshua, he defeated strong and entrenched peoples in order to bestow on Israel the land he had promised to Abraham. The Lord's protection is seen in the cyclical history in the period of the judges, when Israel's apostasy brought subjugation to enemies, which moved Israel to repent and plead for God's help, to which he responded by raising up one Spirit-empowered champion after another. Israel's history reflects in miniature the cosmic conflict between God and Satan, between the woman's offspring and those aligned with the prince of darkness (Gen. 3:15). Generation after generation, battle and bloodshed ensue: Abel vs. Cain, Isaac vs. Ishmael, Jacob vs. Esau, Joseph vs. his brothers, Israel vs. Egypt (and Moab and Ammon and Philistia and Syria and Assyria and Babylon and so on). The conflict is more than interpersonal and international. It is spiritual, but it also entails the whole range of disasters and dysfunctions that have flowed, like toxic waste, from Adam's rebellion.

Old Testament passages that acclaimed the Lord's prowess as his servants' Rescuer and Protector are often linked to Christ in the New Testament. Jesus is the supreme Lord and divine Champion, and the rescue from sin and death that he has achieved for us through his obedient life, sacrificial death, and triumphant resurrection is the ultimate redemption that secures our safety in covenant with God. Consider, for example, two Old Testament passages and their New Testament commentaries.

The "I Am" Who Redeems Israel

The Angel of the Lord, who is the Lord himself, said to Moses at the burning bush: "I have surely seen the affliction of my people . . . , and I have come down to deliver them." When Moses asked, "What is your name?" the answer came: "I AM WHO I AM. . . . Say this to the people of Israel, 'I AM has sent me to you'" (Ex. 3:7–8, 13–14). God revealed his special, covenantal name to confirm his assurance that he had arrived to rescue his enslaved people by his outstretched arm. Centuries later, Jesus told a hostile crowd that he would rescue his followers from death itself: "Truly, truly, I say to you, if anyone keeps my word, he will never see death" (John 8:51). His listeners accused him of claiming to be greater than Abraham, and Jesus confirmed their understanding of his claim: "Truly, truly, I say to you, before Abraham was, I am" (v. 58). They recognized his allusion to the burning bush, but they refused to believe that he was the Lord who had delivered Israel from Egypt. So they grabbed stones to execute him as a blasphemer (see 10:30–33). John's Gospel testifies, however, that Jesus' implied claim to be Israel's divine Redeemer was absolutely true.

The Lord Who Stills Storms

Psalm 107 opens with a summons to praise the Lord for redeeming his people from all sorts of trouble (vv. 1–3), followed by stanzas that describe the plight of those who found themselves wandering homeless in deserts, sitting chained in prison, or depressed and diseased. When they cried out to the Lord, he brought them home, set them free, or healed them. Then we come to a stanza (vv. 23–32) describing sailors who "went down to the sea in ships" and were caught in a storm that threatened to submerge their ships and drown them. When they cried out to the Lord, however, "he made the storm be still, and the waves of the sea were hushed." No wonder "they were glad that the waters were quiet"! Centuries later, Jesus slept in the stern of a fishing boat, as his disciples desperately waged war against a ruthless storm at sea. Expecting to go down and drown, they cried out to Jesus in their distress. He awoke, rose, and rebuked wind and sea; "and the wind ceased and there was a great calm." Yet instead of rejoicing in relief, the disciples "were filled with great fear," wondering, "Who then is this, that even the wind and the sea obey him?" (Mark 4:35–41). Psalm 107 had given the answer: This is the Lord who rescues his storm-tossed people, so that they are not overwhelmed by the threatening seas (see Isa. 43:1–2).

Whenever we run across a text that portrays the conflict between good and evil, between God and Satan, between the woman's offspring and that of the serpent, whatever the immediate enemy (whether Egypt or Edom or Babylon or Satan's temptation to lust or pride), Scripture's testimony to the power of the Lord to rescue and defend his people points to Jesus, whose power to save is most victoriously displayed in the weakness of his cross.

The Lord as Provider: Loving Husband and Faithful Shepherd

Christ the Lord not only created the universe in the beginning but sustains it in the present. In him "all things hold together" because he "upholds the universe"—keeps it in existence and in operation—"by the word of his power" (Col. 1:17; Heb. 1:3). Even more personally, the Lord cares and provides for the people whom he calls close to himself in covenant commitment, Israel in the Old Testament and believers from all nations in the New. The Lord's role as Provider for his dependent people is conveyed in rich metaphors. Let's sample two of these portraits of the Lord as Provider.

The Husband of His Bride

The Lord was the *husband* of Israel, and their covenant at Sinai was their exchange of marital vows (Jer. 2:2–3; 31:32). He had lavished his gifts on his bride to enhance her beauty (Ezek. 16:8–14). But the bride had been unfaithful, playing the harlot with the foreign gods served by the surrounding nations—nonexistent gods that could not provide for their worshipers' needs (Jer. 3:20; Hos. 2:2). The northern kingdom, Israel, and its capital, Samaria, were like a promiscuous older sister who led her younger sister, Judah, into infidelity; and Judah plunged deeper into corruption than either Samaria to the north or Sodom to the south (Ezek. 16:44–51). Yet the Lord's faithfulness as husband to an adulterous wife would eventually overcome Israel's wanderlust and restore the marriage. Hosea spoke words of comfort and reconciliation to Israel in the north:

> And in that day, declares the LORD, you will call me "My Husband," and …
> I will betroth you to me forever. I will betroth you to me in righteousness

and in justice, in steadfast love and in mercy. I will betroth you to me
in faithfulness. And you shall know the LORD. . . . And I will say to Not
My People, "You are my people"; and he shall say, "You are my God."
(Hos. 2:16–23)

The same promise that Hosea spoke to the wayward northern kingdom,
Isaiah delivered in other words to Judah in the south. Looking ahead to the
Babylonian captivity, Isaiah saw that the exiles would resemble a barren
widow, bereft of a husband to protect and provide and of children to offer
hope for the future (Isa. 54:1). Beyond the exile, however, the Lord himself
would build the barren widow's family, giving her many children (vv. 2–3)
and caring for her as her loving husband:

> Your Maker is your husband,
>   the LORD of hosts is his name;
> and the Holy One of Israel is your Redeemer,
>   the God of the whole earth he is called.
> For the LORD has called you
>   like a wife deserted and grieved in spirit,
> like a wife of youth when she is cast off,
>   says your God.
> For a brief moment I deserted you,
>
> . . . .
>
> but with everlasting love I will have compassion on you. (Isa. 54:5–8)

For their wedding, the Lord promised to provide his bride with the garments
of salvation and a robe of righteousness (Isa. 61:10). The God-forsakenness
that Judah's spiritual adultery had brought on herself would be reversed,
displaced by the Lord's delight in her as on a second honeymoon: "and as
the bridegroom rejoices over the bride, so shall your God rejoice over you"
(62:4–5).

In the New Testament, John the Baptist invoked this Old Testament
metaphor, comparing the Israelites who had been prepared through John's
preaching to a bride, Jesus the Messiah to their bridegroom, and himself
to the bridegroom's friend, who is overjoyed by the groom's arrival (John
3:28–30). Jesus applied the image of the bridegroom to himself (Matt. 25:5–
10; Mark 2:19–20). Paul appealed to Christ's loving provision for his church
to illustrate the principle and to motivate Christian husbands to nourish

and cherish their own wives (Eph. 5:25–32). And the book of Revelation pictures the consummation of history as the wedding feast of the Lamb (Rev. 19:6–9), when his redeemed people are presented to him in radiant beauty "as a bride adorned for her husband" (21:2).

In John's Gospel, Jesus transformed water into wine at a wedding feast (John 2:1–11). Jesus' miracles led his disciples to believe in him (v. 11); and they are called *signs* not only because they display his supernatural power, but also because they convey a message from God, pointing to unseen truth about the nature of Jesus' mission. In this case, the Lord's provision of wine to celebrate a marital union signifies the arrival of the ultimate Provider for his people, a feast day foretold by Isaiah centuries earlier:

> On this mountain the LORD of hosts will make for all peoples
>> a feast of rich food, a feast of well-aged wine,
>> of rich food full of marrow, of aged wine well refined.
> . . . .
> And the LORD God will wipe away tears from all faces,
>> and the reproach of his people he will take away from all the earth,
>> for the LORD has spoken.
> It will be said on that day,
>> "Behold, this is our God; we have waited for him, that he might save us."
>>> (Isa. 25:6–9)

The master of the feast spoke words more true than he knew when he praised the groom for saving the best wine for last (John 2:10). The Lord, Israel's husband, had indeed reserved his best provision for the last days. The God for whom believing Israelites had waited had at last arrived, and he was now supplying the wine of joy to those who believed in him.

The Shepherd of His Flock

Another metaphor that conveys the Lord's provision for his people is that of the faithful shepherd, who protects his sheep against predators and provides for them by finding rich and safe pastureland and fresh water. On his deathbed, Jacob spoke of the Lord as his shepherd and invoked the shepherd's protection and provision for his son Joseph (Gen. 48:15; 49:24; see Ps. 80:1). Looking back to the exodus and the Lord's provision and protection in the wilderness, a psalmist evoked the image of the shepherd:

> Then he led out his people like sheep
> and guided them in the wilderness like a flock.
> He led them in safety, so that they were not afraid,
> but the sea overwhelmed their enemies. (Ps. 78:52–53; see also 77:19–20)

King David, called by God from herding sheep and anointed to lead God's people, sang confidently of the Lord, his shepherd, who ensured that he lacked nothing, made him rest in lush pastures and drink from still waters (Ps. 23:1–2), and protected him from violent enemies in the valley of the shadow of death (vv. 4–5).

This rich Old Testament imagery of the Lord as his people's shepherd is the background for Jesus' announcement that he is the Good Shepherd, come at last to lay down his life to secure his sheep's eternal and abundant life (John 10:1–30). Jeremiah and Ezekiel had shown that those who were charged to care for God's flock in the past had proved to be predators consuming the flock or hirelings eager to save their own skins rather than defending the vulnerable sheep (Jer. 23:1–6; Ezek. 34; John 10:8, 10, 12–13). As Lord of the flock, Jesus knows his sheep, calls them by name, and lays down his life for theirs, to secure their safety in his own hand and his Father's hand forever (John 10:17–18, 27–29). His open announcement, "I and the Father are one" (v. 30), which so shocked his listeners that they prepared to execute him for blasphemy (vv. 31–33), was the self-evident conclusion of his shepherding role, which Israel's God had claimed for himself in Ezekiel 34.

Elsewhere in the New Testament as well, Jesus is identified as his people's shepherd, who provides for the flock of God (Acts 20:28–30; Heb. 13:20; 1 Peter 2:25; 5:2–4). Revelation 7 describes the peace and provision enjoyed by those whose robes have been washed in the blood of the Lamb, since "the Lamb in the midst of the throne will be their shepherd, and he will guide them to springs of living water, and God will wipe away every tear from their eyes" (7:17). The words that John heard and recorded blended the promise of the final feast of joy (Isa. 25:6–9, quoted above) with the hope of a new exodus and pilgrimage, led by the Lord through his faithful Servant:

> They shall feed along the ways;
> on all bare heights shall be their pasture;
> they shall not hunger or thirst,
> neither scorching wind nor sun shall strike them,
> for he who has pity on them will lead them,
> and by springs of water will guide them. (Isa. 49:9–10)

118

The Lamb, faithful shepherd to provide his flock's every need, is none other than Jesus, who shed his blood to wash believers' consciences clean in pristine purity.

What does this mean for the many texts in which we see the covenant Lord providing nourishment for his people, whether as husband or as shepherd? They point us to Jesus! He is the bread of heaven, exemplified by the manna in the wilderness. He is the Rock from which living water flows. Just as Jesus implemented the Father's plan for creation, so Jesus implements the Father's gracious provision for us. Wherever the Bible speaks of the Lord's giving his people what we need to survive and to thrive, the text is pointing us to Christ the Lord, "who crowns you with steadfast love and mercy, who satisfies you with good so that your youth is renewed like the eagle's" (Ps. 103:4–5).

The Lord as Commander

Although the covenant Lord demonstrates his faithful generosity to his servants in all the ways we have surveyed—creating us, rescuing us, protecting us, preserving us, providing for us—the Bible never lets us imagine God to be a celestial "genie" who pops out of a bottle, addresses us as "Master," and says, "Your wish is my command." Nothing could be further from the truth! He does not invite us to set the terms of our relationship with him, or allow us to negotiate the terms of our covenant commitments. He calls the shots! He sets the standards and determines the consequences that will flow, whether from loyal obedience or from treasonous disobedience.

Our self-centered hearts would prefer to treat God as our servant, our assistant, or our consultant, available at our beck and call to do our bidding and support our purposes. But that is not at all his role in the covenant relationship that he initiates, imposes, and structures to engage his creatures in loyalty to himself. Two well-known examples, one from the Old Testament and the other from the New, will make the point.

To this day in Jewish synagogues around the world, one can hear the recitation of Israel's foundational confession of faith, affirming the uniqueness and unity of the true and living God who had redeemed his people from slavery in Egypt: "The LORD our God, the LORD is one" (Deut. 6:4). In the treaty structure of Deuteronomy, this self-identification of the Lord is integral to the historical prologue that lays the foundation for the specific directions—commands and prohibitions—to follow in the succeeding chapters. Immediately after this confession of the Lord's identity comes the command to love the Lord with all that you are (heart and soul and might)—that is, the demand of exclusive, sincere, and unreserved devotion and loyalty (v. 5). Here is a divine Commander from whom nothing can be withheld!

Then, to translate this ultimatum for an unreserved pledge of allegiance—the "great and first commandment," as Jesus called it (Matt. 22:37–38)—into concrete, day-to-day terms, it is followed by the directive: "And these words that I command you today shall be on your heart. You shall teach them diligently to your children, and shall talk of them when you sit in your house, and when you walk by the way, and when you lie down, and when you rise" (Deut. 6:6–7). Embed the Lord's commands in hearts (your own and your children's) and inscribe them on heads and hands and homes (vv. 8–9). Thereafter we meet detailed instructions about worship (whom, where, when, and how), discerning God's will, diet, justice, warfare, marriage and sexuality, divorce and remarriage, farming and finance, and other issues. Toward the conclusion of Deuteronomy are the lists of consequences to be expected, depending on the servants' performance in relation to the Lord's demands. One might be inclined to conclude that this Lord assumes the right to micromanage his servants' lives in every sphere. In fact, he does!

Our second example of the Lord's role as Commander shows us that his authority to direct his servants' inner desires and outward behavior remains undiminished as we move into the New Testament. Jesus' demand for exclusive loyalty, expressed in ready and willing obedience without reservation or reluctance, remained unchanged from the *Shema'* of Deuteronomy 6:4–5. Neither parents (who are to be honored) nor children (who are to be cared for) nor one's own life (which may be prudently preserved) may compete with Jesus or trump his claim on a disciple's devotion:

> Whoever loves father or mother more than me is not worthy of me, and whoever loves son or daughter more than me is not worthy of me. And whoever does not take his cross and follow me is not worthy of me. Whoever finds his life will lose it, and whoever loses his life for my sake will find it. (Matt. 10:37–39)

It is hollow and hypocritical to profess allegiance to Jesus in mere words, without heeding his directives for our lives: "Why do you call me 'Lord,

Lord,' and do not do what I tell you?" (Luke 6:46). He is a Commander who expects ready and eager obedience!

On the eve of his crucifixion, Jesus honored his disciples with the status of friends (John 15:15). They were not merely servants, mindlessly following directives, but friends to whom Jesus had opened his heart and revealed his mission from the Father. Yet their friendship did not close the gap between his authority as their Lord and their subordination as those who are bound to obey his word. Just as he did when he met with Moses on Sinai to deliver his commands, so the incarnate Lord still demanded the obedience of his followers:

> Whoever has my commandments and keeps them, he it is who loves me. And he who loves me will be loved by my Father, and I will love him and manifest myself to him. . . . If anyone loves me, he will keep my word, and my Father will love him, and we will come to him and make our home with him. Whoever does not love me does not keep my words. And the word that you hear is not mine but the Father's who sent me. (John 14:21–24)

When we consider the commands that the Lord issues to his servants, we need to understand the right order of events. We are *not* rescued by Christ *because of* our commandment-keeping—far from it! As Paul made clear to the Christians of Ephesus, "For by grace you have been saved through faith. And this is not your own doing; it is the gift of God, not a result of works, so that no one may boast" (Eph. 2:8–9). By "works" and "your own doing," Paul means our efforts to keep the Lord's commandments, which he sets in contrast to "grace" and "the gift of God." Salvation is the Lord's free gift, received by faith that rests in his promise and his work in Jesus Christ. Paul makes the same point in his letter to the believers in Galatia: "we know that a person is not justified by works of the law but through faith in Jesus Christ, so we also have believed in Christ Jesus, in order to be justified by faith in Christ and not by works of the law, because by works of the law no one will be justified" (Gal. 2:16). Three times in this one sentence, Paul stresses that our right standing before God (being justified), which brings God's blessing as its consequence, is not "by works of the law"—not because we have kept God's commands. And three times Paul asserts that we receive right standing in God's sight by believing in Christ Jesus. The structure of the Ten Commandments actually made the same point to ancient Israel: first, the Lord brought the people out of slavery in Egypt (Ex. 20:2); then, as a result, he directed how they should respond to his saving grace in the following commands. The Lord rescued the Israelites from Egypt and gave them Canaan not because they were faithful commandment-keepers, but because he was a faithful promise-keeper (Deut. 9:4–8; see 7:6–11). In Old Testament and New, when the Lord reaches out to engage guilty people as his covenant servants, his gracious rescue always comes first, creating the context for our response in trust and thankful obedience.[1]

In other words, although neither we nor the children of Israel are summoned to keep the Lord's commands *in order to* receive his favor, he rescues his people *so that* we can and want to keep his commandments. By obeying, we express our grateful love to our divine Champion and Commander. Paul makes this point in the very next sentence of Ephesians after his assertion that we are not saved as a result of our works: "For we are his workmanship, created in Christ Jesus for good works, which God prepared beforehand, that we should walk in them" (Eph. 2:10). Not "*from*" our works, but "*for* good works"—works that result from God's creative and renewing power (since "we are his workmanship") in keeping with his eternal plan (since "he prepared beforehand"). This is the order—God's initiative, then our response—that we see throughout the New Testament: "We love because he first loved us" (1 John 4:19). "If God so loved us, we also ought to love one another" (v. 11). "Be kind to one another, tenderhearted, forgiving one another, as God in Christ forgave you" (Eph. 4:32).

What does this perspective on the Lord as Commander mean for the way we understand the many passages in the Bible in which God gives directives for our hidden thought life, our outward behavior, and our relationships with others? First, Jesus is the covenant Lord who links our obedience to his Word directly to our personal loyalty to him. Whenever we hear God issuing commands and prohibitions to his human servants, those are not merely abstract ethical principles. They are the desires and directives of Christ the Lord, who has drawn us to himself and claimed us for himself in sovereign grace. Disobedience to the Lord's commands is not a matter of accidental oversight or inadvertent error, but an expression of high treason, a personal affront to the tripersonal God who comes in Christ to claim us for himself.

---

1. As we will see in the next chapter, the covenants with Israel at Sinai and with believers of every nationality in Christ consistently *begin* with God's acts of initiating grace toward unworthy people because they flow from the complete obedience of Jesus, the last and greater Adam, whose faithfulness as covenant Servant is in sharpest contrast to the first Adam's fall.

Second, the Lord's commands are expressions of his loving loyalty toward us. The psalmists (e.g., Pss. 19, 119) feel such deep delight in the Lord's statutes that many modern independent-minded readers find their affection for God's regulations nothing short of bizarre. If we marvel that anyone could find such pleasure in the rules laid down by Another, it is because we fail to recognize—as the psalmists did so vividly—that God's instructions are good gifts to sustain his abiding communion with those on whom he has set his steadfast love. The aim of the Lord's many "dos and don'ts" is not merely to manage our behavior. It is to reconfigure the longings of our hearts. To be sure, God has not invested the law's directives with the life-giving power to produce such heart-transformation (Rom. 8:2–4; Gal. 3:21). Only his Holy Spirit can enliven our hearts. Yet the commands show the shape of hearts and conduct conformed to the purity and love of the Lord.

Third, the arrival of Christ as the Lord of the covenant at the turning point of history has modified some aspects of his commands for his servants. Over the centuries, the Lord delivered commands and prohibitions in a vast array of situations. We need to take into account both the points of contact and the points of difference between the settings in which the Lord first gave directives and our context today. Many commands reflect the holy character of God and show how his human image-bearers must reflect God's holiness, so they remain unchanged before and after Christ's coming. To Israel at Sinai, God said, "You shall not commit adultery" (Ex. 20:14); and Jesus and his apostles reaffirmed that God still prohibits marital infidelity, and always will (Matt. 5:27–28; 19:18; Rom. 13:9; 1 Cor. 6:9). On the other hand, for Israel God banned a variety of meats as ceremonially unclean (Lev. 11); but New Testament passages show that those dietary laws, which reinforced Israel's distinctiveness from other peoples, were rendered obsolete by Jesus' coming, as criteria for cuisine (Mark 7:19; Acts 10:13–16, 28; 1 Cor. 10:25–26). The Lord's servants must still glorify him even in their eating (1 Cor. 10:31). But now the Lord of the covenant has come and shown us that henceforth the issue is not *what* we eat, but *why*.

The Lord as Judge

Finally, as Lord, our God is the supreme Judge who determines how he will dispense the rewards or the penalties of his covenant, depending on whether his servants have been loyal and obedient, or rebellious and disobedient. We saw this theme in our survey of the consequences of the covenant in the Ten Commandments. It is the Lord who "visit[s] the iniquity" of idolaters on them and their children (Ex. 20:5) but extends his steadfast love to those who love him and show that love by keeping his commandments (v. 6). He is the Judge who renders the verdict on the one who misuses his name, refusing to "hold him guiltless" (v. 7).

Centuries earlier, Abraham rightly called the Lord "the Judge of all the earth," arguing that the supreme Jurist in the cosmos must certainly render just verdicts and mete out equitable punishments (Gen. 18:25). Centuries later, the psalmists rightly extolled the justice by which the Lord judges (Pss. 7:8–11; 50:4–6). Israel's singers eagerly anticipated the future day when the Lord will come to set right what is wrong in human relations:

> Say among the nations, "The LORD reigns!
>   Yes, the world is established; it shall never be moved;
>   he will judge the peoples with equity."
> . . . .
> Then shall all the trees of the forest sing for joy
>   before the LORD, for he comes,
>   for he comes to judge the earth.
> He will judge the world in righteousness,
>   and the peoples in his faithfulness. (Ps. 96:10–13; see 67:4; 75:2; 98:9)

Israel's prophets also foresaw "the latter days," when the Lord would take up residence on his mountain and "judge between the nations, and . . . decide disputes for many peoples" (Isa. 2:2, 4). He will render judgments not only against his people's foreign enemies but also among his wayward people and their leaders (3:13–15). Through Joel the Lord subpoenas the nations to assemble in the Valley of Jehoshaphat, "for there I will sit to judge all the surrounding nations" and will swing his sickle to harvest people, either for rescue or for utter destruction (Joel 3:12–16).

The New Testament speaks of the judging role of Jesus Christ far more frequently than we might expect. The message that John the Baptist received from God and conveyed as the forerunner of the promised Messiah focused on the latter's role as Judge: "His winnowing fork is in his hand, to clear his threshing floor and to gather the wheat into his barn, but the chaff he will burn with unquenchable fire" (Luke 3:17). Jesus identified himself as the Son of Man who would stand at history's end as Judge, dividing the nations as a shepherd distinguishes between sheep and goats (Matt. 25:31–46). In John 5:25–30, Jesus spoke of the authority delegated to him by God the Father both to impart life and to render judgment, preliminarily in the present and finally at the end of time:

> Truly, truly, I say to you, an hour is coming, and is now here, when the dead will hear the voice of the Son of God, and those who hear will live. For as the Father has life in himself, so he has granted the Son also to have life in himself. And he has given him authority to execute judgment, because he is the Son of Man. Do not marvel at this, for an hour is coming when all who are in the tombs will hear his voice and come out, those who have done good to the resurrection of life, and those who have done evil to the resurrection of judgment.
>
> I can do nothing on my own. As I hear, I judge, and my judgment is just, because I seek not my own will but the will of him who sent me.

The apostle Paul announced to the philosophers of Athens that Jesus' resurrection was God's divine certification that he would be the Judge of the world on the day that God appoints (Acts 17:31; see 2 Tim. 4:1, 8). The visions granted to John in the book of Revelation blend motifs from Psalm 2 and Daniel 7 to describe Jesus as the Messiah who will rule all nations with an iron rod (Rev. 12:5; 19:15) and as "one like a son of man" whose dominion includes all peoples (1:13). He will wield his judicial authority among the nations like a harvesting sickle, as Joel had foretold (14:14–16). The Old Testament allusions and vivid imagery of John's visions are clearly interpreted when John sees a white horse and its rider advancing to wage war against Satan and his hosts:

> The one sitting on [the white horse] is called Faithful and True, and in righteousness he judges and makes war. His eyes are like a flame of fire, and on his head are many diadems . . . . From his mouth comes a sharp sword with which to strike down the nations . . . . On his robe and on his thigh he has a name written, King of kings and Lord of lords. (Rev. 19:11–16)

Is it any wonder that the wicked of the earth are seen to flee at the cosmos-traumatizing return of this glorious divine Judge, that they try to hide in caves and under mountains "from the face of him who is seated on the throne, and from the wrath of the Lamb" (Rev. 6:12–17)?

So as we read the Bible, when we come to scenes in which the covenant Lord renders judgment, vindicating the righteous and condemning the wicked, these texts show us the lay of the land that leads to Jesus. This theme of Lord as Judge moves our thoughts forward to the Son of God, to whom the Father has entrusted the authority to execute judgment. To John the Baptist's confusion, at his first coming Jesus did not swing the sickle and wield the threshing fork to inflict the judgment that the wicked deserve. Rather, he came first to bear just wrath on behalf of guilty rebels, rendering them righteous in standing before God's tribunal. But in Christ's case, "justice delayed" is *not* "justice denied." Wherever in Scripture we see God dispensing justice, that text foreshadows, however faintly, the final judgment and directs our gaze to the divine Judge appointed by the Father, Jesus the Son.

Conclusion

We have surveyed four roles associated with the Lord as the dominant partner in God's covenant with his human servants. The Lord prepares and initiates the covenant. The Lord provides for his people. The Lord issues commands to his servants. The Lord judges both his people and their enemies.

Along the way, we have sampled the ways in which New Testament passages pick up these themes and link them to Jesus, the covenant Mediator who reconnects covenant-breaking sinners to their holy God. As the Lord of the covenant, Jesus is to be adored for his preparation and initiation of our bond with the Creator whose image we bear. Both as Creator and as Redeemer, Jesus the Lord takes the first, decisive steps to draw us into covenant communion. Jesus is to be thanked, trusted, and loved for his faithful provision for us, his ever-needy dependents. Jesus is to be obeyed as the Lord who lays exclusive claim to our allegiance through his commandments, expecting glad compliance with his directives for our thoughts, affections, words, deeds, and relationships with each other. And Jesus is to be regarded with reverent fear as the Lord who will, at his return, render just judgment.

As we read Bible texts that show us God the covenant Lord displaying his power, wisdom, authority, and majesty in creating, preserving, providing, rescuing, commanding, and judging, seeing each passage in its widest biblical context will enable us to discover how each of these themes flows down through the history of salvation to find its fulfillment in Jesus, the eternal Son of God.

Putting It into Practice: The Covenant Lord Avenges a Breach of His Holiness (Joshua 7)

Several aspects of the record of Achan's secret sin, Israel's resultant defeat at Ai, and Achan's exposure and punishment shock modern and postmodern minds. First, a naturalistic worldview, reducing all causation to the physical, doubts the claim that Jericho's well-fortified walls suddenly collapsed without siege works or direct assault, merely at the sound of trumpets and victory shouts. Second, there is the shock of the Lord's demand that every living being in Jericho, except Rahab the believer and her household, be slain and all the city's plunder be "devoted" to the Lord through complete destruction (except metals, which were to be gathered into the Lord's treasury) (Josh. 6:17–19). Third, our individualistic sense of fairness objects that one man's sin, unknown to the nation and unrelated to its military actions, should precipitate the death of thirty-six others (7:5). Fourth, the death penalty might seem excessive as a punishment for theft, for which the law of Moses required restitution, not execution (Ex. 22:1, 4, 7). Finally, the destruction of Achan's children and livestock, along with the offender himself and his ill-gotten plunder, again offends our sense of justice. Obviously, the logic of the Lord's conduct in these events will elude us unless we reexamine our culture's assumptions about personal independence and individual rights.

A second challenge is the fact that we have little guidance from the New Testament for viewing the place of these events in the unfolding story of God's covenant relation to his people. Only two verbal echoes of Joshua 7 are found in the New Testament. In Acts 5:2, the sin of Ananias (with his wife, Sapphira) is described with the same Greek word (ESV "kept back for himself") that appears in the Septuagint (Greek) to describe Achan's sin (ESV "took," Josh. 7:1). This is the only appearance of this verb in the Greek Old Testament (it appears once more in the New Testament). Since the situations involving Achan and Ananias have other striking parallels, it is likely that the Holy Spirit intends Acts 5 and Joshua 7 to cast light on each other. The other echo of Joshua 7 is found in John 9:24, where Jewish leaders rebuke a man whose blindness Jesus had healed in words like those of Joshua to Achan: "Give glory to God" (7:19). But there the situation is radically different from that in Joshua 7: the once-blind man, unlike Achan, had already been glorifying God by testifying openly about Jesus. The *verbal* link seems not to signal a *substantive* parallel in this case.

Three dimensions of the covenant Lord's relationship to his servant people appear in this account. First, the Lord acts as *Protector and Provider* for his people by waging war on their behalf against the city of Jericho, the pagan fortress that stood at the gateway to the Promised Land. Not only the mysterious appearance of the commander of the Lord's army (Josh. 5:13–15) but also the bizarre battle plan dictated for Jericho's defeat showed that the Lord himself would combat and conquer Jericho. For six successive days the ark of the covenant, carried by priests and surrounded by trumpeting rams' horns, led Israel's silent troops on a circuit around the city. On the seventh day, at the climax of seven circuits, the Lord's trumpets sounded, Israel's shouts replied, and Jericho's walls fell. Jericho's devastation showed that "the LORD was with Joshua" (6:27) to wage war on his people's behalf.

Second, here we see the Lord as *Commander*. He mandated Israel's odd battle strategy in order to make clear that he alone deserves glory for Jericho's fall. Therefore, he commanded that his people seize nothing in Jericho as plunder. Rather, virtually everyone and everything was to be consumed by fire in accordance with the Lord's demand, beginning the purge of his land from idolatry's defilement. The adage "to the victor belong the spoils" was operative when the Lord, who acted alone to vanquish and destroy Jericho, laid claim to everything in the city as belonging to himself. He had every right to forbid his people from snatching even the smallest plunder from that fallen metropolis.

Finally, we see the Lord wielding sovereign authority as *Judge*. As uncomfortable as it makes many readers, as holy Creator, the Lord had every right to order the extermination of Jericho's pagan population and the incineration of their property. By their idolatry, violence, injustice, and sensuality, they had denied his unique worthiness to be worshiped, defied his standards for human community, and defiled the land that he had promised to Abraham and his offspring. Though not bound to the living God by his redemptive covenant with Abraham, those nations were nonetheless accountable to the Lord as guilty heirs of Adam.

We should note that the laws for Israel's warfare in Deuteronomy 20 made the cities and peoples of Canaan a special case. For the cities of the Hittites, Amorites, Canaanites, Perizzites, Hivites, and Jebusites, whose influence would lure God's people toward abominable practices, the Lord mandated complete destruction of every breathing being and piece of property (Deut. 20:16–18). Other, more distant cities could be offered terms of peace and their wealth seized as plunder by Israelite troops (vv. 10–15). Even from the next Canaanite town, Ai, the Lord's word permitted his people to seize plunder (Josh. 8:27), though the city itself was burned and its inhabitants slain. The devotion to complete destruction by which the Lord judged Canaan's pagan populace was a sobering preview of the final judgment of the wicked at the end of history.

Achan was even more culpable to the Lord's judgment, having experienced God's provision and protection in the wilderness and God's triumph over Jericho. As father in his family, Achan by his contempt for the Lord brought judgment on his whole household, in keeping with the principle of covenant representation that we noticed in the second commandment (Ex. 20:5). And though Achan occupied no special office in Israel, his sin infected the whole community, moving Israel's holy Champion to withdraw his powerful presence and exposing Israel's soldiers to defeat and death in the first assault on Ai.

How do the dimensions of the Lord's roles as *Warrior, Commander,* and *Judge* in this passage fit into the covenantal lay of the land that leads us to Christ? First, as *Warrior* who protects and provides for his people, the Lord shows us that his destruction of Jericho at the outset of the Promised Land's conquest belongs to the larger trajectory of the age-old conflict between the serpent's offspring and the offspring of the woman, announced in Genesis 3:15. Here the Lord's single-handed destruction of his people's foes is signaled by the ark of the covenant, symbolizing God's presence among his people, which leads the charge against the stronghold of paganism that barred Israel's access to her promised inheritance. Jericho's demise showed the truth of David's later announcement in defiance of Goliath: "The battle is the LORD's" (1 Sam. 17:47).

Moses had warned that the gravest threat posed by Canaan's nations was not military but spiritual. Those peoples must be wiped out, "that they may not teach you to do according to all their abominable practices that they have done for their gods, and so you sin against the LORD your God" (Deut. 20:18). Achan's secret sin showed how lethal the hidden spiritual treason of one's heart could be, not only for the individual but also for those connected to him. At the very time when the faith of Rahab, a Gentile prostitute, identified her with the Lord's people and led to her rescue by grace, Achan identified himself with the pagan city by coveting what his Lord had prohibited (Josh. 7:20–21), violating the tenth commandment (Ex. 20:17) and imitating his mother Eve (Gen. 3:6). Having cast his lot with Jericho's idolaters, Achan shared their defeat and destruction.

Later Scripture deepens the insight that the war for our heart's allegiance is far more significant than mere military combat. Our most formidable foes are not "flesh and blood, but . . . the rulers, . . . the authorities, . . . the cosmic powers over this present darkness, . . . the spiritual forces of evil in the heavenly places" (Eph. 6:12). Our divine Champion has defeated these super-villains single-handedly, but with a most surprising strategy: he triumphed over them in his cross (Col. 2:14–15), conquering as a lion by being slain as a lamb (Rev. 5:5–6, 9).

Second, the Lord's role as *Commander* at Jericho points us forward to the commands that Jesus gives for the spiritual warfare in which we are engaged. Christ's battle strategy today seems as unlikely to yield victory as did the weeklong parades around Jericho. "For the word of the cross is folly to those who are perishing, but to us who are being saved it is the power of God" (1 Cor. 1:18). In contrast to his commission to ancient Israelites as they took possession of Canaan, Jesus instructs his armies not to retaliate against those who inflict physical violence, but rather to turn the other cheek (Matt. 5:39). Because his kingship is not derived from the power structures of this world, he forbids his adherents to advance his reign through swords made of mere metal (Matt. 26:51–54; John 18:36). Rather, we are to put on God's own armor: his truth, righteousness, gospel, faith, salvation, Word (Eph. 6:13–17). These "weapons of our warfare are not of the flesh but have divine power to destroy strongholds" (2 Cor. 10:4). Because these strongholds are not walled cities but "arguments and every lofty opinion raised against the knowledge of God," our mission, in dependence on our Lord's power, is to "take every thought captive to obey Christ" (v. 5).

The Lord's prohibition, violated by Achan, also anticipates the command that Christ the Lord gives to those who trust and serve him in the new covenant. In contrast to the Gentile Rahab, who left her pagan past and entered God's covenant by grace through faith, Achan identified with the city of man with its defilement and its destiny of destruction. Today, Christ continues to call people out of pagan pasts into his new covenant. And he calls his covenant people to separate themselves from anything that defiles and deserves destruction. To the church at Corinth, prone to confuse liberty in Christ with license to participate in immorality and idolatry, Christ's apostle issued sharp directives, bolstered by Old Testament texts:

Do not be unequally yoked with unbelievers. For what partnership has righteousness with lawlessness? Or what fellowship has light with darkness? What accord has Christ with Belial? Or what portion does a believer share with an unbeliever? What agreement has the temple of God with idols? For we are the temple of the living God; as God said,

"I will make my dwelling among them and walk among them,
   and I will be their God,
   and they shall be my people [Lev. 26:12].
Therefore go out from their midst,
   and be separate from them, says the Lord,
and touch no unclean thing [Isa. 52:11];
   then I will welcome you,
and I will be a father to you [2 Sam. 7:14],
   and you shall be sons and daughters to me [Isa. 43:6],
   says the Lord Almighty." (2 Cor. 6:14–18)

Finally, as *Judge*, the Lord, who examines hearts, both exposed and condemned Achan's greedy and deceitful disobedience. Here the parallel with the subterfuge of Ananias and Sapphira in the early church is relevant (Acts 5:1–11). By sending his Holy Spirit to indwell his holy people (John 14:17), the risen Christ fulfills his promise to be with his people to the end of the age (Matt. 28:20). The Spirit's divine presence brings great joy (Acts 13:52) but also holy fear (5:5, 11), since God's holiness is always dangerous to those who disregard the Lord's consuming purity and heart-searching omniscience. Ananias was free to keep his property or use the proceeds of its sale as he wished (v. 4). When, however, he brought only a portion of the price received while claiming that it was the whole, he became guilty of lying to the Holy Spirit, to God himself (vv. 3–4). Like Achan, Ananias had secreted away for himself resources belonging to his Lord. Ananias's penalty, like Achan's, was death.

One other dimension of the Lord's action as Judge is worth noting. Achan's secret sin was imputed to all Israel, leading to the nation's shameful and costly defeat at Ai. Thus his covenant treason and its dire result were soberly memorialized in the renaming of that place as the Valley of Achor ("Trouble"). As Achan had brought trouble on Israel, so Israel's divine Judge brought trouble on Achan (Josh. 7:25–26). Consequently, Achan's destruction under covenant curse (along with his household and livestock) placated the

131

Lord's just wrath: "Then the LORD turned from his burning anger" (v. 26). One man—a guilty man—died; and the many were spared. Centuries later, God's prophets announced that this valley would not always bear the tragic title "Trouble": "I will . . . make the Valley of Achor a door of hope. And there she [Israel] shall answer as in the days of her youth, as at the time when she came out of the land of Egypt" (Hos. 2:15). Rather than serving as a grim reminder of sin's consequences, the Valley of Achor would become peaceful pasturelands (Isa. 65:10). Such prophetic previews raise expectations, perhaps offering hints of a time to come when one man—history's only innocent man, Jesus—would receive "trouble" and destruction, so that others might live, and the Lord would turn from his wrath.

Questions for Reflection and Discussion

1. How does the Bible's revelation of the "sovereign, self-existent Creator" who "is distinct from and independent of all things created" *differ from* other conceptions of what is ultimately real (the deities of other religions, impersonal forces and factors in irreligious systems of thought, etc.)?

2. What is there about the true, *triune* God who reveals himself in the Bible—who is one, and is three divine persons—that makes sense of his creating human beings, male and female, in his own image in order to engage them in covenant?

3. When we realize that God created the cosmos to furnish a "very good" (Gen. 1:31) venue for our covenant relationship with our Creator, how does this insight enrich our understanding of the event of creation and our appreciation for the world all around us?

4. As his people's Protector, how did the Lord intervene to rescue Israel from slavery in Egypt? How has he intervened to rescue Christian believers from the enemies and dangers that threaten us?

5. As his people's Provider, what lavish gifts did the Lord shower on Israel his bride when he brought her into the Promised Land? What types of provisions has your heavenly Bridegroom bestowed on you and on his church today?

6. Which concept do you find more appealing: the Lord as Provider/Protector, or the Lord as Commander/Judge? Why? What Scriptures, from New Testament as well as Old, show the Lord to be his people's

Commander, who demands and expects our ready obedience? As you reflect on the Lord's identity and your own personality, can you say how it actually benefits you to have a covenant Lord who demands your submission?

7. What mistakes are often and easily made when we try to relate the Lord's commands to his promises to show us grace? How does confusion on this issue damage our covenant relationship to God? Which Scriptures are helpful to clarify how our obedience is related to God's mercy?

8. The Bible often predicts that the Lord will come *as Judge*. What are some of these prophecies in the Old Testament and the New? Is this prediction "good news"? Why or why not? In other words: To whom is this good news? To whom is it *not*?

9. Was it just for God to allow Israel to be defeated at Ai—and thirty-six soldiers killed—because of one man's secret sin? Why or why not? Why did the Lord have the right to lay claim to *all* the spoils from Jericho's overthrow? What principle bound Israel together, making the nation, tribe, and clan responsible for Achan's contempt for God's command? Does this principle also work in the opposite direction, to spread blessing rather than guilt?

10. How do the fates of Achan at Jericho and of Ananias and Sapphira in Acts 5 parallel each other? What perspective on Christ as Lord do these incidents together provide, perhaps balancing, correcting, or filling out our perceptions of Jesus?

6

Jesus the Submissive, Suffering Servant: Our Covenant-Keeper and Curse-Bearer

WE WANT TO READ the Bible as Jesus showed his disciples how to read it, that is, as the God-breathed record of God's history-long mission to rescue and remake a people to enjoy his favor and display his glory, a quest that reached its climax in Jesus himself. We are following the clues that the risen Christ gave to his friends in the weeks between his resurrection and his ascension to heaven, clues that open up the beautiful unity of the whole Scripture. We have sampled how some Old Testament passages, written centuries before Christ's coming, record events and promises that are explicitly shown, in various New Testament texts, to be fulfilled by Jesus and his saving work for his people. To recall our journey metaphor, we saw that some of the "routes" of God's written Word (Jesus) are as clearly marked as major highways with illuminated "road signs."

For other texts, seeing the path that leads to Jesus is more like the challenge faced by a hiker in a mountain forest, where footpaths are hard to see, but a flowing stream suggests the "lay of the land." In chapter 4, I tried to show that the covenant structure of the Bible is like this lay of the land. The Bible is the true story of a unique interpersonal relationship: the relationship between the infinite, tripersonal Creator, on the one hand, and the finite, dependent human persons whom he created in his image, on the other. It is a love story, so biblical writers in both Old Testament and New use the analogy of human marriage—the lifelong commitment of love and loyalty between husband and wife—to portray the relationship between God and his human image-bearers. Other biblical images give us additional perspectives on the covenant bond between the Lord and his human servants. Since the Lord is not only our Lover but also our Maker, who created us and provides for us, the Bible also compares the Lord's covenant to the relationship of a father to his children. And because God's sovereign will defines our purpose for being and dictates our response and responsibilities, this covenant resembles the bond uniting a monarch and his subjects, a dominant king and his subordinate, dependent allies.

Yet this love story has conflict at its center. Because of the bride's unfaithfulness, the divine Bridegroom must wage war to rescue her, purify her, and make her his own. Because the human children proved disobedient, the Father must send his eternal and beloved Son to obey the commands that we have broken. Because the Lord's subjects have rebelled against their rightful Ruler, enslaving themselves to a crafty and cruel usurper, their only hope of escape from the penalty due their treason is for the King himself to enter history as the loyal Subject and Servant, rendering obedient allegiance on others' behalf. In order for the covenant to bring blessing rather than cursing, for the marriage to bring bliss instead of divorce, for children to enjoy the Father's smile and subjects to receive the King's pleasure, the Lord himself must humbly intervene to shoulder his servants' obligations, fulfilling both his own commitments and their obligations as well. And because God's justice demands that the unfaithfulness of the bride/children/subjects be addressed, not merely ignored, the Bridegroom/beloved Son/Servant King must also endure, on their behalf, the adverse consequence—the curse—that their guilt deserves.

The necessity for the Lord to fulfill both sets of obligations—both his own promises and his Servant's obedience to his commands—explains why the Mediator who brings God and humans together must be both God and man. Paul was most intentional when he wrote, "For there is one God, and there is one mediator between God and men, the *man* Christ Jesus" (1 Tim. 2:5). Elsewhere, Paul taught that Christ Jesus was and is "God over all, blessed forever" (Rom. 9:5), the Lord to whom every knee will bow and whom every tongue will confess (Phil. 2:10–11, alluding to Isa. 45:22–23). But here, when he wrote about Jesus' mission as Mediator, he stressed Jesus' humanity. The epistle to the Hebrews makes the same point in other words. To lead us into the glory that we forfeited, we need a Champion who calls us "brothers" and shares our flesh and blood (Heb. 2:10–15). To regain access to God's holy presence, we need a High Priest like Aaron, from our human brothers and acquainted with our weakness (4:15–5:3). Yet unlike Aaron, the Mediator we need must be not only truly, fully human but also "holy, innocent, unstained," not in need of cleansing for his own sin (7:26–28). The Mediator of the new and better covenant (that bond of steadfast love that cannot be broken even by our worst failures) can only be Jesus, the Son who is both "the radiance of the glory of God" (1:3) and the faithful Servant who came into the world to do God's will and thereby to save and sanctify others (10:5–10).

Two Megacovenants with Two Representative Servants

In chapter 4, we saw that those who have studied the Bible before us have identified two overarching covenants by which God has related to his human creatures over the course of history. First, God made a covenant with unfallen humanity at creation. The terms of this covenant were intimated in the instructions that he gave to Adam and Eve (Gen. 1:28; 2:16–17). Centuries later, Hosea 6:7 compared Israel's covenant-breaking with that of Adam at the dawn of human history. We call this a *covenant of works*, since receiving the blessing symbolized by the tree of life in Eden was contingent on the personal and flawless obedience of Adam as the Lord's covenant servant.[1]

After Adam's failure, God made the second overarching covenant with sinful humanity, encapsulated in God's words of curse on Satan in Genesis 3:15 and subsequently elaborated in the unfolding biblical record. This second covenant, which includes the particular covenants that God established throughout Israelite history (Abraham, Moses, David) and climaxes in the new covenant inaugurated by Christ, is aptly called a *covenant of grace*.[2] In this redemptive bond, not only does God keep his commitment as Lord, ful-

---

1. WCF 7.2: "The first covenant made with a man was a *covenant of works*, wherein life was promised to Adam; and in him to his posterity, upon condition of perfect and personal obedience" (emphasis added).

2. WCF 7.3: "Man, by his fall, having made himself incapable of life by that covenant [of works], the Lord was pleased to make a second, commonly called the *covenant of grace*; wherein he freely offereth unto sinners life and salvation by Jesus Christ; requiring of them faith in him, that they may be saved, and promising to give unto all those that are ordained unto eternal life his Holy Spirit, to make them willing, and able to believe" (emphasis added).

filling his own freely chosen obligations (promises), but also, in undeserved mercy toward his guilty servants, he provides an offspring of the woman whose suffering would undo the damage done by Adam, bestowing life on those doomed to death. Romans 5:12–21 and 1 Corinthians 15:21–22 show that in each of these two "megacovenants," the Creator relates to human beings through designated representatives, men whose choices as covenant servants affect vast multitudes of people:

> Therefore, as one trespass led to condemnation for all men, so one act of righteousness leads to justification and life for all men. For as by the one man's disobedience the many were made sinners, so by the one man's obedience the many will be made righteous. (Rom. 5:18–19)

> For as by a man came death, by a man has come also the resurrection of the dead. For as in Adam all die, so also in Christ shall all be made alive. (1 Cor. 15:21–22)

As he did in 1 Timothy 2:5, Paul highlights the reality of Christ's humanity. Jesus is "the one man" whose obedience makes many righteous, through whom comes the resurrection of the dead. The humanity of Christ as "the second man" (1 Cor. 15:47), "the last Adam" (v. 45), explains how he can act on behalf of other people, so that his fidelity as the Lord's Servant renders them righteous and entitles them to resurrection life.

In this chapter, we explore the privileges and conditions that define the servant's side of God's covenant, and how Christ came to fulfill those conditions and consummate those privileges by keeping the covenant commands and suffering the covenant curse in our place. This perspective on the mission of Jesus—the way he proved faithful as the Servant of the Lord, whereas every other servant, each flawed heir of Adam, has failed and fallen short—gives us a window on the good, the bad, and the ugly in the biblical record of those who have gone before us: Abraham, Isaac, Jacob, Joseph and his brothers, Moses and the Israelites, Joshua, Barak, Deborah, Samson, Ruth and Boaz, King Saul, David, Solomon, and their successors . . . as well as Simon Peter and Andrew, James and John, Barnabas and Paul, and the rest. Sometimes these fathers and mothers of faith shine brightly, living their trust in daring obedience. At those times, they are "sneak previews" of the Coming Attraction—the ultimately and completely faithful Servant of the Lord. On the other hand, too often even the best of God's human servants fall flat on their faces. Moses, the Lord's servant, brought God's covenant to his people from the mountain, bearing their abuse and interceding for their lives (Ex. 32–34). Yet Moses was disqualified from entering the Lord's land because of a brief fit of self-centered impatience, expressed in an action that disobeyed the Lord's direction (Num. 20:2–13). David righteously refrained from killing Saul when the opportunities presented themselves (1 Sam. 24, 26). But David conspired to cover up his own lust and adultery by killing a soldier loyal to him (2 Sam. 11). Peter boldly stood in the face of the Sanhedrin's threats (Acts 4:19–20) but later retreated from the truth, fearing others' disapproval (Gal. 2:12). In every believer who walks across the pages of Scripture we see the dark shadows of Adam's legacy as well as glimmers of the bright beauty of Jesus, the second Adam. Likewise, Old Testament Israel and the multinational church in the New Testament, as expressions of God's covenant community, exhibit a troubling mix of Adam's failure as covenant servant and of Christ's power to reconfigure his people into conformity to his fidelity.

We will survey four features that characterize the servant's role in covenant with the Lord: privilege, provision, probation, and product. We'll see these themes worked out in detail in a moment, but let me explain each briefly here:

- *Privilege*: The Lord's covenant places his servant in a privileged role, a preeminent status in contrast to others.
- *Provision*: The servant depends on the Lord for all that is needed to fulfill his calling and to enjoy the Lord's favor. (This is the "flip side" of the Lord's role in preparing for the covenant, protecting and providing for the servant, as we saw in chapter 5.)
- *Probation*: The servant's exclusive loyalty, trust, and obedience to the Lord are put to the test. (This is implied in the commandments that instruct the servant how to express his loyalty to the Lord, as we saw in chapter 4.)
- *Product*: The servant will receive from the Lord treatment appropriate to the servant's performance in the test of his loyalty, whether well-being in recognition of steadfast obedience or woe as a result of failure and betrayal. (This is another way of viewing the consequences of the covenant, as we saw in chapter 4.)

138

We will explore how these four dimensions of the servant's role come to expression in the two overarching covenants (of works at creation, then of grace after Adam's fall), in which the decisions of two covenant servants, Adam and Christ, so radically affected so many others. Then we will see how these categories also help us to make sense of the checkered record of the Lord's other servants in the Old and New Testaments, both individuals such as Moses and David, and corporate servants such as Israel and the church.

Adam and Christ: The Servant's Privilege as the Image of God

If we have been influenced by modern concepts of personal rights and individual independence, combining privilege with servanthood might seem absurd. Something in every human heart, infected as we naturally are with resistance toward God, objects to the idea that it is a privilege to subdue our will and submit our preferences to someone else. God's Word, however, challenges both our inborn autonomy and our culture's democratic assumptions. In the Bible's presentation of reality, every creature owes its very existence to the Creator and is made for his purposes and pleasure. Then, when our personal Creator condescends to engage human beings, whom he created uniquely in his likeness, as servants in covenant with himself, he sets us apart for a place of distinctive privilege and preeminence.

Genesis 1:26–28 reveals that God created man, male and female, in his image and according to his likeness. God's image and likeness distinguished humankind from other living creatures on earth. Although God authorized sun, moon, and stars to "rule" day and night by marking the boundaries of time periods, only to the first human couple, as the capstone of his creativity, did God delegate authority to reign over all of earth's living creatures, blessing them in his words of commission: "Be fruitful and multiply and fill the earth and subdue it and have dominion over the fish of the sea and over the birds of the heavens and over every living thing that moves on the earth" (Gen. 1:28). These commands not only obligated Adam and Eve to obey the Lord, but also granted our first parents a place of privileged preeminence among the living creatures. As those who bore God's likeness, Adam and Eve resembled God as no other creature on earth does. They could think, speak, plan, engage in interpersonal interaction, and make decisions.

As those created to be God's image, they were to administer God's rule over his whole earthly realm, exercising delegated dominion over

139

fish and the birds of the heavens and every living thing on earth. Ancient kings erected statues of themselves in the distant corners of their realms. Those images symbolized the fact that although the king's palace was in his capital city far away, his authority extended even to his kingdom's most distant boundaries. They warned, in effect, "The king's eyes can see this far (through his spies), and his arms reach this far (through his armies)." Likewise, Adam and Eve were created to be God's living, breathing, active images (not dead, insensible stone or wood) to administer the reign of God over all their fellow creatures. Specifically, Adam's mission (with Eve's help) was "to work... and keep" a special garden sanctuary, Eden, in which God would meet with them (Gen. 2:15, 19–20). As we will see in the following chapters, the terms "work" and "keep" might be better translated "serve" and "guard," the normal senses of these terms. Our first parents' mission in their purity was to exercise rule not as tyrants but as servants of the Lord and caretakers of all they directed. Moreover, just as later Levites would be charged to guard the tabernacle as the Lord's holy residence in the center of Israel's encampment (Num. 1:53; 3:5–10), so Adam had priestly authority to protect the garden from defiling invasion by a subversive enemy, soon to be introduced (Gen. 3:1).

Even after Adam's failure as covenant servant, aspects of humanity's divinely delegated authority over other creatures survive. In a world washed cleaner (not wholly clean, sadly) through the floodwaters of judgment, the Lord reaffirmed to Noah both the command to fill the earth and the authorization to make use of animate creatures as well as plant life (Gen. 9:1–4). The dignity that still sets humans apart as God's image explains why wanton destruction of human life is a heinous offense against the Lord, who engaged Adam and Eve in covenant. That dignity gives grounds for human government, flawed as it is, to administer the Lord's justice to those who assault his servants (Gen. 9:5–6; Ex. 20:13; 21:12–14).

Psalm 8 meditates on the Genesis account of humanity's creation. It overflows with wonder over the privileged place that the Creator has granted to human beings, small as we are in the vastness of the universe:

> What is man that you are mindful of him,
>   and the son of man that you care for him?
>
> Yet you have made him a little lower than the heavenly beings
>   and crowned him with glory and honor.

140

You have given him dominion over the works of your hands;
    you have put all things under his feet,
all sheep and oxen,
    and also the beasts of the field,
the birds of the heavens, and the fish of the sea,
    whatever passes along the paths of the seas. (Ps. 8:4–8)

Although Adam and his children have broken covenant with their Lord, the legacy of our privilege and preeminence among the creatures still survives.

The epistle to the Hebrews invites us to view Psalm 8 and man's privileged position from a different angle, not as a nostalgic memory of a past paradise lost nor as an idealized image of the present, but as a preview of the future, "the world to come," which will be subjected not to angels but to humanity (Heb. 2:5–8). Although "we do not yet see everything in subjection" as all earthly creatures will be someday (v. 8), in one man even now we see the beginning of that privileged destiny. God the Son partook of our human flesh and blood (v. 14), becoming "for a little while . . . lower than the angels" (as the psalm says), and this man Jesus has been "crowned with glory and honor" (as the psalm also says) (v. 9). Hebrews has shown that this Son is divine, the radiance of God's glory and exact imprint of his nature, sovereignly creating, sustaining, and owning the whole cosmos (1:1–3). But to accomplish his *redemptive* mission, "making purification for sins" (v. 3), the Son must embrace our humanity completely, in every respect except sin (4:15; 7:26–27). He must become a second Adam, a last Adam, an infinitely better covenant representative for a new and redeemed human race.

So the first Adam's privileged place among other creatures foreshadows the coming head of the new humanity, who is far more preeminent. This great last Adam is God's

> beloved Son, . . . the image of the invisible God, the firstborn of all creation. For by him all things were created, in heaven and on earth, visible and invisible, whether thrones or dominions or rulers or authorities—all things were created through him and for him. And he is before all things, and in him all things hold together. And he is the head of the body, the church. He is the beginning, the firstborn from the dead, that in everything he might be preeminent. For in him all the fullness of God was pleased to dwell, and through him to reconcile to himself all things, whether on earth or in heaven, making peace by the blood of his cross. (Col. 1:13, 15–20)

Here we see Christ's identity as God, for he has created all things and holds all things together. But we also hear the echo of Genesis 1:26–27 in the title "the image of . . . God." And the Son's true humanity is implied in his being "firstborn from the dead" and "making peace by the blood of his cross." Jesus, who has preeminence over all creatures, is both God and the image of God, the Lord and the Servant of the Lord.

Wherever the Bible gives us glimpses of humanity's dignity and domin-ion, even in the midst of a fallen world and despite its distortions, it bears witness to the legacy of Adam's privileged position as the Lord's covenant servant. In doing so, Scripture also quickens our hope for the greater Adam who was to come, the woman's offspring who has now been born, the image of God who reflects his Father's glory flawlessly and deserves preeminence in all things.

Adam and Christ: The Servant's Provision from the Bounty of God

We have seen that the prologue to the Ten Commandments, the core of the covenant of the Lord with Israel, traces the backdrop of their mutual commitment in God's powerful liberating act in the exodus from Egypt. Provision, which often takes the form of rescue and protection in a hostile world, is one role that the Lord fulfills for his dependent and otherwise defenseless servants. Corresponding to this role of the Lord, then, is the servant's role of receiving and relying on the Lord's strong arm and gener-ous hand.

Even in Eden, before sin and slavery and suffering, God lavishly pro-vided for his servants, Adam and Eve. Not only did he create a universe that was "very good" (Gen. 1:31), but also, specifically for his covenant servants' residence, he planted a garden:

> And out of the ground the LORD God made to spring up every tree that is pleasant to the sight and good for food. The tree of life was in the midst of the garden, and the tree of the knowledge of good and evil.
> A river flowed out of Eden to water the garden, and there it divided and became four rivers. (Gen. 2:9–10)

The creation of the woman was another of God's generous provisions for the man, providing the helper who fit him precisely and the partner in his enterprise to fill the earth through multiplication and to rule it through wise dominion (Gen. 2:18–25). So God furnished a home for his covenant servant, a home that was beautiful to the eye, tasty to the palate, nourishing to the body, well watered, and to be shared by another person who "fit" Adam just right, like him (from his side) yet also refreshingly different from him. If Adam were to fail the test of his allegiance to his covenant Lord (as we know he would and did), it would not be for any lack in the Lord's provision for the servant.

As we turn to Jesus, the last Adam, we find that the Lord also provided for him all that he would need in order to fulfill his role as Servant. At first glance, however, the setting for Christ's service seems so different from the abundant provision enjoyed by Adam. Jesus did not enter a pristine world, an earth that was "very good" and untainted by corruption. Rather, he entered an earth infected with evil, injustice, violence, suffering, and death. Instead of being tested in a garden filled with beautiful trees, Jesus endured trial, first of all, in a wilderness "with the wild animals" (Mark 1:12–13). Instead of enjoying abundant and tasty fruit, Jesus experienced hunger, having fasted forty days, when he faced the trial of his allegiance to the Lord (Matt. 4:2). After the initial temptation in the desert, the devil withdrew from Jesus "until an opportune time" (Luke 4:13); and when that time came, Satan repeated his attack through one of Jesus' closest disciples, Simon Peter (Matt. 16:21–23). Whereas the conditions of Adam's probation were optimal for his fulfilling his servant's role, the outward circumstances that Providence prepared for Jesus' testing were stacked against him on every side.

Yet the New Testament shows us that God provided to Christ precisely what he would need as the Lord's Servant, to sustain the test of his loyal obedience and accomplish his redemptive mission. The Lord God gave his faithful Servant (1) a body to sacrifice, (2) the Holy Spirit, and (3) the mission itself to sustain him to the end.

As we have seen, in order for the eternal Son of God to represent us as the faithful Servant, he had to share our human nature (Heb. 2:5–15; 4:14–5:4). The epistle to the Hebrews shows us that Psalm 40 prophesied this incarnation:

When Christ came into the world, he said,

> "Sacrifices and offerings you have not desired,
>   but a body have you prepared for me.
> . . . .

> Then I said, 'Behold, I have come to do your will, O God,
>   as it is written of me in the scroll of the book.'" (Heb. 10:5–7)

The Father prepared the human body for the Son in Mary's womb, and the Son was born a true human being. In and through that human body, the Son fulfilled the resolve that he announced when he came into the world, "to do your will, O God, as it is written of me in the scroll of the book." Christ's fulfillment of God's will as the Lord's Servant encompassed his entire life of obedience to the covenant commands; but Hebrews focuses on his sacrificial death, using key words from Psalm 40 (*will* and *body*) to direct us to the cross and its atoning effect: "And by that *will* we have been sanctified through the offering of the *body* of Jesus Christ once for all" (Heb. 10:10). The Lord provided for his Servant a human body—a body beset by weakness (4:15) and vulnerable to anguish and death (2:14; 5:7–8). Only through this provision could "the founder of [our] salvation" bring "many sons to glory" (2:10).

Along with the human body in which Christ must obey and suffer, the Lord gave him the strong presence of the Holy Spirit. Here we face mystery. We might expect that Christ's divine nature supplied all the strength that his human nature needed both to resist temptation and to inaugurate God's kingdom in words and deeds of power. As true as this inference is, the New Testament authors emphasize that the Father's bestowal of the Holy Spirit—Jesus' "anointing" as the Messiah—marked the start of his redemptive mission. When Jesus received baptism from John, "the Holy Spirit descended on him in bodily form, like a dove; and a voice came from heaven, 'You are my beloved Son; with you I am well pleased'" (Luke 3:21–22). From that point, then, "Jesus, full of the Holy Spirit, returned from the Jordan and was led by the Spirit in the wilderness for forty days, being tempted by the devil" (4:1). Then, having sustained that trial, he "returned in the power of the Spirit to Galilee.... And he taught in their synagogues, being glorified by all" (4:14–15). In the synagogue of his own hometown, Jesus declared that the Servant's words written in Isaiah 61 had been fulfilled as he read them: "The Spirit of the Lord is upon me, because he has anointed me to proclaim good news to the poor" (4:17–21). Peter later identified the divine source of Jesus' messianic miracles: "God anointed Jesus of Nazareth with the Holy Spirit and with power. He went about doing good and healing all who were oppressed by the devil, for God was with him" (Acts 10:38). The

Lord provided the Spirit to his messianic Son, his faithful Servant, not only to empower his wise words and miraculous works but also to sustain him in his ultimate expression of loyalty, his suffering on the cross to save sinners. If animal sacrifices could bring ritual cleansing, reasons Hebrews, "how much more will the blood of Christ, who through the eternal Spirit offered himself without blemish to God, purify our conscience from dead works to serve the living God!" (Heb. 9:13–14). The Holy Spirit, through whom Christ would be raised on the third day, sustained him in his suffering as the Sacrifice who cleanses covenant-breakers and transforms us into loyal servants of the living God.

Finally, Jesus describes the mission itself as a provision from God. When his disciples tried to press food on him in Samaria, he replied, "I have food to eat that you do not know about." Confused, they speculated whether someone else had brought him a meal, but he made his meaning clear: "My food is to do the will of him who sent me and to accomplish his work" (John 4:31–34). The provision that kept Jesus going was the task laid out for him by God (5:30; 6:38–39), the mission of revealing the Father and rescuing those whom the Father had given to him (17:4–6).

To outward appearances, the Lord's provision for his servants, Adam and Christ, seems so different. God had given Adam all that would be needed to sustain the trial of his loyalty, trust, and obedience, both in his nature as image-bearer and in his environment. Christ entered a world terribly defaced and infected through Adam's failure, a world that seemed to show deprivation rather than provision. Yet in Christ, the second Adam and true Servant, the Lord's provision takes on new depth of meaning. He received from the Father precisely what he needed to sustain his probation and rescue his people. As we will see, this deeper perspective on the Lord's provision for his Servant extends to the experience of Christ's followers, who can rest content in his grace, whether in external plenty or in want (Phil. 4:11–13).

Adam and Christ: The Servant's Probation of Loyalty to God

As we observed in chapters 3 and 4, Paul's discussions of Adam and Christ in Romans 5:12–19 and 1 Corinthians 15:21–22 focus on what we are now calling their *probations* and the resultant *products* of those tests of loyalty. As servants, Adam and Christ each faced the decision whether or not to trust the word of the Lord and therefore obey his commands.

The tree of the knowledge of good and evil tested Adam's willingness to live by the word of his covenant Lord (Gen. 2:16–17), even when that word seemed to contradict the evidence of Adam's and Eve's senses: like other trees in the garden, the tree was visually attractive and its fruit apparently appetizing to eat. Even its name, "tree of the knowledge of good and evil," could be given positive "spin," as Satan's temptation shows. Knowledge is good, after all; and Adam and Eve were made to be "like God" (3:5), as those who were in his image and bore his likeness. In fact, couldn't it be argued that Adam's assignment to "guard" the garden, to protect the purity of God's sanctuary, *required* an ability to distinguish good from evil? But the decisive issue was this: How was Adam to sort out good from evil—by listening to God's voice or by listening to another voice that contradicted God's word and challenged God's motives? A faithful covenant servant would let his every evaluation and decision be controlled by the word of his covenant Lord. Would Adam trust and therefore obey?

In Romans 5, Paul shows that Adam's probation—the testing of his fidelity to his Lord—was not just for himself. He was representing the whole human family, every generation of his descendants down through history. A key aspect of the covenantal lay of the land is the principle of *representative responsibility*, in which one covenant servant is authorized to act on behalf of many others. Paul drives home this principle with sobering repetition:

> Sin came into the world through *one man*, and death through sin, and so death spread to all men because all sinned. . . . Because of *one man's trespass*, death reigned through that *one man* . . . . *One trespass* led to condemnation for all men . . . . By *one man's disobedience* the many were made sinners. (Rom. 5:12–19)

When Adam sinned, you sinned and I sinned, because Adam acted in our place at that fateful moment when he took the fruit from Eve and bit into it, knowing full well that he was turning his back on the good Creator who had done him nothing but good. His failure to pass the test of fidelity to the Lord was our failure.

On the other hand, the last Adam, Jesus, sustained his probation, the testing of his devotion as the Servant of the Lord throughout his life on earth. In the immediate aftermath of his anointing by the Spirit and acclamation by the Father as the beloved and pleasing Son, Jesus was driven by the Spirit into the desert to face temptation by the devil (Luke 4:1–13).

As the faithful Servant, Christ replied to Satan's every stratagem and suggestion by quoting Scripture, affirming his commitment to live by every word that proceeds from God's mouth (Deut. 8:3), to worship and serve the Lord God only (6:13), and not to "put the LORD [his] God to the test" by distrust (6:16). These were all lessons that the children of Israel should have learned in the wilderness, as Moses reminded them on the plains of Moab. These were also lessons that unfallen Adam and Eve knew and should have heeded in Eden.

Later, as we have seen, Satan used Simon Peter to attack Jesus at the focal point of his unique mission as the Lord's Servant, his calling to endure rejection and death in Jerusalem. Mark's Gospel notes a detail of that confrontation: "But *turning and seeing his disciples*, he rebuked Peter and said, 'Get behind me, Satan! For you are not setting your mind on the things of God, but on the things of man'" (Mark 8:33). The sight of his disciples, and beyond them all for whom he would suffer and die, steeled his resolve to follow the bitter path laid out by the Father, as he would later say: "the Son of Man came not to be served but to serve, and to give his life as a ransom for many" (10:45).

Jesus' performance as the Lord's Servant was the opposite of Adam's treasonous failure, as Paul emphasized as he placed these two covenant representatives side by side in stark contrast:

> The free gift by the grace of *that one man Jesus Christ* abounded for many.... Much more will those who receive the abundance of grace and the free gift of righteousness reign in life through *the one man Jesus Christ.*
> ... So *one act of righteousness* leads to justification and life for all men.... By *the one man's obedience* the many will be made righteous ... that ... grace also might reign through righteousness leading to eternal life *through Jesus Christ our Lord.* (Rom. 5:15–21)

If we were dismayed that Adam's offense has rendered us, his children, guilty, how grateful we can be that another Servant, acting on our behalf, withstood the test in complete obedience, so that his one act of righteousness is counted ours by the free gift of grace!

Adam and Christ: The Product of the Test of the Servant's Loyalty

Adam's failure in his test as the Lord's servant produced dire consequences not only for himself and Eve his wife, but for the whole human race. God had said, "In the day that you eat of [the tree of the knowledge of good and evil] you shall surely die" (Gen. 2:17). In keeping with his word, death did indeed begin that very day to work its way into the fabric of human life. Adam and Eve's unbelieving disobedience did not instantly end their physical lives, but death certainly began to permeate their experience. Their openness with each other died: they hid in shame from each other, suddenly embarrassed by their nakedness (3:7). Their delight in their Creator died: they hid in shame from God, the source of life (3:8). They tried to hide from truth through blame-shifting (vv. 12–13). Their future would henceforth be marred by marital conflict and increased pain in their tasks of multiplying (v. 16) and subduing the earth (vv. 17–19). They were banished from the sanctuary of God, and this expulsion from the garden is the worst aspect of the death that God imposed immediately (vv. 22–24). Finally, Adam and his race would return to the dust, from which he had been formed (v. 19). The rest of the biblical record documents the dire product of Adam's failure as covenant servant in the ensuing generations. Murder soon robbed Adam and Eve of one son and sent another, the murderer, into exile (4:1–16). Rebels boasted in their unbridled violence (vv. 23–24). Human wickedness compounded to the point that nothing less than a flood would wash the world clean (well, cleaner) from the pollution (6:1–7). Even after the deluge, the sad story resumed with drunkenness, lust, contempt, and cursing (9:20–25). Through the centuries, the story continued: rape, deception, slaughter, famine, treachery, slavery, abuse, and more.

Yet into the dark prospect of human history following the fall, God's promise of the woman's triumphant offspring injected a glimmer of hope (Gen. 3:15). Paul's comparisons and contrasts between Adam and Christ in Romans 5:12–21 and 1 Corinthians 15:21–22 bring into sharp focus the hints of anticipation strewn throughout the Old Testament, promises that in God's good time another covenant Servant would arise to keep the Lord's commands, deserve the Lord's approval, and confer on others the blessed consequences of his faithfulness. For example, the prophet Isaiah spoke of the Lord's Servant, the object of God's choice and delight, who would be empowered by God's Spirit to establish justice in the earth (Isa. 42:1–4). Unlike Adam, this Servant would listen eagerly to the Lord's word, even when insulted and assaulted by others for his faithfulness (50:4–9). Though deserving vindication from his Lord, this Servant would be wounded for others' transgressions and crushed for their iniquities. As he would undergo the curse that their treason deserved, the guilty would be blessed with God's peace and healing for this Servant's sake (53:4–6).

The New Testament identifies Jesus as the Lord's long-promised Servant (Acts 3:13, 26; 4:27, 30). As the ancient prophet declared the Lord's delight in his Servant (Isa. 42:1), so the Father's voice from heaven announced his pleasure in Jesus (Matt. 3:17; 17:5). Jesus was the Servant who resolutely "set his face" to move submissively toward the rejection awaiting him in Jerusalem (Luke 9:51, alluding to Isa. 50:7). In Jesus, prophecies of the Servant's sufferings have been fulfilled (Luke 22:37; Acts 8:32–35; 1 Peter 2:24–25). And in Jesus, the vindication promised to the Servant for his faithful righteousness has also been fulfilled (Acts 3:13–15). Since he sustained his trial with flawless fidelity, death—the ultimate covenant curse—had no claim on him, no right to keep him in its grip, as Peter announced:

> God raised him up, loosing the pangs of death, because it was not possible for him to be held by it. For David says concerning him,
>
> "I saw the Lord always before me,
>   for he is at my right hand that I may not be shaken;
> therefore my heart was glad, and my tongue rejoiced;
>   my flesh also will dwell in hope.
> For you will not abandon my soul to Hades,
>   or let your Holy One see corruption.
> You have made known to me the paths of life;
>   you will make me full of gladness with your presence."
>   (Acts 2:24–28, quoting Ps. 16:8–11)

Since Jesus represented others as the Lord's Servant, not only did his being "smitten by God" (Isa. 53:4) free them from covenant curse, but also they share his vindication as righteous (52:13). Isaiah foretold that "the righteous one, my servant," would "make many to be accounted righteous" (53:11); and Paul writes that "Jesus our Lord . . . was delivered up for our trespasses and raised for our justification" (Rom. 4:24–25).

As the death that Adam's failure produced was multidimensional, so the life that rewards Christ's fidelity has many facets. Ultimately, as Paul affirms in 1 Corinthians 15, those who are united to Jesus by faith will experience the resurrection of the body into a Spirit-vitalized, corruption-free, overflowingly abundant life, a life befitting the glory and joy of the age to come. But the blessing spills back from the future into believers' present experience through the life-giving presence of the Holy Spirit: "If Christ is in you, although the body is dead because of sin, the Spirit is life because of righteousness. If the Spirit of him who raised Jesus from the dead dwells in you, he who raised Christ Jesus from the dead will also give life to your mortal bodies through his Spirit who dwells in you" (Rom. 8:10–11).

By the power of the Holy Spirit and through the faith he evokes in the human heart, Christians are united with Christ, their representative, as he died under the covenant curse that they deserved and rose again through the covenant blessing that he deserved. But in the mysterious plan of God, our union with Jesus in his death and resurrection effects even more than an exchange of status before the Lord who supremely judges. Not only was Christ, the faithful Servant, charged with and punished for others' infidelity, while they are credited with and blessed for his unswerving devotion; but also Christ's Spirit exerts resurrection power on stone-cold hearts, "dead in . . . trespasses and sins" (Eph. 2:1), bringing them to life and setting in motion a process by which our unfaithful hearts are progressively transformed and transfigured to resemble the devoted heart of Jesus, the true Servant. By sheer grace and his Spirit's sovereign power, the Lord has launched a new-creation project to reclaim, revivify, and re-create covenant-breakers into covenant-keepers, servants whose loyalty brings him delight: "For we are his workmanship, created in Christ Jesus for good works, which God prepared beforehand, that we should walk in them" (v. 10). Our present participation in Jesus' resurrection, signified in our baptism, has ushered us into "newness of life" (Rom. 6:4), setting us free to present ourselves to God as those who have been brought from death to life (v. 13)—to begin to live as servants whose glad submission delights and glorifies our covenant Lord.

We can summarize how Christ's faithfulness as the Servant of the Lord benefits us in three ways: First, because Adam failed in his mission to honor and please our Lord through loyalty, trust, and eager obedience, he brought upon himself and us his children the cursing that the Lord pronounced on servants who repaid his gifts of privilege and provision with unbelief, disloyalty, and defiance. Because the Lord is both just and true to his word, he will not ignore our breach of trust, nor will he fail to impose the dire consequences that he said would follow from disobedience. Therefore, God the Son became our second Adam to endure the Lord's curse on "everyone who does not abide by all things written in the Book of the

Law, and do them" (Gal. 3:10). Although he himself, having become a true human being, lived a life of complete and consistent covenant devotion, in our place he endured the curse that is the inevitable consequence of our violation of the covenant (v. 13). God's righteous wrath inflicted on Jesus the condemnation, forsakenness, and death that he (Jesus) did not deserve, but that we did. Theologians call this Christ's *passive obedience*, not because it was inflicted on him as an involuntary victim (as we sometimes think of passivity) but because it entailed his willing submission to suffering (Latin *passio*) to atone for our violations of the commitment and commandments that God's covenant demanded. Jesus' sacrifice as the Suffering Servant is, as Isaiah 53 states so clearly, the basis on which God forgives us in our justification and extends reconciliation to us. The Lord, who always renders just judgment, has pronounced our debt to his justice "paid in full."

Second, because Adam failed in his mission to honor and please our Lord, he forfeited for himself and us his children the blessing that the Lord of the covenant promised to servants who sustained the test of their loyalty, trust, and eager obedience. Therefore, God the Son became our second Adam to fulfill the conditions of the covenant on our behalf. He entered the world and embraced our humanity to fulfill his Father's will. He obeyed all of God's commands—in his every visible deed, his every audible word, and his every secret motive of the heart. Theologians call this the *active obedience* of Jesus. It is the basis on which God declares us not only forgiven but positively righteous in our justification. On the ground of his complete commitment to the Father's will, Jesus can claim by right all the blessings promised by God to the faithful covenant-keeping Servant. Because he acted on our behalf, as our representative, his flawless obedience and the unimpeachable loyalty expressed in that obedience are reckoned by God as belonging to us as well, and with them the blessings that Christ, the Righteous One, gladly shares with us!

Finally, God the Son, who became our second Adam, is already imparting to believers the eternal life that is his reward for flawlessly keeping his commitment to the Father and his commands. He entered into his reward at his resurrection from the dead by the power of the Holy Spirit. Now he shares his resurrection life with us through that same Holy Spirit, who pursues a quiet but invincible project in our hearts to transform our perspectives, affections, desires, and actions so that they begin to resemble the servant's heart of Christ. For Paul, the contrasts between Adam and Christ lay not only in their opposite decisions with opposite results, but also in the fact that the resurrection life of Jesus, the last Adam, is dynamic and contagious: "Thus it is written, 'The first man Adam became a living being'; the last Adam became a life-giving spirit" (1 Cor. 15:45). We should probably capitalize "Spirit" because Paul's point is that Jesus enlivens, renews, and transforms us through his Holy Spirit. The Spirit comes to us on Christ's behalf to fulfill his promise to be with us always (Matt. 28:20; John 14:17–18). The risen Lord Jesus identifies himself with his Spirit, whose presence sets us free and enables us to see and be transformed by the Lord's glory, "the light of the knowledge of the glory of God in the face of Jesus Christ" (2 Cor. 3:17–18; 4:6). The result is that we begin to live for God by obeying his commands, out of gratitude for grace and love for the Lord who first loved us.

Adam, Jesus, and Other Covenant Servants

On the pages of Scripture, we meet many other individuals who bear the privileged title "servant of the Lord": Abraham, Lot, Moses, Caleb, Joshua, Samuel, David, Solomon, Elijah, Nehemiah, Job, various psalmists, Isaiah and other prophets, Daniel, Zerubbabel, Mary, Peter, Paul, Timothy, Epaphras, James, Jude, and others. Many of these servants exercised a special office among God's covenant community, especially as prophets (Moses, Elijah, etc.) or as kings (David). (In the next three chapters, we will explore the focused responsibilities of the pivotal categories of leaders—prophets, priests, and kings—through whom the Lord administered his relationship to his people.) Others of the Lord's servants are not distinguished by official roles, but their connections to Adam and to Christ make the servant themes that we have surveyed to be very relevant indicators of the ways that their stories fit into the Bible's grand story of Jesus Christ, the Lord who became Servant.

Not only do individuals fill the servant's various roles (for better or for worse), but also Israel as a covenant community is the Lord's servant (Isa. 44:1, 21; Jer. 30:10). By making covenant with Israel at Sinai, the Lord bestowed privilege and preeminence on that company of homeless escapees: "if you will indeed obey my voice and keep my covenant, you shall be my treasured possession among all peoples, for all the earth is mine; and you shall be to me a kingdom of priests and a holy nation" (Ex. 19:5–6). He lavishly provided for his servant people in the land he had promised to their ancestors: "a land flowing with milk and honey[,] . . . a land of hills and valleys, which drinks water by the rain from heaven, a land that the LORD your God cares for. The eyes of the LORD your God are always upon it, from the beginning of the year to the end of the year" (Deut. 11:9–12). In that land, Israel's fidelity as the Lord's servant would undergo testing, and her response to the probation produce either blessing under her Lord's favor or curse under his righteous wrath:

> And if you will indeed obey my commandments that I command you today, to love the LORD your God, and to serve him with all your heart and with all your soul, he will give the rain for your land in its season, the early rain and the later rain, that you may gather in your grain and your wine and your oil. . . . Take care lest your heart be deceived, and you turn aside and serve other gods and worship them; then the anger of the LORD will be kindled against you, and he will shut up the heavens, so that there will be no rain, and the land will yield no fruit, and you will perish quickly off the good land that the LORD is giving you. (Deut. 11:13–17)

Israel's history as the Lord's servant people was checkered at best. Periods of faithfulness, such as the conquest under Joshua, were accompanied by the Lord's favor (Josh. 21:43–45). Immediately thereafter, the era of the judges entailed a downward spiral of Israel's infidelity, leading to the Lord's chastisement through his people's pagan neighbors, resulting in repentance and a respite granted by the Lord through the various judges, followed by another cycle of unfaithfulness, judgment, repentance, and relief. Occasionally one or two of Israel's generations could fairly lay claim to a measure of faithfulness as the Lord's servants (Ps. 44:1–8). On the whole, however, the trajectory of Israel's history moved toward treason rather than trustworthiness, just as the proportions of blessings to curses in Deuteronomy 28 foreshadowed: fourteen verses of blessings, then fifty-four verses of curses. Thus, even faithful generations, like faithful individual servants of the Lord, shared in the nation's wider chastening. They longed for and pleaded for the Lord's rescue and vindication (Ps. 44:9–26; cf. Pss. 13; 80; 89; 119:74–88). Daniel, a righteous individual servant of the Lord, so identified with the unrighteous servant people to whom he belonged that he included himself in their confession of sin: "O Lord, the great and awesome God, who keeps covenant and steadfast love with those who love him and keep his commandments, we have sinned and done wrong and acted wickedly and rebelled, turning aside from your commandments and rules" (Dan. 9:4–5). In enduring the covenant curse of exile in Babylon, Daniel and his three faithful friends not only exhibited fidelity to the Lord but also foreshadowed the completely righteous Servant to come, who would identify with sinners in his baptism (Matt. 3:6, 14–15) and his death (Luke 22:37). Likewise, the members of the faithful generation that sang Psalm 44 affirmed their genuine allegiance in prayer to the Lord who "knows the secrets of the heart" (v. 21): "we have not forgotten you, and we have not been false to your covenant. Our heart has not turned back, nor have our steps departed from your way" (vv. 17–18). Nevertheless, their sufferings, like those of Daniel, actually arose from their fidelity to the Sovereign: "Yet for your sake we are killed all the day long; we are regarded as sheep to be slaughtered" (v. 22). Though faithful to the Lord's covenant and commands, they suffered slaughter, and their deaths were for his sake. What can explain this paradox? Shouldn't we hear and see in this extraordinary congregational psalm the fruit of the Holy Spirit's heart-changing power, applying Christ's resurrection life to his expectant people, even centuries in advance of his suffering and vindication as the preeminent Servant of the Lord?

Paul seems to have seen this psalm in that way, for he views the multiracial church now being assembled after Jesus' death, resurrection, ascension, and sending of the Spirit as standing in solidarity with ancient Israel in its faithful moments. Confronted with a vast array of threats and afflictions, new covenant believers in Jesus can repeat faithful Israel's lament, "For your sake we are being killed all the day long; we are regarded as sheep to be slaughtered" (Rom. 8:36), even as we rest assured that no foe can "separate us from the love of God in Christ Jesus our Lord" (v. 39). Like ancient Israel, and as the fulfillment of ancient Israel, the church now being gathered from all of earth's peoples is the corporate servant of the Lord. Believers are called God's "servants" in the book of Revelation (1:1; 2:20; 6:11; 7:3; 11:18; 19:2, 5; 22:3, 6) and elsewhere, including quotations from the Old Testament that connect the church closely to Israel (Acts 2:18; 4:29; 1 Peter 2:16). As Peter writes to congregations full of people with pagan pasts, he lavishes on them the titles that distinguished Israel's privilege and preeminence: "a chosen race, a royal priesthood, a holy nation, a people for his own possession" (1 Peter 2:9). Believers in Jesus enjoy provision and protection that both resemble and exceed that experienced by Israel at the exodus, when

154

> our fathers were all under the cloud, and all passed through the sea, and
> all were baptized into Moses in the cloud and in the sea, and all ate the
> same spiritual food, and all drank the same spiritual drink. For they
> drank from the spiritual Rock that followed them, and the Rock was
> Christ. (1 Cor. 10:1–4)

The church at "the end of the ages" (1 Cor. 10:11) in "these last days" (Heb.
1:2), like Israel in the wilderness long ago, faces a probation, a testing of
our faith's perseverance: "For we have come to share in Christ, if indeed
we hold our original confidence firm to the end" (3:14). In contrast to the
wilderness generation, who "were unable to enter [the promised inheritance]
because of unbelief" (v. 19), we enter God's rest through faith that holds
fast to Christ throughout life's trials (4:1–3, 11). God's rest is the "product"
of Jesus' successful probation as the Lord's Servant, the promised blessedness that Christ himself has entered through his perfect obedience and
sacrifice (1:3; 10:12–14). By cleansing us of our infidelity and defilement,
Jesus ushers believers into his own reward: "Consequently, he is able to
save to the uttermost those who draw near to God through him, since he
always lives to make intercession for them" (7:25). As the living Savior who
sustained his test, he is able to help those whose faith and faithfulness are
undergoing trial (2:18).

Adam and Christ stand over the whole of human history and the entire
human family as representative servants whose opposite responses to the
Lord's covenant commandments yield opposite results in the lives of others
who populate the Bible's pages. All who are "in" Adam—every human who
ever lived, except Jesus himself—share the guilt of Adam's disobedience,
the disability of Adam's corruption, the curse befitting Adam's treason. Yet
from this cursed covenant community God graciously rescues unworthy
servants, placing them "in" Christ, the faithful Servant of the Lord, whose
death releases them from the curse they deserve, whose obedience imparts
to them the blessing he deserves, and whose Holy Spirit sets in motion a
process of imparting his resurrection life to transform hearts and conform
them to his holiness and steadfast love.

Conclusion

So how does the motif that Jesus is the supremely faithful and Suffering
Servant help us to make sense of the many biblical passages that describe

the covenantal context and conduct of God's finite and flawed human servants, whether individuals or communities, whether in their relative faithfulness (by the sanctifying grace of Christ's Spirit) or in their miserable failures (as fallen children of Adam)? In all the expressions of the covenant of grace down through history, from the first promise of an offspring who would destroy the devil while the offspring himself is wounded, through Abraham, and Moses, and David, and Jeremiah's promise of a new covenant, to its fulfillment in Jesus, the covenant of grace is made with guilty and spiritually disabled covenant servants, with fallen people who can never completely keep its obligations and who therefore always deserve its curse. Nevertheless, God's gracious Spirit mysteriously applies to those who trust his promises the resurrection life of Jesus, the uniquely faithful Servant, even in advance of his obedient life, atoning death, and vindicating resurrection. The Lord speaks in defense of "my servant Moses" (Num. 12:7–8; Josh. 1:2, 7; Mal. 4:4), and "my servant Caleb" (Num. 14:24), and "my servant David" (2 Sam. 3:18; 1 Kings 11:38; Ps. 89:3, 20), not because they were personally sinless but because God's Spirit had begun in them a process of lifelong transformation that made them, to one degree or another, previews of the impeccable commitment and service that God's Son, the final Servant, would fulfill in his incarnation. Of the twelve Israelite spies who scouted out Canaan, only Joshua and Caleb summoned the Israelites to trust the Lord to give them the land that he had promised to Abraham, and their faithfulness almost led to their deaths at the hands of their rebellious kinsmen (Num. 14:5–10). As a result, of the adult generation that left Egypt with Moses, only the faithful Caleb and Joshua, who "wholly followed the Lord," eventually entered the Promised Land (14:30, 38; 26:65; 32:11–12; Deut. 1:36; Josh. 14:6–14).

As we read the historical narratives of the Bible, we should evaluate the human participants in light of the law of the covenant: when they are faithful and obedient, they provide previews of Jesus, the faithful covenant Servant; when they fall short, they show dramatically our need for Jesus to come and offer the joyful obedience that we and they do not and cannot render as we should. At their very best, of course, all the covenant servants who lead up to Jesus offered only flawed faithfulness and relative righteousness. They knew full well that their own fidelity to the Lord's covenant commands could not come close to commending them before the tribunal of God's holy justice. The same psalmist who affirmed his complete and costly devotion to the Lord in words that the New Testament would apply, most fittingly, to Jesus ("For zeal for your house has consumed me, and the reproaches of those who reproach you have fallen on me," Ps. 69:9, quoted in John 2:17; Rom. 15:3) also confessed his own sins and need for forgiveness ("O God, you know my folly; the wrongs I have done are not hidden from you," Ps. 69:5). King David could celebrate in song, "The LORD dealt with me according to my righteousness; according to the cleanness of my hands he rewarded me" (2 Sam. 22:21), for God's sovereign Spirit had begun a good work within David's fallen heart, transforming him into the image of his coming, greater Son (1 Sam. 13:14; 1 Kings 14:8; 15:3). Yet the inspired author of 2 Samuel puts David's claim of innocence into perspective when he goes on to mention Uriah, against whom David sinned so grievously (23:39), and David's foolish pride in the size of his army (chap. 24). As the Spirit of the coming Christ pursued his sanctifying work in Old Testament believers, he crafted them into patterns, types, that—despite all their remaining flaws—sketched the shape of the utterly faithful Servant to come. At their most faithful, the people whom God turned into previews of his Righteous One fell far short of a righteousness that could lay claim to covenant blessing, so they looked ahead in longing hope, clinging to the promise of the one and only Servant whose suffering and perfect righteousness could and would usher them into the blessing of the Lord.

As we read the commands of the Bible, they expose the sobering truth that we have not been faithful covenant servants by keeping the words of the Lord from start to finish, in heart as well as in hand. But there is a Servant who did obey thoroughly, heartily, from start to finish—and Jesus did it all for us! And as we rest in Jesus' righteousness achieved for us, we also trust in the power of Jesus' sanctifying Spirit residing in us, quietly but relentlessly pursuing his mission of transforming our motives, affections, understanding, will, and behavior more and more into the image of Christ.

As we read the Psalms, we hear David and Israel's other inspired singers appeal to the Lord for rescue when they are suffering for righteousness' sake, or for forgiveness when suffering because of their own sins. We hear them rejoicing in the law of the Lord (Ps. 119) and worshiping in the Lord's presence on Mount Zion. And in their voices (whether singing in the minor key of lament or in the major key of praise and thanksgiving), we can also hear the voice of Jesus, the Servant who always delights in the Father's presence but who endured the Father's abandonment as he suffered under our curse.

157

As we read the promises that God makes to those who keep his covenant, we humbly but confidently claim them by faith in Jesus, who deserves every blessing promised and has bound us to himself, making his obedience ours so that we are coheirs with him of all that the Father lavishes on those in whom he is well pleased.

As we read the wisdom of Proverbs or Job or Ecclesiastes, we recall that in Jesus are hidden all the treasures of God's wisdom and knowledge—that he is the Sage wiser than Solomon and his cross is the display of divine folly that mystifies this world's wisdom, directing our line of vision beyond the present age to a new heavens and earth in which God's righteous Servant (and all who belong to him) will be vindicated (with a greater restoration than Job's—namely, Jesus' resurrection from the dead!) and rebellion punished.

Putting It into Practice: The Blessed Servant of God (Psalm 1)

Psalm 1, the gateway to the whole book of Psalms, gives wisdom concerning two ways to live, one "known" (that is, recognized and approved) by the Lord and thus bringing blessedness, and the other leading to condemnation in the judgment and banishment from the congregation of the righteous—in short, perishing (1:6). It is closely linked to the second psalm in several ways. The theme of blessedness opens the first psalm and closes the second (1:1; 2:12). The threat of perishing closes both (1:6; 2:12). And both entail the interplay of portraits of *individual* servants who enjoy the Lord's favor (1:1–3; 2:7–9), on the one hand, with portraits of *groups*, on the other, who either submit to the Lord (the righteous, 1:5–6; kings who serve the Lord and kiss the Son, 2:10–12) or defy him (wicked, sinners, scoffers, 1:1, 4–5; conspiring peoples and their rulers, 2:1–5).

Like other wisdom literature in the Bible, Psalm 1 employs imagery, simile, and contrast. In the imagery we see a tree planted "by streams of water" (v. 3), the ideal location for vitality and fruitfulness in the semiarid Near East. We also see chaff, dry and weightless husks that are separated from the useful grain and discarded, carried away by wind in the winnowing process. The similes compare the man who enjoys and absorbs the Lord's law to the tree, and the wicked to the ephemeral chaff. The contrast, obviously, is seen in the values and the destinies of the righteous servant who treasures the Lord's Word, on the one hand, and wicked sinners who scoff at the Lord and his way, on the other. What we do not find in this psalm, interestingly, is a command or prohibition. Implicitly the psalm counsels us against consorting and siding with those who treat the Lord and his law with contempt, a path that ends in perishing. It also paints so appealing a picture of the blessed life enjoyed by the lover of God's law that we cannot miss its tacit appeal, "Don't you want this blessedness? Here is how it is found."

Since the first psalm stands at the head of a collection of songs in many moods, in both major and minor keys, we must notice that the wisdom it offers has an eschatological, eternal perspective. We do this psalm an injustice and set ourselves up for deep disappointment if we construe it to claim that Bible meditation is a speed pass to prosperity in the present, or that the winds that remove the wicked chaff will blow this week or next. Psalm 1 does not offer a facile, short-term formula that blissfully ignores the harsh realities explored in Psalms 37, 73, and others: in the present, as often as not, the wicked, scoffing sinner seems to be the thriving tree, and the humble servant who treasures the Lord's Torah is swept away by violent aggression. Yet Psalm 1 lifts our sights above the present confusion and conflict to fix our gaze on "the judgment" to come (v. 5), in which the wicked will no longer stand and the righteous will experience the vindication that shows that all along the Lord has "known"—personally attended to and benevolently guarded and guided—their way. The psalm's eschatological perspective is both confirmed and elaborated by a parallel passage in the prophecy of Jeremiah, in which a portrait of the blessed man is preceded by a counterimage of his opposite:

> Thus says the LORD:
> "Cursed is the man who trusts in man
>   and makes flesh his strength,
>   whose heart turns away from the LORD.
> He is like a shrub in the desert,
>   and shall not see any good come.
> He shall dwell in the parched places of the wilderness,
>   in an uninhabited salt land.
>
> "Blessed is the man who trusts in the LORD,
>   whose trust is the LORD.
> He is like a tree planted by water,
>   that sends out its roots by the stream,
> and does not fear when heat comes,
>   for its leaves remain green,

and is not anxious in the year of drought,
>   for it does not cease to bear fruit." (Jer. 17:5–8)

The first psalm and this prophetic poem strikingly illumine and interpret each other, especially in two ways. First, the prophet discloses the motive that underlies the blessed man's delight in the Lord's law—namely, that he "trusts in the LORD." The servant's loyalty to the Lord exhibits itself in reverent attention to his Word, and meditation on the Word feeds trust in the Lord who spoke the Word. Second, the prophet places the blessed life in sharp contrast to the curses incurred by the one who trusts in man and turns from the Lord—who repudiates his covenant commitment as servant. Jeremiah could hardly be more obvious in echoing the opposite outcomes of Israel's probation as the Lord's servant described in Deuteronomy 28. The wisdom of Psalm 1 and Jeremiah 17 is not pragmatic and shortsighted; rather, it exhibits the ultimate outcomes of opposite responses to the role and responsibilities imposed by the Lord on his servants.

Who, then, is the Torah-loving man of Psalm 1? How should we connect the psalm's attractive (vibrant, fruitful tree) and alarming (wind-blown chaff) images to Christ, and to ourselves? The servant themes that we have explored in this chapter provide the clues to this psalm's location in the covenantal lay of the land that leads us to Jesus. This psalm implies Christ's authority as Lord to pass judgment on servants bound to him in covenant, whether in condemnation or in vindication (vv. 5–6); and the second psalm speaks even more explicitly of the authority of the Anointed Son as Judge (2:7–12).

But Psalm 1 also portrays what it means to be faithful as the Lord's servant, both in devotion to the Lord's instruction and in distance from the influence of the Lord's enemies. The psalm presents two mutually exclusive categories of people: on the one hand, the righteous feast their hearts unceasingly ("day and night," v. 2) on the Lord's law; on the other hand are the wicked, sinners, and scoffers who do not do so. A hard look at ourselves in the harsh light of these alternatives leads to the disconcerting conclusion that none of us has been the servant whose life resembles that ever-fruitful tree. Indeed, as Psalm 14 shows:

>   The LORD looks down from heaven on the children of man,
>   to see if there are any who understand,
>   who seek after God.

> They have all turned aside; together they have become corrupt;
> > there is none who does good,
> > not even one. (Ps. 14:2–3)

So from one perspective, it makes sense to understand the "blessed man" of Psalm 1 as finding his truest—in fact, uniquely true—expression in Jesus alone. When he entered the world, it was with the express purpose of accomplishing the Father's will, delighting to follow the Lord's law that was inscribed in his heart:

> Then I said, "Behold, I have come;
> > in the scroll of the book it is written of me:
> I delight to do your will, O my God;
> > your law is within my heart." (Ps. 40:7–8)

He is the ever-fruitful tree, the Righteous One who can stand in the judgment.

Yet "the congregation of the righteous" (Ps. 1:5), whose way the Lord knows, is an assembly of many, not just one. As the Lord's faithful Servant, Jesus would suffer death to bring many others to life—to make others into faithful servants, "whose trust is the LORD" (Jer. 17:7). He would, on the cross, endure the "perishing" reserved for the wicked, his life driven away like chaff before the wind, even though his delight was in the law of the Lord. Yet, though momentarily destroyed on behalf of others, Jesus was raised to everlasting life. In his exaltation he has become the source of abundant life to those who rely on him, who draw nourishment from him through his Word and by his Spirit. He is the source of living water, his life-imparting, fruit-producing Spirit (John 4:10–11; 7:38–39). He is the Vine that nourishes branches, so that they can bear much fruit (15:4–5). As he sustains our lives and fruitfulness by the Spirit's mighty presence, Jesus the Servant transforms us who trust him into those who share his delight in the Lord's law and his blessedness under the Lord's approving verdict and loving care.

Questions for Reflection and Discussion

1. Why does Jesus have to be both God and man in order to be the "one mediator between God and men" (1 Tim. 2:5)? Specifically, why is his real, full *humanity* so necessary in order for us to receive blessings/benefits instead of curses/condemnation through our covenantal relationship to God?

161

2. Some cultures, cherishing ideas of individual freedom and self-determination, are offended by the apostle Paul's statements that Adam's disobedience adversely affected his descendants for generations to come (Rom. 5; 1 Cor. 15). Other cultures have little trouble accepting that Paul's teaching about covenantal representatives accurately reflects the interconnectedness of families, generations, clans, and the human race as a whole. What evidence from other parts of the Bible (and from the way in which families and communities actually function) reinforces the principle of one representative's acting on behalf of others?

3. In what ways did the first Adam's privileged position as the image of God foreshadow the even greater preeminence of Jesus, the second Adam? How do we still share in the privilege and authority of the first Adam? What foretastes do we experience of our share in the privilege of the second Adam, by God's grace?

4. What gifts did God generously provide for the first Adam, to motivate and enable him to stay faithful as covenant servant? How did the circumstances in which Jesus, the second Adam, fulfilled his role as Servant pose greater challenges to his faithfulness than those encountered by Adam? What gifts did God bestow on Christ to equip and fortify him to maintain unswerving loyalty as the Servant of the Lord? What gifts does Christ now share with us to make us into faithful servants?

5. In Adam and Eve's probation as covenant servants, what *decisive issue* did Satan's temptation pose for them? What aspects of Jesus' allegiance to God his Father were put to the test by Satan's three approaches in the wilderness? By Satan's later assaults throughout Jesus' ministry on earth? Which of Satan's strategies are most effective when your own loyalty as covenant servant is put to the test?

6. In what three ways does Christ's faithfulness as the Servant of the Lord benefit us? How does each way address the damage that has come to us because of Adam's failure as covenant servant?

7. Since the Bible's verdict about every human being except Jesus is that "none is righteous, no, not one" (Rom. 3:10), how can other parts of Scripture describe individuals as righteous, even "blameless" (Job 1:8; Luke 1:6)? How are we helped in resolving this dilemma by recognizing that the people who trust God show the influences of both

the first Adam and the second Adam—guilt and spiritual death from the unfaithful servant, and resurrection life from the utterly faithful Servant?

8. Can we expect that the Spirit of the risen Servant of the Lord will actually make progress in conforming us to Jesus' covenant faithfulness in our thoughts, motives, words, and actions? Why or why not? Is it possible to discern in ourselves hints of our growth in godliness without succumbing to self-righteousness and pride? If so, how?

9. Who is the covenant-keeping servant of Psalm 1, who will enjoy blessedness from God in the judgment? Should we give more than one answer to this question? Is "the righteous" a solitary individual servant, or a company of many? Give reasons for your answer.

10. Although Psalm 1 contains no direct command, how does it motivate us to seek blessing from God? What makes the psalm's way of moving us even more potent than a bare imperative?

PART 5

Recognizing the Landmarks

7

Jesus the Final Prophet: God's Word

Landmarks: Between the Road Signs and the Lay of the Land

As we walk with Jesus through the pages of Scripture and the epochs of biblical history, the Spirit of Christ, who foretold and "foreshowed" Christ's sufferings and subsequent glories (1 Peter 1:10–11), guides our pilgrimage in a variety of ways. Some routes have been marked by "road signs." These are the Old Testament prophecies and patterns (types) that the New Testament identifies as foreshadowing and finding fulfillment in Christ, his redemptive mission, and his church. Not only in words but also in historical realities—events and individuals, institutions and offices—the Holy Spirit provides previews of the climax of God's redemptive plan in Jesus.

Other paths are less obvious, but for these we can perceive the covenantal "lay of the land" that structures God's relationship with human beings throughout history. The Creator has interacted with us through covenant from the dawn of creation, through our fall into sin (Hos. 6:7), and then throughout the gradual realization of his plan to restore the broken bond through an offspring of Eve (Gen. 3:15). Some passages focus on the Lord of the covenant, showing his powerful deeds, his faithful promises, and his worthiness to receive our devotion and obedience. Others focus on the servant, showing our responsibility to trust and obey, the blessings promised to loyal servants, or the dire consequences of our rebellion. The Lord's role and the servant's role intersect in the incarnation of God the Son, Jesus Christ, who entered the human family in order to restore and secure the covenant bond between God and us by keeping the commitments of both parties as the just and gracious divine Lord and the loyal and submissive human Servant.

In the next three chapters, we are going to survey a third category of routes that connect the Bible's diverse passages to Jesus. In terms of clarity, these directional indicators fall somewhere between the plain road signs and the subtle lay of the land. On the one hand, the links in this group are not as obvious as the typological ties that the New Testament points out between Old Testament realities and their fulfillment in Christ. On the other, they are not as sweeping and sometimes subtle as the wide landscape of the biblical story of the Lord's covenants with his servant people. This middle level of links often helps us to discern, even in Old Testament texts not explicitly mentioned in the New Testament, the route that leads from a particular passage to Christ.

These directional markers are like landmarks. The direction that a landmark offers is not as unmistakable as a street sign that identifies Main Street or a house number that shows that you have reached your destination. On the other hand, landmarks are easier to see than the gentle slope of a forested hillside, so they give us a more precise sense of where we are and what way we need to go than the lay of the land provides. I think, for example, of Pikes Peak, which dominates the eastern face of the Rockies in Colorado and looms over the city of Colorado Springs, where the prairie meets the mountains. Wherever you are in Colorado Springs or its environs, when you see Pikes Peak, you know that you are looking west and can also estimate where you are in relation to the city's center. Mount Kilimanjaro, Africa's tallest mountain (almost six thousand meters, over nineteen thousand feet), towers over the cities of Moshi and Arusha in northern Tanzania. When the cloud cover clears and you glimpse the mountain's snowy cap, wherever you are in or around those towns, you know that you are looking north toward Kenya, just beyond that majestic mountain. Landmarks come in smaller versions, too: the Eiffel Tower in Paris, the Opera House in Sydney, and the Statue of Liberty just off the southern tip of Manhattan. Each orients travelers to their whereabouts, offering invaluable (though not always precise) direction.

Among the clearest landmarks in Israel's experience are the three categories of leaders established by God to administer his covenant relationship with his people: prophets, priests, and kings. These leaders are sometimes called *theocratic officers* because through them God (*theo-*) ruled (*-cratic*) Israel as a nation, "my treasured possession among all peoples" (Ex. 19:5), uniquely set apart from other nations.

Buffers and Bridges

These leaders stood between the Lord and his people as covenant mediators, functioning both as *buffers* and as *bridges*. They were needed as *buffers* because God is holy and pure clear through, a "consuming fire" (Deut. 4:24) whose purity is dangerous to defiled and sinful people. At Mount Sinai, the Israelites rightly realized that having their holy Lord speak directly to them would destroy them. They needed insulation, as it were, from the Lord's consuming glory, so they pleaded with Moses to stand between them and God's dangerous purity:

> Now therefore why should we die? For this great fire will consume us. If we hear the voice of the LORD our God any more, we shall die. For who is there of all flesh, that has heard the voice of the living God speaking out of the midst of fire as we have, and has still lived? Go near and hear all that the LORD our God will say and speak to us all that the LORD our God will speak to you, and we will hear and do it. (Deut. 5:25–27; see Ex. 19:21–24)

Likewise, Israel's priests served in God's sanctuary, offering sacrifices and incense on behalf of the other tribes. Without the insulation of priestly intercessors, even the prophet Isaiah despaired of life when granted a vision of the Lord, "high and lifted up," in the temple (Isa. 6:1–4).

On the other hand, Israel's prophets, priests, and kings also functioned as *bridges*. Because God is gracious, he intends to restore and retain his bond of love and loyalty even with defiled and defiant people; so he comes to us, speaks with us, reconciles us, rules and defends us, and directs us into paths that please him. Since his personal presence is unbearably pure, he sends prophets to bring his Word. He consecrates priests to approach him with prayer and atoning blood. He anoints kings to execute wise justice among his quibbling people and to wage war against their foes. Through these intermediaries, therefore, the Lord kept his people at arm's length, lest his holiness incinerate them; but he extended his hand to them in words, in atoning mercy, and in strong defense and just governance.

Each of Israel's three theocratic offices operated in a sphere of authority and responsibility distinct from the other offices. Kings who presumed to usurp priestly prerogatives, such as offering sacrifice or incense, incurred the Lord's wrath. King Saul's unauthorized sacrifice deprived him of a dynasty of sons to succeed him on Israel's throne (1 Sam. 13:8–14). Centuries later, King Uzziah's presumptuous trespass into priestly territory was punished with defiling leprosy and lifelong banishment from Israel's assembly (2 Chron. 26:16–21). Genealogical factors worked against priests' assuming the military and political powers of the kings, since priests were to belong to the tribe of Levi, whereas the kings were descended from Benjamin (Saul) and then from Judah (David and his descendants).[1] The focal point of the prophets' calling was neither to offer sacrifices nor to wield the sword. Rather, prophets stood outside the religious and political-military establishments, sent by God to call wayward priests and kings to account for their dereliction of duty. Through Jeremiah, for example, the Lord charged all three groups of leaders with malfeasance:

> The priests did not say, "Where is the LORD?"
> Those who handle the law did not know me;
> the shepherds transgressed against me;
> the prophets prophesied by Baal
> and went after things that do not profit. (Jer. 2:8; see 18:18)

In the spiritual decline leading up to Judah's exile, the priests, who had privileged access to God's presence, were indifferent as to his whereabouts. Kings, charged to shepherd God's people (2 Sam. 5:2; 7:7) and enforce his law, violated its commands without compunction. Even prophets, charged to deliver only the Lord's word, instead claimed to speak for empty idols. This indictment shows not only Jeremiah's prophetic mission as God's spokesman but also the contours of each office's distinctive accountability. The failure of these officers was a negative image of what faithful priests, kings, and prophets should have been and done.

Deuteronomy shows the source of this threefold subdivision of the leadership in Israel. As Moses looked ahead to Israel's life in the Lord's land, he gave directions pertaining to kings (Deut. 17:14–20), to priests (18:1–8),

---

1. In the centuries between the Old and New Testaments, the Hasmoneans, a priestly dynasty, wielded royal power; but that development lies outside the history narrated in the Bible.

and to prophets (vv. 9–22). Kings would wield political and military power, so they must saturate their minds and hearts with the law of the Lord. Priests, who attend the Lord's sanctuary, must "stand and minister in the name of the LORD" (v. 5). The prophet who speaks truth in the Lord's name, not the strategies pursued by pagans, must be Israel's avenue of access into the purposes of God (vv. 9–19).

In Moses himself we see the combination of all three varieties of authority. He was clearly a giant among the Old Testament prophets, receiving the law from the Lord on the mountain and delivering it to the people at its foot. In Numbers 12:6–8, the Lord placed Moses in a class by himself: although the Lord would reveal himself in vision or riddle to other prophets, to Moses the Lord spoke clearly and "mouth to mouth." Moses also had a kingly role both as a warrior and as a judge. Although Moses' brother Aaron would head the hereditary priestly family, Moses also offered sacrifices to "cut" the covenant (Ex. 24) and to consecrate both the tabernacle (Ex. 40) and Aaron and his sons to their office (Lev. 8). In the generations after Moses, the tasks of hearing and speaking God's word, executing God's rule, and serving in God's presence were distributed to different groups of officers—prophets, kings, and priests. Yet God planned that those three spheres of mediation would eventually converge in one person, the "one mediator between God and men, the man Christ Jesus" (1 Tim. 2:5).

Jesus the Final Prophet, Perfect Priest, and King of Kings

In these next three chapters, we will explore in depth the motifs associated with each office in ancient Israel and then see how those themes lead us to Jesus as our comprehensive Mediator. One New Testament passage, the prologue to the epistle to the Hebrews, brings together all three of Jesus' mediatorial roles:

> Long ago, at many times and in many ways, God spoke to our fathers by the prophets, but in these last days he has spoken to us by his Son, whom he appointed the heir of all things, through whom also he created the world. He is the radiance of the glory of God and the exact imprint of his nature, and he upholds the universe by the word of his power. After making purification for sins, he sat down at the right hand of the Majesty on high, having become as much superior to angels as the name he has inherited is more excellent than theirs. (Heb. 1:1–4)

This glorious preamble teaches that Jesus is both God and man. As God, the Son is "the radiance of the glory of God and the exact imprint of his nature." He is the One through whom the Father "created the world" and the One who still "upholds the universe by the word of his power." His divine identity uniquely qualifies him to impart revelation from the Father, and this *prophetic* motif is where the prologue opens: "Long ago . . . God spoke . . . by the prophets, but in these last days he has spoken to us by his Son." God's "last days" speaking through his Son stands in continuity with his speech in times past through prophets, and Hebrews will often quote Israel's ancient Scriptures as being spoken to us today (3:7, 13). But the superior dignity of the Son shows that the revelation he imparts is fuller and final. The theme of God's speaking pervades Hebrews (2:1–4; 3:1, 7–19; 4:1–13; 12:18–29; 13:7–8, 22). Moses was a faithful *servant in* God's house, but Christ was a faithful *Son over* God's house (Heb. 3:2–6, alluding to Num. 12:7). Hebrews 3–4 looks back through Psalm 95 to Israel's wilderness wanderings after the exodus and draws a sobering lesson from the wilderness generation's unbelief, warning new covenant believers, in effect: "Today if you *hear God's voice*, do not harden your hearts as in the day that Israel put God to the test at Massah and Meribah." Hebrews 12:18–29 reminds us that whereas God spoke on earth to Moses, God's voice now addresses us from heaven, where Jesus stands as Mediator of a new covenant. The prophetic office has reached its divinely designed destination and fullness in the Lord Jesus, who declared to us "such a great salvation" (2:3–4).

The title "Son" refers not only to Christ's divine nature but also to his royal calling as the Anointed *King* descended from David. Psalm 2 (quoted in Heb. 1:5) speaks of the Lord's Anointed, the King whom the Lord has installed "on Zion, my holy hill" (Ps. 2:2, 6). In the psalm, the Lord promises to give his Son "the nations [for] your heritage" (vv. 7–8), and Hebrews describes him as the royal "heir of all things" (Heb. 1:2). As King, Jesus "sat down at the right hand of the Majesty on high," the first of many references to Psalm 110 in the epistle (1:3, 13; 5:6; 6:20; 7:3, 11–28; 8:1; 10:12; 12:2). In the psalm, the Lord invites David's Lord to take his throne at the right hand, and then appoints him "a priest forever after the order of Melchizedek," an ancient monarch who held both kingly and priestly offices (Heb. 6:20; 7:1; Gen. 14:18). Hebrews ascribes both royal dominion and military prowess to Jesus as the messianic King (Heb. 2:5–9, 14–15; 3:3–5; 7:1–3, 14).

The motif of Jesus' *priestly* ministry comes as the climax of the description of God's Son, in the words "after making purification for sins, he sat down at the right hand of the Majesty on high" (Heb. 1:3). The author to the Hebrews devotes the largest proportion of his epistle to the theme of Jesus' high-priestly qualifications, the atoning sacrifice of himself by which he cleansed our consciences, and his ongoing intercession as the ever-living Priest in the order of Melchizedek (2:17–18; 3:1; 4:14–16; 5:1–10; 7:1–28; 8:1–6; 9:1–28; 10:1–22; cf. 12:28–29; 13:10–16). In fact, the overarching theme of the entire letter is probably in view when we read in Hebrews 8:1 that "the point in what we are saying" is that we have a High Priest who lives forever to serve in God's heavenly sanctuary (8:1–6). When the prologue speaks of Christ's sitting at God's right hand, this enthronement certainly has royal overtones, as we just noted. But Hebrews will show that the King in view in that psalm is, like the ancient Melchizedek, a King who is also a Priest (7:1–28). The location of the Son's throne at God's right hand shows that the sanctuary in which he serves as Priest is not an earthly copy but the heavenly original (8:4–6; 9:11–12); and his seated posture implies that his work of atoning sacrifice has been accomplished once for all (10:11–12). Thus, the psalm forecasts the reunion and confluence of priestly and kingly offices in the ministry of Christ.

In these four verses and in the letter that flows from them, therefore, we can see the biblical basis for summing up Christ's mission using the categories of Prophet, Priest, and King. And we are not the first ones to approach the Savior's redemptive mission through these three perspectives. This threefold way of looking at Jesus' mission was beautifully articulated by the Protestant Reformers and the generations who followed them. From the 1560s comes the Heidelberg Catechism, primarily authored by Zacharias Ursinus and received by denominations with Reformed roots on the continent of Europe as a faithful summary of the Bible's central truths. In response to question 31 (Lord's Day 12), which asks why Jesus is called "Christ," which means "anointed," the catechism answers:

> Because he has been ordained by God the Father and has been anointed with the Holy Spirit to be our *chief prophet* and teacher who perfectly reveals to us the secret counsel and will of God for our deliverance; our only *high priest* who has set us free by the one sacrifice of his body, and who continually pleads our cause with the Father; and our *eternal king*

who governs us by his Word and Spirit, and who guards us and keeps us in the freedom he has won for us. (Emphasis added)

Eighty years later, an assembly of pastors and theologians gathered at Westminster Abbey in London to reform the worship, instruction, and government of the churches in England, Scotland, and Wales. The Westminster Assembly produced, among other influential documents, two catechisms, larger and shorter, for the instruction of children and adults in the central truths revealed in God's Word. Again the threefold tasks of prophets, priests, and kings were seen as a comprehensive (and biblically grounded!) template to express the various dimensions of Christ's redemptive work. The Shorter Catechism (WSC) teaches: "Christ, as our redeemer, executeth the offices of a prophet, of a priest, and of a king, both in his estate of humiliation and exaltation" (answer 23). It goes on to explain the distinctive tasks of each office:

WSC 24: Christ executeth the office of a prophet, in *revealing* to us, by his word and Spirit, the will of God for our salvation.

WSC 25: Christ executeth the office of a priest, in his once offering up of himself a sacrifice to satisfy divine justice, and *reconcile* us to God; and in making continual intercession for us.

WSC 26. Christ executeth the office of a king, in subduing us to himself, in *ruling* and defending us, and in restraining and conquering all his and our enemies. (Emphases added)

Each office entails a rich and complex combination of privileges, responsibilities, and related themes. But these concise summaries capture clearly the distinctive focus of each "theocratic" office and point us toward how each office finds its final expression in Christ's ministries of *revelation, reconciliation,* and *rule.* Clustered around these central missions accomplished by Christ our Mediator are biblical themes of a vast variety. For an overview of the breadth of motifs that God's Word connects to the offices of Prophet, Priest, and King, see the Appendix: Themes Linked to the Three Theocratic Offices (pp. 271–72).

So we can add detail to our "map" of the covenantal texture of the Bible by attending to the distinctive ministries assigned to prophets, priests, and kings and by noting how Israel's prophetic, priestly, and royal figures functioned (sometimes well, too often poorly) as intermediaries of the Lord's truth, authority, and holy presence to and among his people. Their moments of faithfulness in office provided previews of Jesus' ministries as the final Prophet, perfect Priest, and King of kings; and their failures kept believers' hearts looking forward in hope to his eventual arrival.

Prophets, Priests, and Kings in the Image of God

Before we look more specifically at the prophets' role in revelation and its fulfillment in Jesus, the Word made flesh, we need to consider one more biblical perspective. This perspective will help us to grasp how widely the threefold template of revelation, reconciliation, and rule—the focal points, respectively, of the tasks of the prophets, the priests, and the kings—applies to the breadth of the Bible's contents. These themes emerge not only in passages in which we see these Old Testament theocratic officers (or their New Testament counterparts, such as the apostles, who, like the prophets, convey God's word), but also in texts about ordinary people who had no special calling among God's people. Actually, every biblical passage that is about, or written by, or addressed to human beings—in other words, every single text in Scripture—will exhibit one or more prophetic, priestly, or royal motifs for one simple reason: the tasks distributed among prophets, priests, and kings in most of Israel's history align strikingly with dimensions of humanity's original creation in the image of God. To say it again, *these mediatorial offices "line up" with dimensions of human identity as those unique creatures who are made in the image of God and according to his likeness.*

Two statements in Paul's letters cast light on dimensions of Moses' meaning when he described God's creation of Adam and Eve "in our image, after our likeness" (Gen. 1:26). Paul is actually describing the result of God's gracious work of new creation in the experience of those who trust Jesus, but he echoes the language of Genesis 1 to send the signal that the transformation that the Holy Spirit is now performing in believers restores us to resemble our Creator's attributes in purity, as Adam and Eve did before they sinned. Paul informed the Colossians that they had "put on the new self, which is being renewed in knowledge after the image of its creator" (Col. 3:10). Around the same time, Paul wrote to the Ephesians that Christians have "put on the new self, created after the likeness of

God in true righteousness and holiness" (Eph. 4:24). This new identity, the fruit of our union with Christ the new Adam, stands in contrast to "your old self, which belongs to your former manner of life and is corrupt through deceitful desires," which must no longer define our values or our conduct (v. 22). Thus, says Paul, "the image of [our] creator," in which we are being renewed, includes "knowledge" (Col. 3:10); and "the likeness of God," for renewed believers as for unfallen Adam, includes "true righteousness and holiness" (Eph. 4:24).

Paul's cues in Colossians 3:10 and Ephesians 4:24 were picked up by the historic Reformed catechisms and woven into their descriptions of what it meant for Adam and Eve to be made in the image of God. The Heidelberg Catechism (Lord's Day 3, answer 6) affirms about human beings' original condition at creation: "God created them good in his own image, that is, *in true righteousness and holiness*, so that they might truly *know* God their creator, *love* him with all their heart, and *live with him* in eternal happiness for his praise and glory" (emphasis added). WSC 10 echoes Paul's language as well: "God created man male and female, after his own image, in *knowledge, righteousness, and holiness*, with dominion over the creatures" (emphasis added).

Were these catechisms correct to draw these inferences from Paul? I believe so. The creation accounts in Genesis 1 and 2 imply that having knowledge, righteousness, and holiness were significant dimensions of what it meant for human beings to be made in God's image and likeness. First, Adam and Eve bore the image of a God who spoke repeatedly to create and structure his universe, and then God addressed them in words of blessing (Gen. 1:28–30) and of warning (2:17). They were to receive God's revelation, respond rightly to it, and convey it to others, faithfully performing the prophetic calling to receive and relay true knowledge of God. Second, our first parents were authorized by God to exercise dominion over other living creatures and charged to exercise discernment and reach decisions righteously, in keeping with the Lord's command and prohibition. They were to be righteous kings, exercising their wills in sync with the Great King's direction. Finally, Adam and Eve were privileged to live with God in holiness in God's garden temple, Eden, and to guard this sanctuary from an enemy who would try to defile it. Even before sin made atonement necessary for communion with our holy Creator, Adam and Eve had a priestly role in worship that required holiness of heart.

These dimensions of Adam and Eve's pristine God-likeness—knowledge, righteousness, and holiness—were gravely damaged at the fall into sin. People still bear the image of God after sin enters the picture (Gen. 9:6; James 3:9), but the faculties that make us personal (thought, decision, relationship) are now distorted and misdirected. We still think and understand, but our thoughts are distorted by deceit and darkened by confusion. We still make choices and judgments, but now with biased and selfish motives rather than with wisdom and uprightness. We still interact with other persons, but not in purity and integrity.

Dimension of Image of God — Parties to the Covenant	**TRUE KNOWLEDGE**	**RIGHTEOUS AUTHORITY**	**HOLY RELATIONSHIP**
LORD	Speaks truly, illumines hearts	Rules justly, defends, judges	Consecrates, receives worship
MEDIATORS	Prophet: Hears, delivers the Word to God's people	King: Executes the Word, judges wisely and justly, defends God's people	Priest: Teaches the Word, atones and prays for God's people
SERVANT	Hears and trusts God's Word	Obeys God's Word	Pursues purity and peace in reconciled relation to God and God's people

Fig. 7.1. Covenant Parties, Mediators, and the Image of God

This link between the image of God and the theocratic offices yields three conclusions for our walking with Jesus through his Word: First, every son of Adam and daughter of Eve who appears on the Bible's pages, because he or she is created in God's image and likeness, still shows traces of our human callings to know God truly (prophet), to exercise rule righteously (king), and to relate to our Creator purely (priest). Knowledge is "imaging" or reflecting God in terms of our thought and our speech. Righteousness is imaging God in terms of our decisions through wise choices and just actions. Holiness is imaging God in terms of the personal purity and integrity necessary to engage God in his presence. Second, we can expect to find the

177

themes of knowledge, righteousness, and holiness in biblical persons who are not set apart to office as speakers of God's word (prophets, apostles, preachers), or defenders and judges of God's people (kings, judges, elders, etc.), or attendants and intercessors in God's sanctuary (priests, Levites, etc.). In ordinary people and in passages not directly tied to Israel's officers, therefore, we can expect to catch glimpses of these landmarks. When we do, we will note that the uneasy blend of faithfulness and failure that we see in sinful bearers of the divine image invites us to look to a Redeemer who would be the final Prophet, righteous King, and perfect Priest as the complete Mediator of a new covenant. Hence our third conclusion: because every son of Adam and daughter of Eve shares in our first parents' guilt and defiled nature, none of those whom we meet on Scripture's pages flawlessly fulfills humanity's prophetic, kingly, and priestly callings until we come to the incarnation of the beloved Son, who is "the image of the invisible God" (Col. 1:13–15).

Let us now look more closely at the prophetic office, and see how the distinctive characteristics of this calling, with its focus on revelation and knowledge, provide a preview of Christ's mission as the supreme Word of God, the final Revealer of the Father. In the next two chapters, we will do the same for the offices of priest and king.

The Prophet's Mission: To See and to Hear

The contrast between the prophets' mission and the priests' duties is often drawn in these terms: Prophets speak *from* God *to* people, while priests speak *from* people *to* God. Prophets preach, and priests pray. On the whole, that is a helpful way of looking at these two offices, as the WSC's description of Christ's prophetic and priestly ministries shows. Yet these generalizations make the boundary between the prophet's task and the priest's a bit too sharp. Actually, prophets pray for people as a part of their official activities. We hear Moses interceding before the Lord for the very survival of idolatrous Israel (Ex. 32:30–34; 33:12–23), and God earlier advised a Philistine king to ask for Abraham's prayers, "for he is a prophet" (Gen. 20:7). On the priestly side of things, although receiving *new* revelation from God was not integral to the priestly office, priests were authorized and accountable to be caretakers and conveyers of God's law: to keep it safe, read it publicly, apply it in judicial matters, and teach it to others (Deut. 17:8–13; 31:9–13; Ezra 7:1–10; Neh. 8:1–8; Mal. 2:4–7). Nevertheless, although the Bible shows prophets praying and priests preaching, the *focus* of the prophet's office is bringing God's word to his people.

In order to bring the Lord's word to his servant people on earth, the prophet must first receive the message from the Lord himself. God's law condemned those who claimed to speak in his name but did so at their own initiative, without his authorization (Deut. 18:20–22). The apostle Peter stressed that true prophecy arises not from the prophet's own interpretation of God's will but from the Holy Spirit's initiative (2 Peter 1:20–21). So before prophets can speak God's word or perform miraculous signs to show the divine authority of their message, they must hear the Lord speak and, often, be granted the privilege of beholding his glory, at least in a visionary mode. Before prophets speak and show, they must hear and see.

Prophets were summoned into God's heavenly royal throne room, to receive their messages from the divine King of kings. Often these royal audiences were conducted by means of visionary experiences in which prophets were called to serve as the Lord's spokesmen. Certain prophets—notably Isaiah (Isa. 6) and Ezekiel (Ezek. 1) in the Old Testament and John in the New (Rev. 1:10–20; 4:1–6)—described visions in which the prophets were mysteriously "caught up" into heaven (see 2 Cor. 12:1–3), to behold God's glory and to be struck with fear at the Lord's consuming holiness. Sometimes the Lord displayed his glory not just to the prophet's mind but in ways that others also perceived, visually or audibly or both (Dan. 10:5–8; Acts 9:7; 22:9; 26:13–14). False prophets, on the other hand, presumptuously invented their own visions and messages: "For who among them has stood in the council of the LORD to see and to hear his word, or who has paid attention to his word and listened?" (Jer. 23:18). The genuine prophet, having *seen* and *heard* in the Lord's heavenly council, brings God's word to his people.

The preeminent example of a prophet's privileged audience with the Lord himself occurred when God gave his law to Moses on Sinai. God's heavenly court descended as an ominous cloud onto the top of the mountain, so that it shuddered and blazed with fire (Ex. 19:16–20). Moses climbed up to meet with God and receive the law, and then to bring it back to the frightened people at the foot of the mountain. He glimpsed the back of the Lord's glory; and when he returned to the Israelites, his face radiated the splendor of the Creator who had spoken to him (Ex. 33:18–23; 34:4–8, 29–35). Moses' superiority to other prophets is linked to his experience on that mountain:

> Hear my words: If there is a prophet among you, I the LORD make myself known to him in a vision; I speak with him in a dream. Not so with my servant Moses. He is faithful in all my house. With him I speak mouth to mouth, clearly, and not in riddles, and he beholds the form of the LORD. Why then were you not afraid to speak against my servant Moses? (Num. 12:6–8)

The face-to-face mode of the Lord's self-disclosure set Moses apart from the prophets who would follow.

The New Testament guides us from Sinai to Jesus along three trails, one leading from Moses to Christ as the consummate Prophet, a second connecting the radiance of the Lord's glory to Christ the incarnate Son, and a third (alongside the second) relating Moses to us, who now behold the Son's divine glory by faith and bring his words to others. First, Jesus is the Messenger from the Father who is like, but even greater than, Moses. God promised his people that he would raise up a spokesman who had the same intimate access to God that Moses had enjoyed: "The LORD your God will raise up for you a prophet like me from among you, from your brothers—it is to him you shall listen" (Deut. 18:15). The apostle Peter declared that this prophecy found fulfillment in

> the Christ appointed for you, Jesus, whom heaven must receive until the time for restoring all the things about which God spoke by the mouth of his holy prophets long ago. Moses said, "The Lord God will raise up for you a prophet like me from your brothers. You shall listen to him in whatever he tells you." . . . And all the prophets who have spoken, from Samuel and those who came after him, also proclaimed these days. (Acts 3:20–24)

When Jesus was transfigured on the mountain, Peter, James, and John had heard God identify him as the long-promised Prophet. Narrating the Father's words, Luke's Greek (differing from the ESV rendering) reproduces the exact word order of Deuteronomy 18:15, showing the allusion to that Old Testament text: "This is my Son, my Chosen One; *it is to him you shall listen*" (Luke 9:35). Jesus is the preeminent Prophet like Moses. Yet as Hebrews 3:5–6 shows, Jesus is far better than Moses, worthy of greater honor as a Son excels a servant and as the Creator excels his creation.

Second, when Moses was ushered into the Lord's presence on the mountaintop, the glory that he saw was actually the glory of Christ the

Son. The infinite superiority of Jesus the Son as Revealer of the Father is implied in the prologue to John's Gospel:

> And the Word became flesh and dwelt among us, and we have seen his glory, glory as of the only Son from the Father, full of grace and truth. . . . For the law was given through Moses; grace and truth came through Jesus Christ. No one has ever seen God; the only God, who is at the Father's side, he has made him known. (John 1:14–18)

Jesus' glory is "full of grace and truth." These words echo God's description of himself as his stunning radiance passed by Moses on the mountain: "The LORD, the LORD, a God merciful and gracious, . . . *abounding in* ['full of'] *steadfast love* ['grace'] and *faithfulness* ['truth']" (Ex. 34:6). John further comments on the connection and the contrast: "the law was given through Moses; grace and truth came through Jesus Christ." Jesus the Son reveals God the Father in a fullness far beyond Moses, the greatest ancient prophet. As the second person of the Trinity, he knows the Father as no mere creature ever could and makes the Father known as no one else can. Jesus himself made this very claim: "All things have been handed over to me by my Father, and no one knows the Son except the Father, and no one knows the Father except the Son and anyone to whom the Son chooses to reveal him" (Matt. 11:27). Just as Moses, Isaiah, Ezekiel, and other prophets were qualified to deliver God's self-disclosure because they had seen his glory and heard his words, so Jesus the Son "bears witness to what he has seen and heard" (John 3:32). But Jesus is no mere human carried up from earth to heaven and then returning to speak what he has received. Rather, he is the One "who comes from heaven" (v. 31), so he can "speak of what I have seen with my Father" (8:38).

The third trail that leads from Moses' sight of God's glory at Sinai and its fulfillment in the new covenant appears in 2 Corinthians 3. Here the parallel is not between Moses and Christ, but between Moses, on the one hand, and gospel heralds and all believers in Christ, on the other. Just as Moses removed the veil over his face when he met with the Lord, so now "through Christ [the veil that hides God's glory] is . . . taken away. . . . When one turns to the Lord [as Moses did], the veil is removed" (2 Cor. 3:14–16). Since the glory that made Moses' face glow at Sinai was the glory of God's Son, we who now "see" Jesus by believing in him through the good news of his grace share Moses' prophetic privilege. Under the new covenant, our gaze at God's glory is better than Moses' experience at Sinai in at least two remarkable ways, both mentioned in verse 18: "And *we all*, with unveiled face, beholding the glory of the Lord, are being transformed into the same image *from one degree of glory to another.*" First, Moses *alone* ascended the mountain to see God's bright splendor while receiving God's word, but now *"we all"*—everyone who trusts Christ—are privileged to take in his divine glory through the eyes of faith. Second, the glory of Moses' face gradually faded; but now, as we fix our hearts' gaze on Jesus' splendor, we are gradually transformed to resemble his perfection more and more, "from one degree of glory to another." By the power of "the Lord who is the Spirit" (v. 18), the glory of God working in us and reflected through us grows and grows.

Let's consider just one more example of how God commissioned messengers by letting them see his splendor and hear his words. Isaiah saw the Lord high and exalted, with the train of his royal robe filling the temple (Isa. 6:1–10). Isaiah was overwhelmed by his sense of guilt and defilement, but a seraph symbolically cleansed his lips with a burning coal from God's altar and pronounced him forgiven. In gratitude for such grace, seen, felt, and heard, Isaiah volunteered to bring the Lord's message to Israel, a daunting assignment:

> And he said, "Go, and say to this people:
>
> "'Keep on hearing, but do not understand;
> keep on seeing, but do not perceive.'
> Make the heart of this people dull,
>   and their ears heavy,
>   and blind their eyes;
> lest they see with their eyes,
>   and hear with their ears,
> and understand with their hearts,
>   and turn and be healed." (Isa. 6:9–10)

John's Gospel quotes this sobering prediction to explain why so many who saw Jesus' signs did not believe in him. John concludes his quotation: "Isaiah said these things because he saw his glory and spoke of him" (John 12:37–41). It was *Jesus'* glory that Isaiah saw when he was called, centuries earlier, to speak God's convicting and comforting words. Jesus is not just one more messenger who has seen God's glory and heard God's word. He is the God whose glory the prophets saw, and he is the Word of God whom the prophets heard from the Father's throne. Believers who see "the light of the knowledge of the glory of God in the face of Jesus Christ" (2 Cor. 4:6) by trusting the gospel's promises enjoy prophetic privilege, which entails prophetic duty.

To Speak and to Show

Having seen the Lord's glory and heard his words, Israel's prophets were to speak God's word and to confirm their message with miraculous signs to be seen. We will survey the content conveyed in the prophets' words in the next section. Here we explore how the actions of the prophets, especially the miracles that God performed through them, reinforced their authority as his messengers and illustrated their message. Miracles are associated in the Bible with the prophetic office far more frequently than they are with priests or with kings. To be sure, God's Spirit gave Samson—a "royal" figure as Israel's judge and champion—physical strength far beyond the ordinary. But Israel's kings and priests did not typically perform miracles. Rather, the messengers who carried God's word were those whom God armed with signs to confirm the divine origin of their words.

At the burning bush, Moses asked how he could persuade the elders of Israel that the Lord had really appeared to him and authorized him to go to Pharaoh to demand the Israelites' release. God gave Moses three signs— the rod-turned-into-serpent, the leprosy that appeared and disappeared instantaneously, and the water-turned-into-blood (Ex. 4:1–9). When Egypt's pharaoh hardened his heart against the Lord's word, ten signs—plagues of increasing severity—showed both the Egyptians and the Israelites that the God of the slave people could easily overpower the deities served by their oppressors, confirming the Lord's word through Moses.

The miracles that God worked through prophets were not merely acts of raw power to compel awe. The form of the miracle reinforced the message delivered in the words that the Lord gave to his prophets. So the plagues on Egypt were signs of God's sovereignty over the idols that the Egyptians worshiped: the Nile god, deities of crops and herds that depended on the river, the sun god Ra, and finally the allegedly semidivine Pharaoh himself (who could not protect his own firstborn son). Also associated with Moses' ministry were miracles of judgment and salvation in Israel's decades of wilderness wandering: water from a rock, manna descending in dew morning by morning, and venomous vipers' bites cured by a glance at the bronze replica of a snake. We have seen in earlier chapters that these provisions from the Lord previewed and would find fulfillment in Christ.

Centuries later, God sent the miracle-working prophets Elijah and Elisha to press his demand for his people's loyalty and trust. The signs by which these prophets showed God's mercy to the needy outcast foreshadowed the signs that would attest to the Messiah and his mission. When drought brought famine to the northern tribes (in keeping with the covenant curse of Deuteronomy 28:23–24), the Lord sent Elijah into Gentile territory, to a penniless Gentile widow in the Phoenician hamlet of Zarephath. The Lord rewarded her faith in his word by sustaining the food supply for herself, her son, and her guest—the prophet (1 Kings 17:8–16). When the child died, the God of life answered his prophet's prayer and restored the boy to life, so Elijah "delivered him to his mother" (v. 23). Later, the Lord performed similar miracles of provision and resurrection through Elijah's successor, Elisha (2 Kings 4).

When we turn to the New Testament, we see an outbreak of God's miraculous interventions surrounding the ministry of both Jesus and his apostles. The unique authority of Jesus to reveal God the Father was attested by his deeds: "Go and tell John what you have seen and heard: the blind receive their sight, the lame walk, lepers are cleansed, and the deaf hear, the dead are raised up, the poor have good news preached to them" (Luke 7:22). Those who had seen and heard him spoke of Jesus as "a prophet mighty in deed and word before God and all the people" (24:19). Their description of Jesus resembles the words by which Stephen would characterize Moses: "mighty in his words and deeds" (Acts 7:22). Peter and other apostolic preachers pointed to Jesus' miraculous deeds as God's own confirmation of Jesus' authority and mission: "Men of Israel, hear these words: Jesus of Nazareth [was] a man attested to you by God with mighty works and wonders and signs that God did through him in your midst, as you yourselves know" (2:22). Jesus himself had presented his miracles as his credentials: "For the works that the Father has given me to accomplish, the very works that I am doing, bear witness about me that the Father has sent me" (John 5:36). John and the other Gospel writers recorded Jesus' signs in order to elicit trust in him: "Now Jesus did many other signs in the presence of the disciples, which are not written in this book; but these are written so that you may believe that Jesus is the Christ, the Son of God, and that by believing you may have life in his name" (20:30–31). Since miracles are signs that convey a message, they are linked to words. Jesus explained their symbolic message: he multiplied bread to feed over five thousand in the desert, and then explained that he himself is the "bread of life" (6:35, 51). He identified himself as "the resurrection and the life," promising that those who believe in him will never die; then he raised Lazarus from the dead (11:25–26).

The signs that showed Jesus to be God's final Word (John 1:1–3, 14; Heb. 1:1–2) resembled signs performed by Old Testament prophets too consistently to be mere coincidence. The thousands fed by five loaves and two fish in a deserted place should bring to mind God's miraculous gift of manna to sustain Israel in the wilderness (John 6:30–32). In describing how Jesus raised the son of a widow in the small Galilean town of Nain, and "gave him to his mother," Luke chose words that demanded that we see the parallel and fulfillment of Elijah's raising of the son of the widow of Zarephath (Luke 7:11–17). Jesus' feeding of the five thousand is linked not only with the manna of Moses' day but also with the multiplication of loaves to feed a crowd through the prophetic ministry of Elisha (2 Kings 4:42–44). Yet Jesus' multiplication of bread transcends Elisha's provision: Elisha fed one hundred with twenty loaves, whereas Jesus fed five thousand with five! In fact, Jesus himself drew the lines of connection between the miracles of Elijah and Elisha—performed, shockingly for Gentiles!—and his own mission:

> But in truth, I tell you, there were many widows in Israel in the days of Elijah, when the heavens were shut up three years and six months, and a great famine came over all the land, and Elijah was sent to none of them but only to Zarephath, in the land of Sidon, to a woman who was a widow. And there were many lepers in Israel in the time of the prophet Elisha, and none of them was cleansed, but only Naaman the Syrian. (Luke 4:25–27)

The authority of Jesus' apostles was likewise confirmed by signs. The author to the Hebrews reminds his readers that the message of new covenant salvation "was declared at first by the Lord, and it was attested to us by those who heard, *while God also bore witness by signs and wonders and various miracles* and by gifts of the Holy Spirit distributed according to his will" (Heb. 2:3–4). Although some of the Corinthian believers critiqued Paul's speech and sufferings, he reminded them: "The *signs of a true apostle* were performed among you with utmost patience, with *signs and wonders and mighty works*" (2 Cor. 12:12).

Although the vast majority of the signs performed by Jesus in person and through his apostles displayed God's mercy and power to rescue people in need, the Lord's new covenant messengers were also authenticated by occasional miracles of judgment. Jesus pronounced a curse on a fruitless fig tree one day, and by the next it had withered and died (Mark 11:12–14, 21–22). His curse on that inanimate tree was not an expression of pique over unsatisfied hunger, but a prophetic sign of judgment to come on spiritually fruitless Israel (Luke 13:6–9, 33–35; see 19:41–44). The harmful miraculous signs that accompanied Jesus' apostolic messengers served functions similar to the judgment wonders of the Old Testament prophets. In their greed and hypocrisy, Ananias and Sapphira, like Achan at Jericho (Josh. 7:1, 10–26), conspired to keep a portion of what they had claimed to devote to the Lord; for their contempt toward the Holy Spirit, the Lord struck them dead (Acts 5:1–11). Temporary blindness befell those who opposed Christ and his truth, casting Saul the persecutor and Elymas the false prophet into darkness for a time (9:8–9, 17–18; 13:10–12). The outward imposition of physical blindness signified the rebels' sightless hearts and minds. For Saul, physical blinding served a redemptive purpose, accompanying the restoration of spiritual sight that was integral to his call as Jesus' witness.

In fulfillment of the ancient prophets' mission to speak the Lord's word and show the Lord's power, Jesus, the Father's final Word, came bringing the Father's message and doing the Father's works of healing and rescue. He "began to do and teach" throughout his life on earth, culminating in his death, resurrection, and ascent to God's right hand (Acts 1:1). From his heavenly throne and by his outpoured Holy Spirit, he continued his prophetic ministry of deeds and words through his apostles.

The Prophet's Message: Prosecution

The message that the Lord conveyed through prophets can be summed up in the contrasting terms *prosecution* and *promise*. Especially after Moses, Israel's prophets had the disquieting task of prosecuting the Lord's legal charges against his treasonous people. The prophetic books teem with descriptions of Israel's and Judah's infidelities and of the covenant curses that God's unfaithful servants were experiencing and would experience, just as the Lord had said they would (Deut. 28). On the other hand, the prophets were also sent with words of hope, with promises of future redemption to comfort those same disloyal people, when God's Spirit would come to turn their hearts to himself in humble repentance. Jeremiah's call to prophetic office shows both sides of the message that he was to speak:

> Then the LORD put out his hand and touched my mouth. And the LORD said to me,
>
> "Behold, I have put my words in your mouth.
> See, I have set you this day over nations and over kingdoms,
> to pluck up and to break down,
> to destroy and to overthrow,
> to build and to plant." (Jer. 1:9–10)

On the one hand, the words that the Lord placed in his prophet's mouth would pronounce judgment: to "pluck up," "break down," "destroy," and "overthrow." On the other, God's word through Jeremiah would offer hope of building and planting. Isaiah brought to King Hezekiah a sobering announcement of the future plundering of the temple, humiliation of the royal heirs, and exile of the people from the Lord's land (Isa. 39:5–7). On the heels of that dire prediction, however, the Lord gave his prophet a very different message to deliver, promising a terminus to the coming exile: "Comfort, comfort my people, says your God. Speak tenderly to Jerusalem, and cry to her that her warfare is ended, that her iniquity is pardoned" (40:1–2). After Israel's devastation and dispersion, the Lord would lead his hurting and humbled people home, and "the glory of the LORD shall be revealed" for all to see (vv. 3–5).

The song of Moses had invoked the sky above and the earth below as witnesses to the Lord's covenant with Israel, witnesses who would testify against a disloyal people by withholding rain from the sky and produce from the earth (Deut. 32:1; see 30:18–19; 31:28). Later prophets summoned heaven and earth to the witness stand, to testify for the prosecution of the guilty nation:

> Hear, O heavens, and give ear, O earth;
> for the LORD has spoken:
> "Children have I reared and brought up,
> but they have rebelled against me." (Isa. 1:2)

In summoning the mountains to bear accusing testimony against Israel, Micah used a specific legal term (*rib*), rendered "indictment" in the ESV, to speak of the Lord's lawsuit charging his people with treason:

> Hear, you mountains, the indictment of the LORD,
>> and you enduring foundations of the earth,
> for the LORD has an indictment against his people,
>> and he will contend with Israel. (Mic. 6:2; see Hos. 4:1–2; 12:2)

Judah's persistent and perverse refusal to hear the Lord's prosecutors as they brought his indictments led, in the end, to Judah's banishment from the Lord's land altogether. The inspired author of the books of Chronicles summarized the whole history of the prophets' prosecutorial efforts and the resistance of God's people, issuing eventually in exile:

> The LORD, the God of their fathers, sent persistently to them by his messengers, because he had compassion on his people and on his dwelling place. But they kept mocking the messengers of God, despising his words and scoffing at his prophets, until the wrath of the LORD rose against his people, until there was no remedy. (2 Chron. 36:15–16)

Jesus himself is the climactic Prophet-Prosecutor sent by the Father to summon his people to repentance. In the aftermath of his cleansing of the temple from distracting merchandisers, the authorities challenged Jesus to identify his authority to purge God's place of worship. Instead of answering them directly, he posed a counterquestion that put his critics into a dilemma (Mark 11:27–33). He went on, however, to imply his answer to the question of his authority in a parable about tenant farmers who wickedly refused to pay a vineyard owner the rent that they owed him (12:1–12). This story is laced with allusions to the Old Testament. The owner's preparation of the vineyard echoes the image of Israel as a vineyard that received the best care but yielded bitter grapes (Isa. 5:1–7; see Ps. 80:8, 14). The owner sends servant after servant, season after season, to collect his rent; but the tenants mistreat them all in defiance of the owner, a fictional echo of the summary indictment we heard just now in 2 Chronicles 36. Finally, the owner has "one other, a beloved son" (Mark 12:6). When he sends him last, the tenants murder him—the very outcome that Jesus' opponents were plotting at the moment and would achieve by the week's end (12:12; see also 3:6; 11:18).

Through these Old Testament echoes, Jesus shows that his authority to cleanse the temple is based on his dignity as Son, the Father's last and best Messenger. He brings to a finale the succession of messengers whom God had sent to convict disloyal stewards of his vineyard and to claim its fruit.

After his resurrection and ascension, Jesus continued his "prosecutorial" mission through the presence of his divine Spirit of truth and the words of his human spokesmen. Concerning the Spirit, Jesus promised:

> And when he comes, he will convict the world concerning sin and righteousness and judgment: concerning sin, because they do not believe in me; concerning righteousness, because I go to the Father, and you will see me no longer; concerning judgment, because the ruler of this world is judged. (John 16:8–11)

Through his Spirit-anointed messengers, Christ continued to indict people for their sin and call them to repent. The apostle Peter bluntly confronted his hearers in Jerusalem with their culpability for the death of Jesus:

> The God of Abraham . . . glorified his servant Jesus, whom you delivered over and denied in the presence of Pilate, when he had decided to release him. But you denied the Holy and Righteous One, and asked for a murderer to be granted to you, and you killed the Author of life, whom God raised from the dead. To this we are witnesses. (Acts 3:13–15)

Through their evil action, however, God fulfilled his promises to rescue them from the punishment they deserved, so Peter commanded them: "Repent therefore, and turn again, that your sins may be blotted out, that times of refreshing may come from the presence of the Lord, and that he may send the Christ appointed for you, Jesus" (Acts 3:19–20).

The words of the soon-to-be-martyred Stephen sound even more like the indictments brought by Old Testament prophets:

> You stiff-necked people, uncircumcised in heart and ears, you always resist the Holy Spirit. As your fathers did, so do you. Which of the prophets did your fathers not persecute? And they killed those who announced beforehand the coming of the Righteous One, whom you have now betrayed and murdered, you who received the law as delivered by angels and did not keep it. (Acts 7:51–53)

Stephen stood in the company of the ancient prophets and of Jesus the beloved Son, witnesses sent by God to bear witness against a recalcitrant people. The prophets' indictment of sin and warning of impending judgment led to their own suffering at the hands of defiant people. The Servant of the Lord who daily heard his Master's word and delivered it to others resolutely set his face like flint to endure disgrace from those who struck him, spat on him, and pulled out his beard (Isa. 50:4–7). As they delivered their unpopular message, Christ's spokesmen shared in the sufferings of Jesus the preeminent Prophet-Servant, as Paul wrote:

> Now I rejoice in my sufferings for your sake, and in my flesh I am filling up what is lacking in Christ's afflictions for the sake of his body, that is, the church, of which I became a minister according to the stewardship from God that was given to me for you, to make the word of God fully known. (Col. 1:24–25)

The Prophet's Message: Promise

God sent his prophets to his people not only with the bad news of their rebellion and the cursed consequences it would reap, but also with unimaginably good news: comforting promises of hope and assurances that even their worst wickedness could not thwart his steadfast love and determination to reclaim, restore, and transform their wayward hearts. Not surprisingly, the prophets' promises of coming salvation focused on a specific individual, whom they identified in various ways and whose redemptive mission they saw from various perspectives. When he appeared, he would be an Anointed King, a descendant of the great King David. In keeping with his royal role, he would rescue God's people from enemies, defend them, and rule them, as a shepherd protects and leads his sheep (Isa. 9:6–7; 16:5; Jer. 23:5–6; Ezek. 34; Amos 9:11–12). The prophets also forecast the mission of the promised Savior in priestly terms. His suffering, like that of a lamb at slaughter, would atone for others' transgressions and bring about their peace with God (Isa. 53:4–7). As a result, the defilement that disqualified even the priests who stood in God's presence would be purged when "I will bring my servant the Branch . . . , and I will remove the iniquity of this land in a single day" (Zech. 3:8–9).

The prophets also framed the work of the coming Deliverer in prophetic terms, portraying him as the climactic herald of the good news of peace between God and his people. Isaiah, for example, foresaw a Messenger hastening over mountaintops to herald hope to a downcast people:

> How beautiful upon the mountains
>> are the feet of him who brings good news,
> who publishes peace, who brings good news of happiness,
>> who publishes salvation,
>> who says to Zion, "Your God reigns." (Isa. 52:7)

The apostle Paul tells us that Jesus is that preacher of peace: "For [Christ] himself is our peace, who has made us both one and has . . . reconcile[d] us both to God in one body through the cross . . . . And he came and preached peace to you who were far off and peace to those who were near" (Eph. 2:14–17). In the synagogue of Nazareth, Jesus identified himself with the Servant of the Lord of Isaiah 61:1–2, who was anointed with God's Spirit for the *prophetic* task of proclaiming the good news of relief to the poor, healing to the heartbroken, and liberty to captives (Luke 4:17–21).

Many lines of connection could be traced between the Old Testament prophets' promises of salvation, on the one hand, and Jesus' and the apostles' proclamation that God's new-creation work has now begun. We are going to focus on just one surprising correspondence that Jesus himself draws between himself and the prophet Jonah, a messenger whose mind-set contradicted his Master, a courier who resented the message he carried, since it offered grace to cruel, godless Gentiles. At first hearing, God's charge to Jonah does not sound like the summons to bring good news to its intended audience: "Arise, go to Nineveh, that great city, and call out against it, for their evil has come up before me" (Jonah 1:2). Jonah, however, knew the long-suffering mercy of his God. He realized that this divine warning implied the Lord's readiness to forgive and spare the populace of that wicked city, if they were to repent. That was why, when God told him to go east to Nineveh, Jonah headed west, across the Mediterranean Sea. When Nineveh repented and the Lord relented, the prophet angrily protested against God's mercy: "O Lord, is not this what I said when I was yet in my country? That is why I made haste to flee to Tarshish; for I knew that you are a gracious God and merciful, slow to anger and abounding in steadfast love, and relenting from disaster" (4:2). Ironically, Jonah was quoting the Lord's self-description at Sinai, after he had spared the idolatrous Israelites from utter destruction (Ex. 34:6–7). Because of God's steadfast love, Jonah's ancestors survived at

Sinai, so the prophet lived to begrudge that same grace to Israel's archenemy. The Lord who had spared the prophet's life in the sea sent that same reluctant and resentful spokesman to proclaim good news to a pagan nation.

Jonah's attitude toward both God and others was the negative image of God's final Messenger, Jesus. Jonah in his vengeful longing for God to destroy Nineveh, without forewarning or opportunity to repent, was shamefully unlike Jesus. Yet when Jesus was asked for a sign to verify his authority as God's spokesman, he answered: "An evil and adulterous generation seeks for a sign, but no sign will be given to it except the sign of the prophet Jonah. For just as Jonah was three days and three nights in the belly of the great fish, so will the Son of Man be three days and three nights in the heart of the earth" (Matt. 12:39–40; see also 16:4). Despite their differences, in two respects Jonah was strikingly like Jesus. First, both Jonah and Jesus came back from "the dead" in three days. Jonah was narrowly spared from death by drowning in the sea, "entombed" in a great fish, and then returned to the land of the living three days later. Jesus literally endured anguished death on the cross, was entombed in the earth, and then rose from the dead the third day. Second, both were "raised from the dead" in order to preach repentance and offer salvation to pagans outside God's covenant community. In fact, the Ninevites' humble repentance in response to God's word, brought by God's "resurrected" prophet, put to shame the unbelief of Jesus' Jewish contemporaries: "The men of Nineveh will rise up at the judgment with this generation and condemn it, for they repented at the preaching of Jonah, and behold, something greater than Jonah is here" (12:41). And the Ninevites' repentant faith provided a preview of the Gentiles to whom Jesus "came" after his resurrection, by his Spirit and through his apostles, to preach "peace to you who were far off" (Eph. 2:17).

Conclusion

The epistle to the Hebrews has shown us that with respect to listening to God's messengers, the stakes are higher now than ever before. "Long ago, at many times and in many ways, God spoke to our fathers by the prophets, but in these last days he has spoken to us by his Son" (Heb. 1:1–2). Now God's Word is clearer, more "three-dimensional," more directly personal because "the Word became flesh" (John 1:14). For that very reason, as Hebrews stresses, refusing to hear God's voice now in his Son has the direst of eternal consequences: "See that you do not refuse him who is speaking. For if they did not escape when they refused him who warned them on earth, much less will we escape if we reject him who warns from heaven" (Heb. 12:25). The salvation announced by Jesus in this "year of the Lord's favor" (Luke 4:19) brings the prophets' promises to fulfillment; but also, for that reason, the consequences of persistent unbelief and rebellion are even more dire.

So as we read the books of the prophets, with their words of warning and indictment and comfort and hope, we must recognize that wherever and however and through whomever the Word of God comes to us, it is Jesus who is exercising his office of Prophet, "revealing to us, by his word and Spirit, the will of God for our salvation" (WSC 24). Wherever in the Bible we meet themes such as the Word of God, the miracles that verify true prophets, the Spirit's initiative to bring God's Word, and even the general themes of speaking and hearing, there the landmark of Jesus' mission as the Great Prophet points the way to how those passages connect to Jesus, the Word made flesh. As we walk with Jesus through the pages of his Word with our eyes attuned to the landmark of the prophetic office, we will approach the Bible with questions such as these in mind: Is there a prophet of God in this text, a spokesman who brings—or should bring—God's truth to God's people? Is the prophet faithful to his mission of revelation, or unfaithful, or a mixture of faithfulness and unfaithfulness? How does his faithfulness preview Jesus? How does his failure reveal the need for Jesus, the final Word, to come? Are the prophet's words reinforced by miraculous signs? Do those signs correspond to signs performed by Jesus, the final Word? Does this prophetic word press God's lawsuit against guilty people and predict coming judgment? How do such words accuse us, too, and so turn us to Jesus, who bore our judgment? Does this prophetic word promise God's mercy and relief in the face of present suffering? How is Jesus the full and final "Yes" to all of God's prophetic promises of salvation? Since the New Testament apostles are extensions of Jesus' prophetic ministry, how do their words and miraculous signs point us back to Jesus, who commissioned them to speak his Word to the church?

Putting It into Practice: God's Despairing Spokesman (1 Kings 19)

In the aftermath of the Lord's great victory over the 450 prophets of Baal at Mount Carmel, we are surprised by Elijah's response of fear, discouragement, and complaint toward the Lord. Baal, the Canaanite storm god, had remained mute and impotent as his worshipers slashed their bodies hour after hour. When it became Elijah's turn to show what the Lord could do, the prophet's simple prayer brought a blazing bolt of fire from heaven, and a waterlogged sacrifice and altar went up in smoke and steam in an instant. The Israelites responded as they should, exclaiming, "The LORD, he is God; the LORD, he is God" (1 Kings 18:39). The prophets of Baal were slaughtered that very afternoon. And in mercy the Lord relieved the drought that had lasted three and a half years, sending rain in torrents. But Israel's king, Ahab, reported the events to his pagan queen, Jezebel, and she sent a death threat to Elijah. Unexpectedly, the prophet of the Lord, who had courageously withstood 450 prophets, "was afraid, and he arose and ran for his life" (19:3). Elijah had stood tall and strong for the Lord and his word at Carmel, a fitting preview of the incarnate Word who would stand alone amid a raging mob of vicious enemies, abandoned by his feeble friends. But now the prophet's faith faltered and he came to the brink of hinting that the Lord who commissioned him had failed to back him in a crunch.

Elijah had had "enough" (1 Kings 19:4). He was conflicted, wanting the Lord to take his apparently fruitless life (v. 5) but complaining that others wanted to do so (vv. 10, 14). When he reached Mount Horeb, Elijah twice stated the root of his discouragement in identical words: "I have been very jealous for the LORD, the God of hosts. For the people of Israel have forsaken your covenant, thrown down your altars, and killed your prophets with the sword, and I, even I only, am left, and they seek my life, to take it away" (vv. 10, 14). He had zealously kept his covenant commitment as the Lord's servant, not only as any Israelite should but also in his special office as God's messenger. He used the title "the God of hosts," appealing to the Lord's role as Protector and Defender both of his own glory and of his faithful servant. In the age-old warfare between the serpent and the offspring of the woman (Gen. 3:15), it seemed to Elijah that the woman's offspring had been reduced to a single faithful individual—"I, even I only, am left." When the prophet's foes prevailed, the Lord's cause would be lost.

The Lord would correct his downcast prophet's bleak misperception, expanding his horizon to take in the community of the faithful who surrounded him. But the Lord would also direct his sight forward in time, to those whom God would use to advance his agenda in the next generation. In fact, Elijah's experience lies along a prophetic path that leads from Sinai to Calvary, from Moses to Jesus. The echoes of Moses' ministry in this text are many: The angel of the Lord provided bread and water in the wilderness, so that the servant of the Lord could travel forty days and nights (reflecting Israel's forty years). Both prophets stood on Horeb, the Mount of God where Moses saw the Lord's glory and received the Lord's covenant for Israel. Both hid their faces as the Lord's glory passed. To both the Lord demonstrated his presence in wind, earthquake, and fire, but for Elijah there was a difference: the Lord was not in the wind, earthquake, or fire, but rather in "a low whisper" (1 Kings 19:11–12).

It is not as though those terrifying displays of destructive power were unfit to convey the presence of the Almighty Creator, who is jealous for his own glory (Ex. 19:16–20). But Elijah needed to hear another side of the God of hosts, a whisper that bordered on silence (see Job 4:16; Ps. 107:29). If he had been expecting either a popular uprising or an immediate divine act to dethrone and destroy Ahab and Jezebel, the prophet must learn to await God's timing. Can you hear in Elijah's lament an advance echo of the misgivings of John (Luke 7:18–19), the prophet who would come "in the spirit and power of Elijah" (1:17), announcing the Lord's arrival with "unquenchable fire" (3:17), only to find himself imprisoned by a corrupt king and his bloodthirsty wife (Matt. 14:1–12)? The Lord assured Elijah that in due time he would bring judgment on the wicked, using both godless (Hazael, Jehu) and godly (Elisha) instruments (1 Kings 19:15–17). For John's encouragement, on the other hand, Jesus pointed to displays of grace already taking place (healing for the disabled, good news to the poor) as demonstrating the quiet way in which he was inaugurating his messianic kingdom.

Moreover, unbeknownst to Elijah, he was not as alone in his zeal for the Lord as he supposed. The Lord had kept a faithful remnant of seven thousand for himself even in the apostate northern kingdom (1 Kings 19:18). What Elijah had failed to see in his frustration with God's quiet methods was that Elijah was not, after all, the solitary offspring of the woman who would have to do battle, one on one, with the serpent. He was zealous for the Lord, to be sure, but he was not the One who was actually entitled to say, "Zeal for your house will consume me" (John 2:17, quoting Ps. 69:9). The day would come when the enemies of God would circle like jackals around the solitary faithful Servant of the Lord as he died, alone, on a cross. Because Jesus the woman's offspring (seed) died and dropped into the ground, a countless crop of children are being born by grace into the family of God (John 12:24). Jesus is God's gentle whisper, crucified in weakness but raised in power. His voice now addresses us, not on the earthly Sinai but from the heavenly Jerusalem, summoning us to persevering faith to hear and speak his Word, which quietly achieves the purposes for which the Lord sends it (Isa. 55:10–11).

Questions for Reflection and Discussion

1. What is it about God's character and our character that requires that we have *buffers* to insulate us when he comes close, as well as *bridges* to span the distance between our Creator and us? In what ways did Israel's priests and prophets, especially, function as buffers and bridges between the Lord and the people?

2. What are some Old Testament passages that describe the duties and privileges of prophets, priests, and kings? What three distinct spheres of authority and responsibility were identified with Israel's prophets, priests, and kings, respectively?

3. Which words in the opening of Hebrews (1:1–4) reveal Christ's prophetic role in revealing God's truth? his priestly role in atoning for sin? his kingly role in ruling? Later in Hebrews, where do these themes reappear?

4. How do the Heidelberg and Westminster Shorter Catechisms characterize Jesus' mission as our Redeemer and Mediator? Is there warrant in the Bible for summing up Jesus' redemptive work using these three categories? Why or why not?

5. How can the roles of Israel's prophets, priests, and kings be correlated with aspects of our identity as people created in the image of God, mentioned in Ephesians 4:24 and Colossians 3:10 and illustrated in Genesis 1–2? What do these connections imply about *every human being*, whether or not he or she holds a special "office" in the community of God's people? In what ways do you "image" God as prophet, priest, and/or king in everyday life?

6. How is Jesus' ministry of *revealing God and his Word* like that of Moses and other prophets, and in what ways is it better than that of the prophets who came before him?

7. What were God's purposes in working miraculous signs through such prophets as Moses, Elijah, and Elisha? What were the purposes of Jesus' miracles?

8. How is the fact that God often sent prophets to Israel bearing messages of *prosecution* related to the covenantal relationship that constitutes the Bible's "lay of the land"?

9. How should we understand the oracles of indictment and coming judgment delivered by the prophets, God's prosecuting attorneys, in light of the first and second comings of Jesus Christ, and the Spirit's ministry in the church between those comings?

10. How were Jonah's mission, message, and experience a "sign" pointing to Christ? How did Jonah's attitude contradict that of Christ? How can we put these contrasts together? Most importantly, how do the similarities and the differences between these two spokesmen—Jonah and Jesus—help us to understand how other prophets (for example, despairing Elijah in 1 Kings 19) function as previews—but *only* previews—of God's last best Word?

8

Jesus Our Great High Priest:
God's Presence

A Cluster of Landmarks

In the previous chapter, we began to observe "landmarks" that the Lord has embedded in the covenantal terrain and trajectory of his holy words and mighty works in Scripture. These landmarks help us to see the routes that lead us most naturally to Christ from the many passages that describe various types of leaders whom God appointed to stand between himself and Israel, his beloved but guilty people. Those leaders—prophets, priests, and kings—functioned as buffers, insulating sinful people from the Lord's dangerous holiness, his white-hot consuming purity. But they also functioned as bridges, linking the Lord with those same people, who desperately needed his presence, protection, compassion, and direction. God sent prophets such as Moses and Elijah to speak his words. Through those words, the Lord summoned his people to trust and obey, conforming their thoughts to his truth and their desires to his revealed will. Prophets emerged from the presence of the Lord, having seen his glory and heard his words, to speak God's message and to show its meaning in miraculous signs. They prosecuted the Lord's lawsuit and pronounced his verdict and sentence against unrepentant traitors. But they also promised relief and restoration in the future for broken people who longed in humble hope for healing from their God. Yet the prophets themselves, even the best of them, failed to fully trust and obey the Word of God that came to them and through them. Only when the Word who was with God in the beginning, who was and is God, "became flesh and dwelt among us" (John 1:14) did we hear the voice of the Creator through a thoroughly faithful spokesman, Jesus.

In this chapter, we examine a second landmark, the priestly office that stood at the center of Israel's worship. Gathering to worship the Lord in his presence defined Israel's identity, setting Israel apart from every other nation as the one people on earth among whom the Creator of the universe had come to reside. But should we speak of the Old Testament priesthood as a single landmark? So wide an array of themes cluster around the priests' ministry in the Lord's presence that we do better to think of them not as a single peak (Pikes Peak or Kilimanjaro) but as a whole range of mountain majesties.

The Westminster Shorter Catechism (answer 25) describes Jesus' priestly office in these words: "Christ executeth the office of a priest, in his once offering up of himself a sacrifice to satisfy divine justice, and reconcile us to God; and in making continual intercession for us." Notice four themes in this summary:

(1) "his once offering up of himself a *sacrifice*,"
(2) which, in a sin-infected situation, was needed to accomplish a first purpose for sacrifice, namely, to "*satisfy divine justice*," removing sinful people's guilt,
(3) thus achieving a second purpose, to "*reconcile us to God*," making it possible for us to approach and enjoy God's presence in peace, and finally
(4) Jesus' "making *continual intercession* for us" to God the Father.

So the catechism focuses on the priestly role in atoning for sins through sacrifice, removing the obstacle to our intimate communion with God, and in praying on behalf of others. These tasks are at the heart of a priest's distinctive calling.

Yet in Old Testament Israel, the priests' sphere of responsibility was much broader than this description, and so is the priestly work of Jesus. The presence of God in his holiness, living in the midst of unholy people like us, was the focus of the priests' calling. Priests were to serve and protect the *sanctuary* in which the Lord dwelt among his servants. They enforced the *separation* that set apart holy things and people from those that were defiled, unfit to be near God. Human sin and our need for atonement placed *sacrifice* "front and center" among the priests' tasks, and the sacrifices that they offered related not only to the forgiveness of sins but also to the resulting consecration of God's servants and their communion with their Lord. Finally, associated with their ministry of sacrifice was the priests' service of *supplication*, as they approached the Lord's presence to intercede with him on others' behalf, as the catechism notes.[1]

So the role of Israel's priests was complex. They were associated with a variety of institutions and regulations. They were in charge of the tabernacle and the temple, along with the sacrifices that were offered in these sanctuaries. But their duty to protect the Lord's holy home among his people also linked them with regulations about ceremonial defilement and rituals for cleansing, with the kosher dietary laws, and with the calendar of annual feasts. The laws about sabbatical years and the Jubilee year were grounded in the truth that the Lord had set apart the Promised Land as his own property, a holy territory in the midst of a sin-cursed world. Through these aspects of the ancient priests' calling to attend to the holy presence of the Lord, we will glimpse the paths that lead from a wide range of ceremonies and statutes to their fulfillment in Christ, who is the Great High Priest (Heb. 4:14) and the final atoning Sacrifice (10:12–14), the person who is himself the Lord's temple (John 2:21–22) but who also builds believers into "a holy temple in the Lord[,] . . . a dwelling place for God by the Spirit" (Eph. 2:21–22; see 1 Peter 2:4–5). Let us survey the cluster of themes that distinguish the priestly landmark that points us to Jesus and to the "kingdom of priests" (Ex. 19:5) that he is gathering through his atoning and consecrating sacrifice.

Sanctuary: The Presence of God

Since Adam's fall, sin has disrupted our relationship to God. Genesis 3 shows this breach of communion not only in our first parents' attempt to hide when they heard the sound of the Lord's arrival, but also in their banishment from the garden of God. Now, therefore, the priests' central mission as mediators between the holy Creator and sinful people is to offer sacrifice and prayer that will lead to atonement for sins and reconciliation

---

1. As we observed from Jeremiah 2:8 and 18:18, another role of the priests, as the caretakers of God's commandments, was to provide ongoing instruction in the law and its application to relationships within the Lord's community (Deut. 17:8–13; Mal. 2:4–7). Since this ministry of God's written Word overlaps with the prophets' mission to bring new words from God, for the sake of space and simplicity we will pass over the priests' task of teaching in this chapter.

of sinners with God. But that task is based on the foundational privilege of priests, which is to stand in God's presence, to worship and serve him, and to lead others in the privilege and joy of worship. In order for the priests to offer a sacrifice to atone for sins, there must be a sanctuary in which they can approach God.

The presence of God creates holy space. Throughout the Bible, the arrival of the Lord makes places holy, whether or not a physical structure or sanctuary is involved. His purity poses a danger to polluted people, so those who find themselves suddenly standing on holy ground react in fear. Jacob, fleeing from his brother, spent a night at Luz. There the Lord appeared to him in a dream, standing at the top of a staircase that reached from earth to heaven. On that staircase the Lord's angels ascended to hear his will and descended to earth to carry it out. When Jacob awoke, he was afraid: "Surely the LORD is in this place, and I did not know it. . . . How awesome is this place! This is none other than the house of God, and this is the gate of heaven" (Gen. 28:10–17).

Centuries later, Moses was tending flocks near Mount Horeb when he spotted a bush that burned constantly without being consumed by the flames. As he approached, the Lord told him to remove his sandals because he was standing on holy ground. The desert floor had been sanctified as sanctuary by the presence of the Lord in the burning bush (Ex. 3:1–6). When Moses later returned to the mountain with the newly liberated Israelites, God gave him the blueprints for a tent in which the Lord would live in the midst of Israel's nomadic camp, traveling right along with his pilgrim people. And when that tabernacle was completed, the Lord visibly showed that he was moving into it when "the cloud covered the tent of meeting, and the glory of the LORD filled the tabernacle. And Moses was not able to enter the tent of meeting because the cloud settled on it, and the glory of the LORD filled the tabernacle" (40:34–35).

Subsequently, when the temple was built at King Solomon's direction, the display of God's terrifying, purifying presence produced the same overpowering phenomenon: "And when the priests came out of the Holy Place, a cloud filled the house of the LORD, so that the priests could not stand to minister because of the cloud, for the glory of the LORD filled the house of the LORD" (1 Kings 8:10–11). Solomon knew well that even heaven itself cannot contain the Lord, so he realized, "How much less this house that I have built!" Yet the Lord had placed his "name" in this earthly temple, making it the singular place on earth for creatures to commune with their Creator. So Solomon dared to ask the Lord to listen "in heaven your dwelling place" to people's pleas directed toward the sanctuary on Mount Zion, and to answer their requests in his grace (vv. 27–30).

In the beginning, the whole heavens and earth were "very good" (Gen. 1:31), so in one sense the whole universe was a cosmic sanctuary in which the Creator's majesty was displayed and his creatures brought him glory. On the other hand, the charge given to Adam to "keep"—to *guard* or *protect*—the garden of Eden (2:15) foreshadowed the duty of later priests and Levites to *guard* the tabernacle from being entered by anyone who did not belong in its holy space (Num. 3:5–10). In a special sense, then, Eden was a sanctuary—a holy place—consecrated by the Lord's presence to meet with his image-bearers. When Adam and Eve failed in that priestly-military task of protecting God's garden sanctuary from Satan's insidious invasion, God replaced them with guardians who would be impervious to temptation, posting at the garden's gate "the cherubim and a flaming sword that turned every way to guard the way to the tree of life" (Gen. 3:24). Adam and Eve, now themselves stained by sin, were not allowed to trespass on holy ground and seize a reward—eternal life—to which they had no right (3:24).

The cherubim reappear in the designs and descriptions for the tabernacle and the temple, in which the Lord focused his presence among his people. Golden statues of cherubim faced each other on the lid on the ark of the covenant, their wings overshadowing the central mercy seat, the throne above which the Great King ruled and met with Moses (Ex. 25:18–22). Except when it was carried, covered, ahead of the Israelites as they trekked through the desert, this ark was to be kept inside the tabernacle's inner chamber, the Most Holy Place. It was behind a veil into which images of cherubim had been skillfully woven (26:31–33). These images reminded the priests day by day and especially the high priest on the Day of Atonement that God's holy presence could be approached only with due reverence for his dangerous purity. When the Lord settled down among his people in the temple, two additional statues of cherubim symbolized the Lord's spiritual attendants who guarded access to his presence: "In the inner sanctuary he made two cherubim of olivewood, each ten cubits high. . . . And the wings of the cherubim were spread out so that a wing of one touched the one wall, and a wing of the other cherub touched the other wall; their other wings touched each other in the middle of the house" (1 Kings 6:23–27). Under the outstretched inner wings of these cherubim the ark of the covenant—the throne of the Lord—was placed, "so that the cherubim overshadowed the ark and its poles" (8:6–7).

The primary responsibility for guarding the purity of the Lord's holy place fell not to golden replicas of God's terrifying heavenly courtiers, but rather to the tribe of Levi and to Aaron's priestly family. In Israel's wilderness campsites as the people traveled from place to place, the arrangement of the tribes placed twelve tribes (including the two tribes descended from Joseph, Ephraim and Manasseh) in groups of three around the four sides of the Lord's tent in the center of the camp (Num. 2). Inside that ring of twelve, separating the other tribes from God's tent, were three clans of Levites on the northern, western, and southern sides, with Aaron and his family on the east, sentries guarding the way into the courtyard surrounding the tabernacle proper (3:21–39). This arrangement not only maintained the purity of the Lord's precincts but also protected his people from his consuming holiness: "But the Levites shall camp around the tabernacle of the testimony, so that there may be no wrath on the congregation of the people of Israel. And the Levites shall keep guard over the tabernacle of the testimony" (1:53).

Clearly, the holy space, set apart by the Lord's radiant and fiery presence, is a dangerous place for guilty sinners to approach or enter! Yet drawing near to God is our very purpose for being as his covenant servants, our greatest need and our highest privilege. We cannot live *without* intimate engagement with God, for we were made in his image for his friendship; yet in our sin, we cannot live *with* him in his daunting holiness. How can this dilemma of the sanctuary—that it is vital to our identity, yet lethal to us in our impurity—be resolved? Central to the answer is our next priestly theme, sacrifice; but before we turn there, we need to see how the sanctuary motif finds fulfillment in Jesus and the church that he is constructing as his living temple.

The New Testament shows that the Old Testament sanctuaries, tabernacle and temple, have now found fulfillment through Jesus and his redemptive work in four distinct but interrelated ways:

(1) Jesus is the true sanctuary in which God dwells with humanity.
(2) At his ascension, Jesus entered the heavenly sanctuary on our behalf.

(3) Jesus now brings us into that heavenly sanctuary through his sacrifice, by our faith.

(4) Jesus is building us together into a new sanctuary.

John's Gospel in particular announces clearly that *Jesus is the true
sanctuary in which God dwells with humanity.* The Gospel's prologue (John
1:1–18) introduces Christ as the Word who was with God and was God,
who created everything and in whom the light of God's life shines. Then in
verse 14 we read: "And the Word became flesh and dwelt among us, and we
have seen his glory, glory as of the only Son from the Father, full of grace
and truth." We have already pondered the allusions to Moses' prophetic
ministry in these concluding statements of John's prologue (vv. 14–18). Now
notice the priestly implication of the verb *dwelt.* The Greek verb (*skēnoō*)
that lies behind this translation is related to the noun *tent* (*skēnē*), which
refers to the Lord's tabernacle in the midst of Israel's camp in the books
of Moses (Ex. 25–40; Lev. 1–19; etc.) and the New Testament (Acts 7:44;
Heb. 8–9; see Rev. 15:5).

The second chapter of John records Jesus' cleansing of the Jerusalem
temple, purifying it for its purpose as a place for worshipers to meet with
God. When observers demanded a miraculous sign to prove his authority to purge the sanctuary, he replied, "Destroy this temple, and in three
days I will raise it up" (John 2:19). Some mistook his meaning to refer to
the architectural complex that the long-deceased King Herod had started
renovating four decades earlier; but John notes that after Jesus' resurrection,
his disciples came to understand that "he was speaking about the temple
of his body" (v. 21), which he would let others destroy in his zeal for the
Lord's house (v. 17, quoting Ps. 69:9). Jesus' zeal for the Lord's house was a
priestly action, for the priests were to keep the Lord's dwelling place pure,
guarding it from spiritual pollution. We will revisit this theme when we look
briefly at our "practice" passage, 1 Samuel 2:27ff., at the end of this chapter.

The epistle to the Hebrews shows Christ as fulfilling the sanctuary
motif in another way: At his ascension, *Jesus entered the heavenly sanctuary
on our behalf.* Hebrews notes that the earthly tabernacle was constructed to
replicate a design that had been shown to Moses on Mount Sinai (Heb. 8:5,
quoting Ex. 25:40). The tent that the Lord's glory indwelt on earth was a
copy of a heavenly original that Moses saw amid the cloud of glory that
descended on the mountaintop. Now, as a result of his innocent sacrifice

on the cross, his resurrection to "indestructible life" (Heb. 7:16), and his ascension to God's right hand (8:1), Jesus has entered as our High Priest into that heavenly sanctuary, to present his blood for our atonement and to pray for us before the throne of grace (9:11–14; 7:25). Our situation is somewhat like that of ancient Israel on the Day of Atonement. Our Great High Priest has entered the Most Holy Place with atoning blood (his own!) that is infinitely more conscience-cleansing than that of slain animals. We now await his return from the heavenly inner sanctum, to lead us into the fullness of the inheritance that he has secured for us (9:24–28). Until then, our hope is secure, since it is bound to him as he stands in the original sanctuary on our behalf: "We have this as a sure and steadfast anchor of the soul, a hope that enters into the inner place behind the curtain, where Jesus has gone as a forerunner on our behalf, having become a high priest forever after the order of Melchizedek" (6:19–20).

Even as we wait for Jesus our High Priest to emerge from the heavenly sanctuary, our situation is far better than Israel's. The sacrificial blood that our High Priest presents to God accomplishes far more than symbolic and ceremonial cleansing. It goes deep to purge our conscience of guilt (Heb. 9:13–14) and never needs to be repeated (10:1–4). As a result, we are not simply standing outside like the ancient Israelites, awaiting a high priest's return from the inmost chamber of the Lord's tent. Because we are united to him by faith, Jesus actually *brings us into the heavenly sanctuary through his sacrifice.* He consecrates us, people who were once defiled and distant, to become priests who can draw near and offer sacrifices that please our God.

> Therefore, brothers, since we have confidence to enter the holy places by the blood of Jesus, by the new and living way that he opened for us through the curtain, that is, through his flesh, and since we have a great priest over the house of God, let us draw near with a true heart in full assurance of faith, with our hearts sprinkled clean from an evil conscience and our bodies washed with pure water. (Heb. 10:19–22)

Through Jesus' sacrifice, we approach God's throne of grace to seek and find the help we need (Heb. 4:14–16). We also offer worship that brings pleasure to the Father's heart: "Through [Jesus] then let us continually offer up a sacrifice of praise to God, that is, the fruit of lips that acknowledge his name. Do not neglect to do good and to share what you have, for such sacrifices are pleasing to God" (13:15–16).

Finally, *Jesus is building us together into a new sanctuary*. The physical structures (tabernacle and temple) that the Lord set apart as his holy meeting places with his people were not only copies of his true residence in heaven. They were also previews of the Lord's future plan to take up residence not in a tent composed of pelts and ornate curtains, nor in a building of wood overlaid with gold, but in a community of living, breathing people, his church. Peter writes to Christian believers:

> As you come to him, a living stone rejected by men but in the sight of God chosen and precious, you yourselves like living stones are being built up as a spiritual house, to be a holy priesthood, to offer spiritual sacrifices acceptable to God through Jesus Christ. (1 Peter 2:4–5)

Paul, too, announces the amazing truth that now, through Christ, Gentiles are incorporated into "a holy temple in the Lord[,] . . . a dwelling place for God by the Spirit" (Eph. 2:21–22). The Lord's sanctuary is no longer a structure in a single city. The sanctuary is Christ's people, and from this holy space the Lord's glory radiates to the surrounding world. This same reality is expressed in the vision of the New Jerusalem in the book of Revelation. This city is called the bride of the Lamb, so it portrays the church. Its symbolic dimensions show its shape to be the same as that of the Most Holy Place in the tabernacle and the temple, its height and length and width all equal (Rev. 21:16). Its gates bear the names of Israel's twelve tribes, and its foundations bear the names of the Lamb's twelve apostles. This is a vivid image of the people of God, appropriately announced by a voice from God's throne: "Behold, the dwelling place of God is with man. He will dwell with them, and they will be his people, and God himself will be with them as their God" (21:3).

Separation: The Purity of God

Another feature central to the priests' calling is holiness, separation from anything and everything that would introduce defiling impurity into the presence of God. Because the Old Testament sanctuaries (tabernacle and temple) were "holy," anything that the law defined as tainted and tainting (for example, touching a dead body or suffering from abnormal medical conditions) excluded Israelites from entering the courts of the Lord. They had to wait for a prescribed time, undergo inspection and be pronounced "clean," and often go through further cleansing rituals. Uncircumcised Gentiles could not enter the temple at all. They needed to become proselytes, submitting to the Lord's covenant through washing, circumcision, and sacrifice. Even Israelites, if they did not belong to the consecrated tribe of Levi, could enter only the open courtyard outside the tabernacle and later the temple.

This theme of holiness—separation from what defiles, whether symbolic (ceremonial laws) or moral—extends beyond the holy *spaces* of the sanctuaries to include holy *time*, regulations defining holy *living conditions*, and the setting apart of a holy *people*. So Israel's priesthood stood at the center of a vast network of rules pertaining to purity, all of which find their fulfillment in Christ, our Great High Priest, and his flawless holiness that has invaded our defiled world.

The Lord separated *holy time* from the Israelites' everyday tasks, so that they could focus their attention on their covenant communion with him. These "oases" in the calendar came at various frequencies. By his example at creation, the Lord had set apart one day in seven as a Sabbath, a day to cease from labor, consecrated not only for Israel's refreshment but also for worship and communion with him (Ex. 20:8–11). In addition to this weekly holy time, Israel was to observe feasts throughout the year to celebrate his saving actions (Passover/Unleavened Bread, Booths/ Ingathering), his generous provision (Firstfruits, Weeks), and his gracious forgiveness (Trumpets, Day of Atonement) (Lev. 23). Three annual feasts (Passover, Weeks, Booths) were to be observed by pilgrimage to and assembly at the Lord's sanctuary (Ex. 23:14–17). Beyond these annual feasts, the Lord established for his holy land a seven-year cycle reflective of the weekly cycle for his people:

> For six years you shall sow your land and gather in its yield, but the seventh year you shall let it rest and lie fallow, that the poor of your people may eat; and what they leave the beasts of the field may eat. . . .
>
> Six days you shall do your work, but on the seventh day you shall rest; that your ox and your donkey may have rest, and the son of your servant woman, and the alien, may be refreshed. (Ex. 23:10–12)

The sabbatical year was to provide rest for the land and relief for the poor, just as the weekly Sabbath offered refreshment to workers, their dependents, and their animals. After seven sabbatical years, every fiftieth year was an especially holy celebration of relief and release (Lev. 25:8–22): "And you shall consecrate the fiftieth year, and proclaim liberty throughout the land to all its inhabitants. It shall be a jubilee for you, when each of you shall return to his property and each of you shall return to his clan. . . . For it is a jubilee. It shall be holy to you" (vv. 10, 12). Across Israel's calendar the Lord interspersed holy moments and seasons of rest and joy in his presence: days and seasons and years set apart from the mundane as holy to himself and refreshing to his people.

The New Testament shows Jesus as bringing surprising fulfillments to this network of Israel's "holy times." From Luke's Gospel, we learn that Jesus' public ministry opened with his announcement that the eschatological fulfillment of the day of Jubilee had dawned. In the synagogue of Nazareth, he read Isaiah's prediction of the final Jubilee:

> The Spirit of the Lord is upon me,
>> because he has anointed me
>> to proclaim good news to the poor.
> He has sent me to proclaim liberty to the captives
>> and recovering of sight to the blind,
>> to set at liberty those who are oppressed,
> to proclaim the year of the Lord's favor. (Luke 4:18–19, quoting Isa. 61:1–2)

Then he announced that he had fulfilled this Scripture as he read it. He was the Spirit-anointed herald (Luke 3:22; 4:1, 14), who proclaimed good news to the poor and release to captives in the new year of the Lord's favor. The system of sabbatical years, with the Jubilee year as its capstone, found fulfillment in the arrival of God's royal reign, the era of redemptive release inaugurated by God's Messiah.

The New Testament shows us that Israel's annual feasts were designed to foreshadow Christ and his redemptive achievement. Passover, which recalled Israel's deliverance from slavery and death in Egypt, was fulfilled in Jesus:

> Cleanse out the old leaven that you may be a new lump, as you really are unleavened. For Christ, our Passover lamb, has been sacrificed. Let us therefore celebrate the festival, not with the old leaven, the leaven of malice and evil, but with the unleavened bread of sincerity and truth. (1 Cor. 5:7–8).

Because shed blood more precious than a lamb's has set us free (see 1 Peter 1:18–19), "leaven" is to be purged from our lives. This is not the yeast that makes dough rise, but rather the malice that taints our hearts and relationships. The Feast of Weeks (Pentecost) or Firstfruits, seven weeks after Passover, was the fitting moment for the ascended Messiah to pour out his Spirit and to begin harvesting "firstfruits" of all the nationalities across the whole world (Acts 2:1–11). During the Feast of Booths, as Israelites encamped again outside their homes to commemorate their ancestors' forty years in tents, Jesus evoked wilderness memories of the rock struck at Massah and the pillar of fire, identifying himself as the source of living water (John 7:37–39) and the divine light that illumines and protects (8:12). The sobering Day of Atonement ritual summoned Israel to repentance and graphically portrayed the cost of the people's forgiveness by God, the shedding of a substitute's blood. Now Jesus our Great High Priest has made such repeated sacrifices obsolete by his once-for-all offering of himself, our sinless Substitute (Heb. 9:7; 10:1–10).

How did Jesus fulfill the weekly Sabbath? In the generations after the Jews' return from Babylonian exile, rabbinical traditions grew up to define with great precision any action that even ran the risk of violating the Sabbath commandment. Jesus, on the other hand, exerting his authority as Lord of the Sabbath, defined the day's holiness positively rather than negatively (Mark 2:28). His focus was not on what the Lord's holy day was separated *from* but rather on what it was to be set apart *for*. Jesus showed the Sabbath to be God's remedy for what threatens human life in the image of God, such as hunger (Luke 6:1–5), or a withered hand (vv. 6–11), or demonic enslavement (13:10–13). The Sabbath is the ideal day for Israel's Lord and Liberator to set Abraham's children free!

The epistle to the Hebrews ties the theme of the Lord's rest following his work of creation (Heb. 4:4, quoting Gen. 2:2) with the promise of entering God's rest implied in Psalm 95. When the conquest of the Promised Land under Joshua was essentially complete, Israel received "rest on every side" (Josh. 21:44–45). Yet still in David's day, many years later, in Psalm 95 the Lord was still urging his people to enter his rest through receiving his word in faith (Heb. 4:7–8). This invitation is still extended to us today: "So then, there remains a Sabbath rest for the people of God" (v. 9). In Jesus' first coming, the final Jubilee of release and relief has dawned; but as pilgrims, we are still en route to "a better country, that is, a heavenly one" (11:16), to our full enjoyment of "God's rest" (4:8–11). So our labors cease one day in seven, and we gather to worship in the presence of the risen Christ through his blood (12:22–24). We treasure this holy time as a foretaste of the ultimate holy place toward which we trek: "For here we have no lasting city, but we seek the city that is to come" (13:14).

Related to the priestly separation theme are the law's many regulations that demand and define *holy food, farms, clothes, bodies, buildings,* and so on. Through his commandments, the Lord embedded in the visible, touchable, everyday experience of the Israelites the recurring message that they were set apart from the other peoples on the earth to approach his holy presence in worship. He prescribed the people's kosher diet (Lev. 11) and prohibited them from planting different grains in the same field or wearing clothing made of wool and linen together (Deut. 22:9–11). Other laws specified how priests should diagnose ritual uncleanness incurred though bodily conditions (skin blemishes or fluid discharges) or contact with corpses, and how such defilement could be removed to restore those affected to the worshiping congregation (Lev. 12–15). Even buildings might suffer "leprous disease"—perhaps mold or mildew—that would, unless remedied, make its residents ritually unclean, unfit to commune among God's holy people (14:33–57).

With the coming of Christ, the obligation to stay separate from defilement continues, but the practice of this principle shifts from the external to the internal, from the physical to the spiritual. With respect to the dietary laws, for instance, Jesus teaches that in God's eyes people are defiled not by what enters the mouth but by what comes out of it (Mark 7:14–19). What taints is not what the mouth *ingests* (even nonkosher foods), but what it *expresses,* corrupt thoughts and motives spilling out of a corrupt heart in destructive words. Likewise, as we have seen, Paul reinterprets the law prohibiting the use of leaven at Passover and the festal week that followed it: the yeast to be avoided (year-round, by the way) is not a grocery ingredient, but malicious motives that corrupt relationships in the church of Christ (1 Cor. 5:6–8). Paul wraps up an extended discussion of dietary disputes with the conclusion: "Whether you eat or drink, or whatever you do, do all to the glory of God" (10:31). Although the New Testament does not specifically comment on every type of regulation in the books of Moses (such as laws defining separation in clothing or farmland), the way that the dietary regulations find fulfillment in the call to holiness of heart shows the path that links

210

"You shall not wear cloth of wool and linen mixed together" (Deut. 22:11) to Jesus, the Great Priest who is "holy, innocent, unstained, separated from sinners" (Heb. 7:26).

The description of Jesus as "separated from sinners" might surprise us, since his critics charged, for good reason, that he was "a friend of tax collectors and sinners" (Luke 7:34; see 15:1–2). What his opponents failed to see was that such contact did not stain Jesus, but rather cleansed others. Whereas the law of Moses treated leprosy's defilement as contagious, so that the touch of an "unclean" person infected others, when God's Holy One arrives, it is his purity that is contagious. Rather than Jesus' being defiled by contact with a leper, the touch of Jesus' absolute purity and power cleansed the leper and qualified him again to approach God in grateful worship (5:12–15). The touch of a woman who had suffered a defiling condition for years did not pollute Jesus, but instead made her well and "clean" (8:43–48).

The detailed, life-pervading regulations by which God's law insisted on Israel's separation from anything unfitting for his holy presence were the outworking of Israel's identity as a *holy people*, consecrated for communion with the Lord. As his stunning divine glory descended on Sinai and traumatized both the mountain itself and the people who stood at its foot, the Lord declared: "Now therefore, if you will indeed obey my voice and keep my covenant, you shall be my treasured possession among all peoples" (Ex. 19:5). Repeatedly the Lord reinforced his demand of purity—ethical, ceremonial, dietary, and every other form—with the refrain, "Be holy, for I am holy" (Lev. 11:44; 19:2; 20:7, 26; see 1 Peter 1:16).

As we begin to grasp the spiritual depth of the Lord's demand for thoroughgoing holiness, we feel a tension built into the New Testament's description of Christians. On the one hand, Paul calls Christians "saints," that is, "holy ones," and sometimes speaks as though we are already "sanctified" (1 Cor. 1:2). On the other hand, like ancient Israel, Christian believers—including, perhaps especially, those in Corinth!—are *far from* subjectively holy. The New Testament authors rebuke a host of grievous violations of God's purity on the part of the followers of Christ, insisting that we put to death and remove from our lives a wide range of evil attitudes and action: "sexual immorality, impurity, passion, evil desire, and covetousness, which is idolatry[,] . . . anger, wrath, malice, slander, and obscene talk from your mouth. Do not lie to one another" (Col. 3:5–9). So which is it? Are we God's holy people or not? Are we already purified as priests or aren't we?

211

The answer to our dilemma—which is painfully experiential, not just intellectual—is that the holiness of the saints is (1) a status that God has already graciously conferred *on us* because we are "in Christ," (2) a new identity that the Holy Spirit has implanted *in us* as a tiny seed of holy life because we are "in Christ," and (3) a lifelong process that the Spirit carries out *in us* because we are "in Christ." In Christ, who is our sanctification (1 Cor. 1:30), we have *a holy status* and are authorized as priests to draw near to God's throne of grace, to serve him as his royal priesthood, his holy nation (1 Peter 2:9). Hebrews captures the tension and dynamic in a few words, referring to both the instantaneous and the progressively sanctifying power of Jesus' sacrifice: "For by a single offering he *has perfected* for all time those who *are being sanctified*" (Heb. 10:14). *Perfected* in Hebrews has a special priestly sense, essentially meaning "consecrated to come into God's holy presence" (5:9–10; 7:19). Because of Christ's once-for-all sacrifice, we can now draw near to God's throne of grace as "perfected" priests, despite our personal struggles with sin. Yet at the same time, believers "are being sanctified"; and because they are still in that process, they must encourage each other constantly (3:13; 10:24–25).

The apostle John, who insists that believers confess honestly that we "have . . . sin" and do sin (1 John 1:8–10), also insists that Christians' lives are no longer characterized by an unremitting indulgence in unholy motives, thoughts, or behaviors. This is because the Spirit of God, as he unites people to Christ by faith, instills in them *a new, holy identity*: "No one born of God makes a practice of sinning, for God's seed abides in him, and he cannot keep on sinning because he has been born of God" (3:9; see 5:18). Even to the church at Corinth, still so stained by serious sins, Paul wrote assurance that, despite their sensual living before the gospel reached them, "you were washed, you were sanctified, you were justified in the name of the Lord Jesus Christ and by the Spirit of our God" (1 Cor. 6:11). Paul appeals to this new identity when he directs believers, "Put on then, as God's chosen ones, *holy* and beloved, compassionate hearts, kindness, humility, meekness, and patience" (Col. 3:12).

Paul describes the Holy Spirit's lifelong project of eradicating every impurity from our motives, choices, words, and actions in words such as these:

> And I am sure of this, that he who began a good work in you will bring it to completion at the day of Jesus Christ. (Phil. 1:6)

> Now may the God of peace himself sanctify you completely, and may your whole spirit and soul and body be kept blameless at the coming of our Lord Jesus Christ. (1 Thess. 5:23)

This process entails conflict between the holy purposes of God's Spirit and the lingering lust for pollution that is our ugly legacy from Adam; but in the end, the victory will belong to God's invincible Spirit (Gal. 5:16–17, 22–24; see Rom. 6:10–14). In this assurance, Christians are summoned to pursue holiness "without which no one will see the Lord" (Heb. 12:14). (Notice that holiness, separation from sin's defilement, leads to priestly access into God's presence to "see the Lord.") In fact, it is precisely because of the Holy Spirit's ongoing presence and power that believers can and must engage in this pursuit, relying on his grace: "as you have always obeyed, so now . . . work out your own salvation with fear and trembling, for it is God who works in you, both to will and to work for his good pleasure" (Phil. 2:12–13).

Sacrifice: The Peace and Pleasure of God

This theme brings us to the center of Christ's work as our Great High Priest: his sacrifice of himself to atone for our sins, remove our spiritual defilement, and bring us to God. In the Old Testament sanctuary, sacrifices served several functions. Sin and guilt offerings symbolized the death that must occur to atone for sin. Whole burnt offerings represented the worshipers' wholehearted consecration to God. Firstfruits and thank offerings expressed worshipers' grateful acknowledgment that everything was a gift from their generous God. Peace or fellowship offerings, in which most of the sacrificial animal was eaten by the worshipers with God's priests and Levites, showed that atonement would lead to communion between the Lord and his people. Let's sample how these diverse types of sacrifices, with their various purposes, pointed the way to Jesus and his priestly mission.

Atonement Sacrifices to Remove Guilt and Deflect Wrath

As early as the aftermath of the fall, Scripture hints that only the death of a substitute can avert the ruin that sinners bring on themselves by violating the Lord's law. Adam and Eve's effort to cover their shame with fig leaves was futile, but the Lord mercifully clothed them in the skins of animals (Gen. 3:7, 21). The text does not directly portray the animals' death,

213

but it suggests that only God can cover our shame, and that this covering must entail the loss of a substitute's life.

Our rebellion and the impurity it produces make it both unfitting and dangerous for us to approach God's holy presence. Therefore, as soon as the tabernacle was built and consecrated (Ex. 25–40), Leviticus gives instructions regarding various types of sacrifice to be offered by Israel's priests. Sacrifices related to atonement for disobedience (sin offerings and guilt offerings) are prominent in these regulations (Lev. 4–7). The most dramatic ritual related to the guilt-purging aspect of sacrifice was the Day of Atonement, when two goats were set apart, one to be sacrificed and the other to be banished into the desert (Lev. 16). The first showed that the shedding of blood was necessary to remove sinners' guilt and avert God's curse; and the sending out of the second goat signaled the result of that sacrificial death, that Israel's sin and guilt were sent far away, no longer obstructing communion between the Lord and his people.

Yet the Day of Atonement ritual had to be observed annually and other sacrifices offered more frequently because, as Hebrews says, "it is impossible for the blood of bulls and goats to take away sins" (Heb. 10:4). The shed blood of animals, mere bulls and goats, could symbolize, visibly and externally, the price that would need to be paid to deal with human sin. But those animals, though physically flawless, could not really endure the personal God's judgment against personal creatures who have moral responsibility because they are made in God's image. The ancient sanctuaries' guilt offerings and sin offerings, as well as the Day of Atonement, were all "shadows" embedded at the heart of Israel's worshiping community to show the shape, as it were, of the one final Sacrifice who would cleanse worshipers' consciences before the heart-searching gaze of God. Jesus offered himself, history's only innocent human covenant-keeper, as the final sin offering that cleanses our consciences once for all (Heb. 9–10). Jesus' sacrifice accomplishes the deep, conscience-cleansing, lasting atonement that the animal sacrifices could not (9:12–14).

Consecration Sacrifices to Express Complete Devotion

From the dawn of human history, Scripture shows us offerings intended to express worshipers' devotion of themselves and their produce to the Lord. The biblical text identifies the offerings presented by Cain and Abel, Adam and Eve's sons, as "firstfruits" offerings—vegetables or grains from Cain, a firstborn lamb from Abel—presented in testimony to the truth that the entire harvest and flock belonged to the Lord (Gen. 4:3–4; Ex. 22:29–30). The flaw of Cain's offering, which provoked the Lord's rejection, does not seem to be that it was vegetable produce rather than a slain animal. Both would later be acceptable as firstfruits offerings under the law given through Moses (Ex. 23:19; Lev. 2:12–16). The flaw was Cain's heart, as becomes clear in his sullen and finally violent reaction to the Lord's preference for his brother's offering (Gen. 4:5–8). At this early point in history, then, we see offerings that were supposed to express worshipers' consecration of themselves and their resources to the Lord.

When the Lord pitched his tent in the midst of Israel's camp, he gave instructions for whole burnt offerings and for firstfruits and grain offerings. Whole burnt offerings yielded "a pleasing aroma to the LORD" because they symbolized the devotion of the worshiper to God (Lev. 1). Nothing was held back to be eaten by priests or people, but all was consumed by fire on the altar. Firstfruits and grain offerings were not related to the atonement of sin, since no bloodshed was involved in these offerings of harvested crops (Lev. 2). They signified the worshiper's acknowledgment that his whole harvest, even that retained to feed one's own family, was God's gift, to be used for God's glory.

A special application of the use of sacrifice to symbolize complete consecration to the Lord's service was the ritual by which Aaron and his sons were set apart as priests to stand in the Lord's presence on behalf of all Israel (Lev. 8:14–30). The ritual involved washing, a sacrifice to atone for their sin, and donning vestments fit for the Lord's holy presence. Anointing with oil symbolized Aaron's need for God's power and favor in order to perform his priestly duties (v. 30). As those set apart from their Israelite kinfolk to serve in the Lord's presence, the priests were prohibited from practices that would render them ceremonially defiled (for instance, contact with a dead body, 21:1–15). Consecration to the Lord's service was comprehensive and life-consuming!

Christ's death on the cross was our atoning sacrifice, but it was also his own sacrifice of utter consecration to his Father and to his mission from the Father. In his High Priestly Prayer, Jesus spoke to his heavenly Father about his own consecration and that of the people whom the Father had given to him: "For their sake I *consecrate* myself, that they also may be sanctified [*consecrated*] in truth" (John 17:19). Jesus uses the same Greek verb in both clauses. His point is that he has totally devoted himself to his priestly service to the Father on our behalf, in order that he may also devote us completely to his Father, so that we may stand in humble wonder in his presence, and there glorify and enjoy him forever. The epistle to the Hebrews explains Psalm 40 as foretelling the coming of Christ into the world to replace whole burnt offerings and other sacrifices. In their stead, Christ came to offer the very body that the Father had prepared for him through his incarnation:

> Consequently, when Christ came into the world, he said,
>
> "Sacrifices and offerings you have not desired,
> but a body have you prepared for me;
> in burnt offerings and sin offerings
> you have taken no pleasure.
> Then I said, 'Behold, I have come to do your will, O God,
> as it is written of me in the scroll of the book.'" (Heb. 10:5–7)

In these words (Ps. 40:6–8), Hebrews explains, we hear Christ's voice announcing that he has come to replace both the atoning and the consecrating sacrifices of the Old Testament by the once-for-all sacrifice of his own body, offered in keeping with God's will (Heb. 10:8–10).

Consecration offerings also find fulfillment in Christians' donations (such as contributions to help defray Paul's expenses), which are "fragrant offering[s]" that please God (Phil. 4:18), just as the "pleasing aroma" of wholly consumed animal sacrifices and grain offerings delighted the Lord (Lev. 1:9, 13, 17; 2:1–3). In fact, any and all good deeds of compassion that meet others' needs are "sacrifices pleasing to God" (Heb. 13:16). Although Christ's death is the final and fully sufficient *atoning* sacrifice once for all, Christians still have "sacrifices" to offer. We do so not to address our guilt, but to express our gratitude to the Lord who died once for all for us and the fact that, having been bought at so great a price (1 Cor. 6:20), we belong to him and are set apart for his use. God's mercy in Jesus moves us to offer our very selves in total consecration to him: "I appeal to you therefore, brothers, by the mercies of God, to present your bodies as a living sacrifice, holy and acceptable to God, which is your spiritual worship" (Rom. 12:1).

Communion Sacrifices to Celebrate the Reunion That Results from Atonement

The peace offerings described in Leviticus 3 and 7:11–18 symbolized the ultimate objective of the sacrificial system: the reestablishment of communion between Israelite worshipers and the Lord. For these sacrifices, the slain animal's blood was sprinkled on the altar, and its fat and internal organs consumed by fire. But the rest of the meat was to be eaten either by the priests (7:31–36) or by the worshiper himself with his family (7:15–16). After Israel entered the Promised Land, the Lord directed his people to gather at his temple, bringing the tithes of their crops and the firstborn of flocks and herds. "And you shall eat there before the LORD your God and rejoice, you and your household" (Deut. 14:22–26; see 12:5–7).

Through these sacrifices, Israelites enjoyed food and fellowship in communion with their Lord. These offerings find fulfillment in the Lord's Supper that Jesus instituted for his church to observe until he returns in glory. The elements of the Supper, bread and wine, symbolize Jesus' body and blood, sacrificed once for all on the cross. Receiving these simple elements by faith in the Savior whose death they represent is, as Paul says, a "participation" in the body and blood of Christ (1 Cor. 10:16), sharing table fellowship with the Lord himself (v. 21). So the elements of the Lord's Supper obviously point us back to Jesus' sacrifice, his body given for us and his blood shed for us. But they also point us to the present and to the future: to present communion with our crucified and risen Lord and with each other as members of his one body through the Holy Spirit, and to the future when our fellowship by faith will give way to fellowship by sight (11:26).

The book of Revelation shows us the final fulfillment of Israel's feasts of restored reunion with the Lord. In Revelation 7, John sees saints in heaven standing before God's throne and serving him night and day, in robes made radiantly white by washing in the blood of the Lamb (Rev. 7:14–15). The purifying power of Jesus' sacrifice opens the way to their communion with the living God. The Lamb's provision for his saints in heaven—relieving their hunger and thirst, guiding them to springs of living water (vv. 16–17)—anticipates the great wedding celebration when the Lamb returns at the end of the age to take his bride to himself (19:9).

Israel's peace offerings and joyful feasting in the courts of the Lord testified in advance to the wonderful reality that Christ's sacrifice on our behalf not only atones for our sin and consecrates us to God's service, but

217

also ushers us into the Father's banquet, to enjoy his company as he feeds us from his bounty.

Supplication: Prayer to God

Interestingly, in the Old Testament we actually read about the prayers of prophets more often than we encounter intercessions spoken by priests. In a dream, God counseled the Philistine King Abimelech to ask for Abraham's prayers, "for he is a prophet" (Gen. 20:7). Moses, whose primary calling was prophetic (though he performed priestly and even royal actions), interceded for relief from judgment both for Egypt's pharaoh and for the guilty but penitent Israelites (Ex. 8:8, 12, 28, 30; 9:28, 33; Num. 21:7). Later prophets also prayed for the Israelites and their kings (1 Sam. 12:19, 23; 1 Kings 13:6), as well as for Gentiles in need (1 Kings 17:20–22).

Despite the frequency of prophets' prayers in Scripture, the Shorter Catechism has good grounds to associate intercession in a special way with Jesus' fulfillment of the priestly office. The role of the priests to pray for their fellow Israelites is entailed in the privilege of serving on others' behalf in the sanctuary of God. When the temple was consecrated, King Solomon asked the Lord, who had placed his name in that earthly "house" (1 Kings 8:29), to hear from heaven when his people (as well as foreigners) "pray toward this house" (vv. 33–34, 38–39, 42–43). The animal sacrifices that the priests offered, especially sin and guilt offerings and the annual Day of Atonement sacrifices, were unspoken petitions for the Lord's forgiveness.

Priests entered the outer chamber of the sanctuary daily, and one of their tasks was to offer incense every morning and every evening on the golden incense altar (Ex. 30:1–10; 40:5). The books of Moses do not explicitly discuss the function of the incense burned on this altar (though see Lev. 16:13), but later Scripture associates the smoke of the incense with the prayers of worshipers (Ps. 141:2; Rev. 5:8; 8:3–4). When John the Baptist's father, Zechariah, was chosen to offer the daily incense in the temple, the people outside were at prayer (Luke 1:8–10). The angel Gabriel, appearing beside the incense altar, assured Zechariah that his prayer had been heard and would be answered (vv. 11–17). In view of the priest's representative role, it is unlikely that the prayer in question was only Zechariah and Elizabeth's personal petition for a son. In fact, Zechariah's unbelief when Gabriel announced that they would be parents in their old age shows that he had long abandoned hope that God would grant such a petition. Rather, the pleas of both priest and people were for deliverance "from the hand of our enemies" (v. 74), and the mission of Zechariah's son, John, would be to prepare for the Lord who was about to come to bring that rescue.

The garments worn by the high priest as he entered the Most Holy Place on the Day of Atonement symbolized the calling of the high priest to represent his fellow Israelites before the Lord through sacrifice and prayer. On his shoulders were ephods containing two onyx stones, on which were etched the names of Israel's twelve tribes. Thus, as the Lord looked down from heaven, he would see (as it were) the names of six tribes on one of the high priest's shoulders and the names of the other six on the other shoulder: "And Aaron shall bear their names before the LORD on his two shoulders for remembrance" (Ex. 28:12). On Aaron's chest was the breastpiece that had twelve stones, each bearing the name of one of the twelve tribes: "So Aaron shall bear the names of the sons of Israel in the breastpiece of judgment on his heart, when he goes into the Holy Place, to bring them to regular remembrance before the LORD" (Ex. 28:29). Thus, as he passed through the inner veil and approached the ark of the covenant, the names of Israel would be visible from God's throne, the mercy seat. These features of Aaron's priestly garments emphasize that when he carried the blood of the slain goat into the Most Holy Place, to sprinkle it on the atonement lid that covered the ark of the covenant, he was by that act interceding for forgiveness for all Israel.

One more feature of the priests' role that fits under the general category of prayer is their pronouncement of blessing on the Lord's people. The direction and authorization is given in Numbers 6:23–26:

> Speak to Aaron and his sons, saying, Thus you shall bless the people of Israel: you shall say to them,
>
> The LORD bless you and keep you;
> the LORD make his face to shine upon you and be gracious to you;
> the LORD lift up his countenance upon you and give you peace.

This is not a conventional prayer, since it is actually addressed to the people receiving the blessing ("you") rather than to the Lord himself. Moreover, it entails more than intercessory petition. It is God's priestly representatives' actually laying claim to the people who belong to the Lord and bringing them under his protective favor, as the Lord's commentary shows: "So shall they put my name upon the people of Israel, and I will bless them" (Num. 6:27). Yet at a later point in Israel's history, during the reform and purification of temple worship initiated by King Hezekiah, the priests' blessing of the people would be described as prayer: "Then the priests and the Levites arose and blessed the people, and their voice was heard, and their prayer came to his holy habitation in heaven" (2 Chron. 30:27). The blessing pronounced by the priest Eli on Elkanah and his wife Hannah as they visited their son at the Lord's tent annually was certainly prayerlike: "May the Lord give you children by this woman for the petition she asked of the Lord" (1 Sam. 2:20). In the Bible, where we hear priests blessing others (such as the priest-king Melchizedek's blessing of Abraham in the name of God Most High, Gen. 14:19–20), we hear anticipations of the intercessory ministry of Jesus, our Great High Priest.

The main reason that the catechism associates intercession—prayer or supplication on others' behalf—with Jesus' priestly calling, no doubt, is that the New Testament itself does so. Hebrews 7 draws a series of contrasts between (1) the Levitical priesthood in the order of Aaron and (2) Christ's priesthood in the order of Melchizedek. The priests belonging to the tribe of Levi and descended from Aaron entered their office on the basis of genealogy, whereas Christ, in the order of Melchizedek, became a priest by God's immutable oath and his own indestructible (resurrection) life, as Psalm 110:4 had announced (Heb. 7:5–6, 14–17). Death prevented Aaron and his descendants from continuing in their priestly role, but Christ "holds his priesthood permanently, because he continues forever" (vv. 23–24). In his permanent tenure as Priest, Jesus brings believers comprehensive salvation and access to God, "since he always lives to make intercession for them" (v. 25). Christ's prayers for us are integral to the activities that he carries out in his eternal priestly office (see also Rom. 8:34). Jesus' prayers for us are wiser, more compassionate, and longer-lasting than the prayers of Aaron and his sons. John gives us a window on the perpetual priestly ministry that Jesus conducts for us in heaven in John 17. Christ prays for our protection from the evil one and for our unity, which will testify to the watching world that the Father has indeed sent Jesus as the Redeemer into the world.

Christian believers' privilege and responsibilities in prayer are based on the priestly sacrifice and intercession of Jesus on our behalf. Because we have in God's very presence a Priest who has experienced our weakness and temptations but also endured every test with pure faithfulness and innocence, we can "with confidence draw near to the throne of grace, that we may receive mercy and find grace to help in time of need" (Heb. 4:16). Moreover, we have a priestly calling to pray for others, just as Aaron and his sons interceded on behalf of the other Israelite tribes. The radical cleansing that Christ achieved is vividly demonstrated in the experience of the Gentile Christians to whom Paul wrote Ephesians. Early in the letter, he called them to remember that they had once been "far off" (Eph. 2:13), excluded from God's people and walled out of his holy sanctuary, "separated from Christ, alienated from the commonwealth of Israel and strangers to the covenants of promise, having no hope and without God in the world" (v. 12). Now, however, Christ has broken down the wall that kept Gentiles out (v. 14). Former pagans are not only admitted to God's house but actually built into its composition (vv. 20–22). At the conclusion of the letter, Paul spells out the implications of this inclusion in terms of priestly intercession, asking his Gentile readers—who are now "in Christ"—to become his priestly intercessors, as they also pray for all the saints

> at all times in the Spirit, with all prayer and supplication. To that end keep alert with all perseverance, making supplication for all the saints, and also for me, that words may be given to me in opening my mouth boldly to proclaim the mystery of the gospel. (Eph. 6:18–19)

Christ, the final and eternal High Priest, has consecrated a whole kingdom of priests, who not only offer sacrifices of praise to God but also speak supplication and petition for others.

Conclusion

When we read biblical texts that contain the themes and motifs associated with priestly service and the purification necessary for approach into the presence of God—for the joy of worship before the throne of God—we should be asking these questions: How does this text relate to the priestly service of Jesus, to his supremely worthy sacrifice of himself, to his present priestly intercession for his people, and to his Spirit's relentless labor to purify believers and build us into the new, living temple? How does the wide spectrum of Scripture's priestly passages that touch on themes such as sanctuary, separation, sacrifice, and supplication unveil Jesus' multifaceted ministry as our Great High Priest:

- to cleanse our consciences and free us from the threat of eternal death by offering up himself as our once-for-all, atonement-achieving Substitute and Sacrifice?
- to qualify us to draw near to God in adoring worship and confident prayer?
- to make us his new and living sanctuary, where our corporate unity and purity display his glory?
- to consecrate us to his service even in the nitty-gritty of daily life, where we eat and drink and do all things as holy servants to exhibit God's glory and reflect his love toward others (1 Cor. 10:31; 8:13)?

Paul uses priestly-sacrificial imagery to sum up the appropriate response that we must make to the mercies of God in every aspect of our lives, everywhere and every moment of every day: "I appeal to you therefore, brothers, by the mercies of God, to present your bodies as a living sacrifice, holy and acceptable to God, which is your spiritual worship" (Rom. 12:1). We offer ourselves in response to Jesus' priestly offering of himself.

Putting It into Practice: The Priest Who Despised the Lord (1 Samuel 2:27–36)

The boy Samuel, the answer to his mother's prayers, was being raised at the tent of God by the old priest Eli. Samuel was apparently descended from the tribe of Ephraim (1 Sam. 1:1) or possibly Judah ("Ephrathite" could refer to a citizen of Bethlehem Ephrathah, Gen. 35:19, the village where David would be born, 1 Sam. 16:1). But as he "was ministering before the LORD, [he was] clothed with a linen ephod" (2:18)—traditionally the garment of Levites and priests. Although Samuel might have belonged to the "wrong tribe" to perform tabernacle duties, he was devoted to the Lord, and thus far more fit spiritually than Eli's own sons, Hophni and Phinehas, who defied God by demanding and eating the fat that should have been consecrated to the Lord and by having sex with women at the entrance to the tent of meeting (2:17, 22). Although Eli had pleaded with his wicked, worthless sons to stop their evil practices, they would not listen to him; and he did nothing more.

Clearly, this situation involves the responsibility of the priests to guard the sanctity of the Lord's dwelling place, and in so doing to protect his sinful people from the danger of the Lord's consuming holiness. Eli's last plea to his sons was: "If someone sins against a man, God will mediate for him, but if someone sins against the LORD, who can intercede for him?" (1 Sam. 2:25). By providing cities of refuge throughout the land and a place of refuge at his altar for the person who had inadvertently harmed a fellow Israelite, the Lord offered protection from justice by human avengers (Num. 35:9–34). But Eli's sons had defiantly insulted the Lord himself, and no one was left to shield them from his holy wrath.

Although Hophni and Phinehas would indeed bear the justice they deserved, the Lord was most angry with their father, Eli, the priest who ineffectually tried to protect God's sanctuary with a meek appeal that was easily ignored. God sent a prophet ("man of God") with a message of judgment on Eli and his priestly house:

> Thus the LORD has said, "Did I indeed reveal myself to the house of your father when they were in Egypt subject to the house of Pharaoh? Did I choose him out of all the tribes of Israel to be my priest, to go up to my altar, to burn incense, to wear an ephod before me? . . . Why then do you scorn my sacrifices and my offerings that I commanded, and honor your sons above me by fattening yourselves on the choicest parts of every offering of my people Israel?" Therefore the LORD, the God of Israel, declares: "I promised that your house and the house of your father should go in and out before me forever," but now the LORD declares: "Far be it from me, for those who honor me I will honor, and those who despise me shall be lightly esteemed. Behold, the days are coming when I will cut off your strength and the strength of your father's house, so that there will not be an old man in your house. . . . And I will raise up for myself a faithful priest, who shall do according to what is in my heart and in my mind. And I will build him a sure house, and he shall go in and out before my anointed forever." (1 Sam. 2:27–35)

The Lord's previous promise refers to his earlier covenant with the descendants of Levi, making them custodians and guardians of his sanctuary (Ex. 32:28–29), and his promise that Aaron and his descendants would be priests perpetually (Ex. 27:21; 29:9; Num. 25:10–13; Ps. 106:30–31).

Eli's refusal to use whatever force was necessary to restrain his sons' contempt for the Lord's sanctuary showed that Eli honored his sons above the Lord (1 Sam. 2:29). Despite his pious-sounding entreaty to his sons, by idolizing them he had scorned the God who had consecrated him to serve in his holy presence. Eli was not a worthy descendant of Phinehas the

Zealot, so the Lord would cut off Eli's sons in their prime and ultimately bring his priestly "dynasty" to an end in sorrow. The solitary survivor left alive to weep his eyes out in grief would be Abiathar, who alone escaped the slaughter of priests who helped David (22:22) and who would later be banished for supporting insurrection against David's royal heir, Solomon (1 Kings 1:5–10; 2:26–27). Zadok, a priest who stayed loyal to David and Solomon, was a preliminary fulfillment of God's promise to raise up a faithful priestly replacement for Eli (1:32–40; 2:35).

Yet the Lord's promise to replace Eli and his descendants looked beyond Zadok, as the heightened wording of 1 Samuel 2:35 shows: "And I will raise up for myself a faithful priest, who shall do according to what is in my heart and in my mind. And I will build him a sure house, and he shall go in and out before my anointed forever." Hebrews 2:17 alludes to this promise, explaining that Jesus "had to be made like his brothers in every respect, so that he might become a merciful and *faithful high priest* in the service of God, to make propitiation for the sins of the people." Hebrews will stress that before Aaron and his sons could offer sacrifices for the atonement of the Israelites' sins, they had to offer sacrifices for their own (5:1–3). Jesus, on the other hand, was and is without sin (4:15; 7:26), coming into the world "to do your will, O God" (10:7, quoting Ps. 40:8)—in the words of 1 Samuel 2:35, to "do according to what is in my heart and in my mind." Whereas Aaron and his sons were prevented by death from continuing in their priestly office and duties, Jesus holds his priesthood permanently because he lives forever (Heb. 7:23–24)—in the words of 1 Samuel 2:35, to "go in and out [as priest] forever."

Now, it is true that the prophet's announcement of the faithful priest to replace Eli's house is framed in terms of the Old Testament situation in which priests and anointed rulers belonged to different tribes. In that context, obviously, the faithful priest was Zadok (and his priestly successors) and the Lord's anointed was Solomon (and his royal successors in the dynasty of David). But here is where the *ultimate* fulfillment transcends the Old Testament expectation: the *finally* faithful Priest *actually is* the Anointed King, the Messiah. As Hebrews shows from Psalm 110, God promised to send an eternal Priest "after the order of Melchizedek" (Heb. 7:11), Abraham's mysterious contemporary in whom the offices of priest and king converged (Gen. 14:18–20). Melchizedek was both a true priest of God Most High and the king of Salem ("Peace") (Heb. 7:1–3), designed by God's providence in history to be an earthly replica of the eternal Son and a prototype of the royal-priestly mission that the Son would accomplish in his incarnation.

So Jesus is the final, faithful Priest promised by that ancient prophet who confronted Eli. Jesus is the replacement of the whole line of Levi and Aaron. Like Samuel, he came (it seemed) from the wrong tribe. But the Melchizedek promise "trumped" the genealogical qualification of the old order: the final, eternal Priest would actually be an eternal King as well. Jesus loved and honored his parents, as the law demanded. But unlike Eli, who idolized his sons, Jesus was always conscious of his primary accountability to his heavenly Father—even at the age of twelve. Jesus showed his zeal for the purity of God's sanctuary by cleansing it of profit-making merchandise and marketers (John 2:14–17). His zeal would be the "last straw" for the members of the temple hierarchy, pushing them to finalize their conspiracy to do away with him through Gentile, Roman hands (Mark 11:15–18).

By his death, Jesus purified a whole new temple—a meeting place of God with his people not constructed of fabric or wood or stone or gold, but a dwelling of God composed of . . . his people! We are his dwelling place, and among us Jesus serves as the merciful and faithful High Priest, zealous to make us wholly pure for the glory of his Father.

Questions for Reflection and Discussion

1. What are some key events in Old Testament history that illustrate that God's presence on earth creates "holy space" and that his presence poses a danger to polluted people? How would you describe what the Bible means by God's "holiness"? Why were people like us filled with fear for their lives when God drew near?

2. When we compare Genesis 2:15 with 3:24 and Numbers 1:53; 3:5–10, what threat was implied in Adam's task to "keep" ("guard") the garden of Eden?

3. In what four ways has Jesus fulfilled and is he fulfilling the purposes of the Old Testament sanctuaries (tabernacle and temple)? What are some New Testament passages that show these themes? How does each aspect of Jesus' sanctuary-related mission benefit Christians today?

4. From weekly Sabbaths (rest for people and animals) to sabbatical years (rest for farmland) to the Jubilee (rest from slavery and debt), the Lord embedded into Israel's calendar foretastes of hope for relief and release. How do Jesus' reading of and comment on Isaiah 61 (Luke 4:18–19)

guide us to God's bigger purpose for separating these *holy times* from seasons of everyday labor?

5. Are believers in Christ today obligated to observe the law's regulations about separation with respect to foods (kosher/clean diet), clothing, and skin conditions? What New Testament passages help us to answer this question? If such rules do not apply physically today, what was God's purpose in issuing them to Israel, and what message do they still convey to us?

6. Are Christians God's *holy people* (saints)? In what sense have we already been separated from sin's defilement, and in what sense are we still awaiting the completion of the Spirit's sanctifying (holy-making) work in us? What Bible passages speak to this issue?

7. What were the three general categories of sacrificial offerings presented in the Old Testament sanctuary (tabernacle, temple)? What did each category express and accomplish in the worshipers' relationship to God?

8. Which category of sacrifice has been fulfilled uniquely, completely, and once for all by Jesus? In what ways do Christians still offer worship that fulfills the meaning and purpose of the consecration and communion sacrifices? What New Testament texts show this?

9. How did the high priest's garments, as he entered the Most Holy Place on the Day of Atonement, symbolize his responsibility to intercede for his fellow Israelites? Who is the High Priest who now *continually* prays for his people? Does the Bible give us hints of what he is asking on our behalf? In what passages?

10. How has Jesus' completion of his unique, atoning mission as Priest laid the groundwork for our ongoing priestly ministry of praying for others?

9

Jesus the King of Kings: God's Rule

The Royal Executive of God's Righteous Rule

In the previous two chapters, we looked at prophets and priests, through whom the Lord spoke to his people and provided the purification that prepared them to approach his presence. Since guilty people could not bear to have their holy Sovereign come close to speak to them (Ex. 20:19), he summoned prophetic messengers into his presence (on Mount Sinai, in his temple, or via heavenly vision) to hear his word. Then he sent them out to declare that word as his agents and instruments of *revelation*. Since the stain of their sin had to be purged if they were ever to approach his presence as his "kingdom of priests" (19:5–6), he set apart the family of Aaron as priests, to enter his sanctuary and offer sacrificial blood to atone for their own and others' misdeeds. Priests were to be the Lord's agents and instruments of *reconciliation*, serving in his holy presence with offerings that would cleanse other worshipers and consecrate them to draw near as well.

Now our attention turns to kings (and other military and judicial leaders), whose mission from the Lord was both to *rescue* and protect his people and to *rule* them with justice and wisdom. As was true of prophets and priests, the kingly or royal office was an institution through which the Lord administered his covenantal bond with his human image-bearers. Specifically, through kings, judges, military commanders, and governors, God exerted his power to defend his people and executed his authority to govern and judge them. Since God's comprehensive plan for history is unified by a single goal, the restoration of cosmic wholeness under one perfect divine-human Ruler (Eph. 1:9–10), these royal functions and those charged to fulfill them also served as "landmarks," signaling paths that were leading into the future, trails that would eventually converge in one Great Revealer-Reconciler-Redeemer-Ruler: Jesus Christ, the final Prophet, the Great High Priest, and the King of kings.

The Lord, the King over All Kings

In nations in which political leaders are chosen through a democratic electoral process and with a balance of power among different branches of government, the idea that a king could wield authority as an absolute monarch might seem amusingly primitive or shockingly distasteful. Over the past several centuries, in significant parts of the world political leaders have come to be viewed as public "servants," answerable to those who elected them to office and subject to replacement if found wanting by the citizens whom they govern. Lord Acton's famous observation has been repeatedly confirmed over the ages: "Power tends to corrupt, and absolute power corrupts absolutely." To curb such absolute power, governmental systems have been developed in which some leaders make laws, while others wield weapons to enforce those laws, and still others assess the laws' justice and assess the guilt or innocence of those accused of violating them. Such checks and balances are prudent restraints on fallen and self-interested human beings. But such limits on people in power are relatively recent and not altogether successful. In the ancient world and still frequently today, absolute sovereigns both define law and enforce it.

To grasp what the Bible means by kingship, we have to set aside our modern democratic assumptions. The ancient world, into which God spoke his word, was governed by kings who actually ruled, whose will and word were law for their subjects. Even tyrants, of course, were not immune to assassination plots; but as long as they lived and grasped the scepter, they wielded enormous power over their domains, for the weal or the woe of their subjects. The monarchs who dominated the ancient Near East and its rising and falling empires—Egypt, Assyria, Babylonia, and so on—held the power of life and death over their people, and often demanded of their subjects not only compliant submission and political loyalty but also religious devotion. When Scripture speaks of the Lord as King, and as King over all of earth's kings, his universal and eternal dominion is in view.

The authority of Israel's kings was circumscribed by the fact that their calling was to reflect and assist Israel's true King, the Lord God himself. Israel's covenant Sovereign had delivered to Moses on Sinai the constitution that would shape Israel's community life, establishing boundaries on behavior and establishing processes for maintaining justice and resolving conflicts. He demanded that each king of Israel, as his vicegerent, saturate his mind and heart in this body of divine law, "that he may learn to fear the LORD his God by keeping all the words of this law and these statutes, and doing them, that his heart may not be lifted up above his brothers" (Deut. 17:18–20). A completely different tribe (Levi) had been called by God to minister in his sanctuary, and kings were banned from usurping priestly privileges (2 Chron. 26:16–21). These and other limitations on Israel's human kings reinforced the fact that *this particular people* already belonged to an absolute Monarch, to the living God, the uniquely holy and righteous "Judge of all the earth" (Gen. 18:25). Israel's supreme King really was an *absolute* Monarch with comprehensive power over his subjects in life and death and everything in between, and he alone could be trusted not to be corrupted by his absolute power.

Now, the Bible speaks of God's kingship in two different, though related, senses. On the one hand, God is the sovereign Creator and Controller of absolutely everything that happens in the universe that he has created. "The LORD has established his throne in the heavens, and his kingdom rules over all" (Ps. 103:19). "For God is the King of all the earth; sing praises with a psalm!" (47:7). Even the arrogant pagan monarch Nebuchadnezzar was compelled at last to confess the truth about the God of Daniel and his Jewish friends:

His dominion is an everlasting dominion,
    and his kingdom endures from generation to generation;
all the inhabitants of the earth are accounted as nothing,
    and he does according to his will among the host of heaven
    and among the inhabitants of the earth;
and none can stay his hand
    or say to him, "What have you done?" (Dan. 4:34–35)

On the other hand, Scripture realistically records that rebellious humans—both pagan foreigners and the Lord's covenant people—defy and resist God's righteous rule. Although their worst actions are still within God's sovereign plan (Gen. 50:20; Acts 2:23), they do not yield *willing* obedience to the *revealed will* of their Creator-King. For that reason, God's Word also promised that God's kingdom reign would come in the future, when the King arrives in person to erase all opposition to his dominion and to bring peace and safety to his loyal subjects. Israel's psalmists lamented the shame endured by David's royal descendants and asked the Lord "how long" it would be until the promised kingdom would arrive (Ps. 89). During Judah's exile, Nebuchadnezzar's dream (Dan. 2:44–45) and Daniel's vision (7:13–14, 27) previewed and promised the future arrival of God's everlasting kingdom in history. God's people were still longing for the arrival of the Messiah, the Anointed King descended from David (John 1:19–20, 41; cf. 4:25; 7:25–31, 40–42), when John the Baptist appeared and announced, "The kingdom of heaven [the last-days reign of God] is at hand" (Matt. 3:2; see Mark 1:15). Although many failed to recognize Jesus as the Messiah, his power to rescue from demons and disease showed that the kingdom of God had arrived (Luke 11:20; 17:20–21). It would come "with power" within the lifetime of those who heard Jesus' words (Mark 9:1). When Jesus rose from the dead and ascended to heaven, God fulfilled his promise to put David's descendant on his throne by seating Jesus at his right hand. That kingdom event in heaven was signaled on earth on the day of Pentecost, when the Holy Spirit descended to empower the church to bear witness to all nations (Acts 2:30–36). As a result of Christ's incarnation, suffering, and heavenly exaltation, "the salvation and the power and the kingdom of our God and the authority of his Christ have come, for the accuser of our brothers has been thrown down, who accuses them day and night before our God" (Rev. 12:10). This redemptive reign of God, inaugurated by Jesus the Anointed King in his first coming, still awaits its consummation in the future, when he will return in glory and "the kingdom of the world has become the kingdom of our Lord and of his Christ, and he shall reign forever and ever" (11:15). Yet John the forerunner spoke truth: the Messiah's arrival and actions in obedience, suffering, and exaltation launched the long-awaited reign by which God would set wrong right once for all. As we are about to see, the kings, judges, commanders, and governors that populate Scripture's pages were, at their best, faint reflections of the son of David who would be the Son of God, the human Ruler so unique in his righteousness that he alone can be trusted to wield absolute power without succumbing to its corrupting influence.

Kingship and the Image of God

In Scripture, kingship themes are not limited to monarchs on thrones or on fields of battle. They appear in a variety of individuals and relationships. This shouldn't surprise us, since we have seen both in Genesis and in the New Testament (Eph. 4:24; Col. 3:10) that human beings, created in God's image, were designed to resemble their Creator in knowledge, righteousness, and holiness—to relate to God as prophets (knowing God truly), as priests (worshiping God in holiness), and as kings (exercising delegated authority righteously).

As prophets, our first parents were endowed with intelligence and language, to hear God's word and to speak it to each other. As priests, they were privileged to enjoy God's presence in his garden sanctuary. Likewise, as kings, they were given dominion, to rule over other creatures on earth; and they were accountable to creation's King for how they exercised the authority that he had delegated to them: "fill the earth and subdue it and have dominion over the fish of the sea and over the birds of the heavens and over every living thing that moves on the earth" (Gen. 1:28). Adam's royal authority is specifically shown in the fact that God, who named created spheres in Genesis 1 (labeling the light "day" and the darkness "night"), in Genesis 2 allows Adam to assign names to the animals (2:19–20). This is Adam's first recorded act as assistant to the Great King. This naming is an exercise in true "knowing" (prophetic), but it is also an exercise in wise "ruling" (kingly).

Although Adam and Eve had authority over the other creatures, they were not absolute monarchs, but were obligated to recognize the limits of their domain. Accountability is implied in the terms that summarize Adam's tasks: he is to "work" (or "serve") the garden and to "keep" ("guard") it (Gen. 2:15). The Hebrew verb *'abad*, meaning "work" or "serve," signals that Adam's labors in the garden—shoveling, pruning, replanting, harvesting, training dogs or horses or whatever—were not to be carried out in such a way that the lower creatures, whether plants or animals, were simply exploited for humanity's whims. The lower creatures could be used by their king, but not abused: the king must view his rule as "service." The verb *guard* has military overtones that are not only priestly (guarding the purity of a temple, Num. 3:5–10) but also kingly. An enemy was "waiting in the wings," a threat not to be named until Genesis 3:1—an enemy who intended to assault this garden fortress of purity and peace. Adam must

231

be on his guard to protect the sanctuary from invasion and to repel the invader. As the caretaker of God's garden, Adam is accountable to the Great King for the integrity of this palace. The boundary of Adam and Eve's royal authority and the reality of their accountability to their supreme Sovereign is shown especially in the limit that he imposed on their almost-universal dominion: "You may surely eat of every tree of the garden, but of the tree of the knowledge of good and evil you shall not eat, for in the day that you eat of it you shall surely die" (Gen. 2:16–17). Their authority carried with it the requirement to rule righteously, in submission to the Creator who had delegated dominion to them through adherence to his word.

When we reflect on this kingly perspective on the image of God, we hear echoes of that royal dignity and duty in various interpersonal relationships, even in our fallen world. Parents in families, masters in the workplace, officers in armies, and rulers in states all reflect, at least faintly, that blend of authority over others and accountability under God that once distinguished the primeval royal couple, Adam and Eve. Wherever in the Bible we see leaders distinguished from subordinates, sovereigns from subjects, we glimpse traces of humanity's royal identity and destiny. Glimpses of the kingly themes profiled above (combat, authority, leadership, justice, and wisdom) in various individuals and relationships are landmarks that point us back to humanity's original creation in the image of God. And by pointing us back, these landmarks point us forward to Christ the perfect King and to our re-creation in his royal image.

Kingship Themes

As we survey the role of kings in the Scriptures, certain themes emerge as distinctive to this office. If prophets are mediators of *revelation* and priests are mediators of *reconciliation*, kings are mediators of God's *rule* over his people. Through Israel's kings, when they fulfilled their calling, the Lord of the covenant provided rescue and protection, leadership and justice. We could sum up the calling of the king by saying that he fights for God's people with courageous faith, leads them with accountable authority, and judges them in wise justice.

All these themes are found together in the image of the shepherd, which appears often in the Old Testament as symbolizing the king's role and responsibility. David, who set the standard for Israel's kings (1 Kings 11:4; 15:3; etc.), had shepherded sheep before his anointing (1 Sam. 16:11;

17:34–36). Thus, God's providence had prepared the pastoral (shepherding) image to portray the duties of rulers. In Ezekiel 34, for example, the Lord rebukes the leaders who had failed miserably to shepherd his flock. The shepherds' responsibilities—the kings' duties—included finding and gathering scattered sheep (vv. 11–12), leading them to good pastureland (vv. 13–14), rescuing them from predators (v. 8), strengthening the weak and bandaging the wounded (v. 16), and even disciplining strong rams that bullied fragile ewes and lambs (vv. 17–19). What a comprehensive portrait of the royal calling!

Think of the first two generations in the dynasty that would lead to Jesus the Messiah: David was the epitome of the warrior-king, courageously defending God's people in reliance on the Lord, both in his combat with the Philistine champion Goliath and throughout his royal career. He was a commander whom his troops gladly and loyally followed. Solomon, whose reign was peaceful (his name comes from the Hebrew word *shalom*, meaning "peace"), was the apex of royal wisdom applied in rendering just judgment, famous throughout the ancient Near East for his sagacity and learning. Admittedly, these generalizations about David and Solomon are not the whole story. At crucial moments in their reigns, David grievously abused his military power and betrayed his subjects' trust and Solomon the sage played the fool by letting pagan wives lure his heart into the absurdity of idolatry. So neither David nor Solomon turned out to be the courageous conqueror and just judge that God's people need in a king. Both are only broken landmarks along a trail that leads, in due time, to the true and final Messiah. But David's and Solomon's respective strengths show the royal profile of that King to come.

The Westminster Shorter Catechism (answer 26) summarizes the Bible's teaching on the kingly work of Christ in this way: "Christ executeth the office of a king, in subduing us to himself, in ruling and defending us, and in restraining and conquering all his and our enemies." Here we see military themes: Christ as King is "subduing" and "defending us," and he is "restraining and conquering all his and our enemies." We also hear the motif of "ruling," which combines commanding, leading, and judging. So kings are defenders and leaders and judges. The warrior theme (David) is intrinsic to the king's calling, and Jesus is the ultimate royal Champion who defends his people and disarms their enemies—paradoxically, through the apparent weakness of his cross. The wisdom theme (Solomon) is also royal, for discerning insight, when combined with integrity of character, qualifies the king to render just verdicts. As we will see, Jesus' parables (Ps. 78:2, quoted in Matt. 13:35), like Solomon's proverbs, are the fruit of royal wisdom (1 Kings 4:32; Prov. 1:1, 6). And Jesus will judge the nations at the end of time (Matt. 25:31–46; Acts 17:31), rendering his verdicts "not . . . by what his eyes see, or . . . by what his ears hear, but with righteousness he shall judge the poor, and decide with equity for the meek of the earth" (Isa. 11:3–4).

The King Wages War in Courageous Faith

From the time that sin entered human experience through the fall of Adam and Eve, conflict has characterized our history. In his word of judgment against Satan, who spoke through the serpent, God announced the enmity that he would place between the woman's offspring and Satan and the grave wound that each would inflict on the other (Gen. 3:15). The patriarch Abraham waged war to rescue his nephew Lot from pagan captors and acknowledged the victory that God had granted by offering tithes as the Lord's plunder to the priest Melchizedek (14:13–24). Supported by Moses' prayers, Joshua led Israel into battle against pagan foes in the wilderness (Ex. 17:8–16) and in the conquest of the Promised Land (Josh. 8, 10). After Joshua's death, during the period described in the book of Judges, Israel's national history ran in cycles of apostasy, affliction, repentance, and rescue (Judg. 2). The people would abandon their devotion to the Lord and worship the gods of the pagan peoples around them instead. The Lord, in turn, would deliver them over to be plundered and oppressed by those peoples. Their distress moved them to temporary repentance, and the Lord raised up "judges," who took up arms to deliver their people (though some did adjudicate cases of justice, 4:4–5). Thus, the Lord was Israel's royal Defender, who rescued his people when they humbled their hearts and sought his face in repentance. The Israelites needed no other king than the Lord himself, if only they would trust and obey. Yet God had promised through Moses to give them a human king (Deut. 17), and earlier prophecies likewise hinted that a scepter-bearing monarch would eventually arise within Israel (Gen. 49:8–12; Num. 24:15–19). The refrain at the end of Judges shows that they did indeed need a human monarch to direct their unruly hearts toward submission to their divine King: "In those days there was no king in Israel. Everyone did what was right in his own eyes" (Judg. 21:25).

The prophet Samuel was Israel's last judge. As Samuel prayed and sacrificed, the Lord himself fought for his people with a deafening thunderclap that routed Philistine armies that were poised to assault the Israelites assembled at Mizpah (1 Sam. 7). But Israel had grown weary of political and military instability, imagining that national security could be found in a central ruler and a royal dynasty that would transcend generations. The opportunity to demand a king came as Samuel grew old, for his own sons followed the wicked paths of the priest Eli's sons, with whom Samuel had grown up years earlier. They were unfit to succeed him as judges, abusing justice and exploiting people. So Israel asked for a king, as God had promised. But they specifically wanted kingship because they imagined that this centralized and hereditary institution would guarantee their security like that of the nations around them. When Samuel protested against their misguided request, they replied: "No! But there shall be a king over us, that we also may be like all the nations, and that our king may judge us and go out before us and fight our battles" (8:19–20). Samuel's primary function as judge was not military but juridical; he made an annual circuit among four cities, to hear and adjudicate disputes throughout Israel (7:15–17). Yet notice that the Israelites wanted a king who would lead them into battle—in fact, who would "fight . . . battles" on their behalf.

Saul was the Lord's answer to their request, and he seemed to start well: tall, strong, humble (1 Sam. 9:1–2, 21). When the Spirit came upon him at his anointing, he began to lead the Israelites in battle against their enemies (10:10; 11:1–11; 13:1–4). But Saul soon showed that his heart was not single in its commitment to keep the word of the Lord. Nervous as he watched his army melt away, he rushed into offering sacrifice to prepare for battle, rather than waiting as instructed by the Lord's prophet Samuel (13:8–14). That disobedience, which seemed necessary and minor to Saul, was enough to bring about his rejection by the Lord: "But now your kingdom shall not continue. The LORD has sought out a man after his own heart, and the LORD has commanded him to be prince over his people, because you have not kept what the LORD commanded you" (v. 14). Later, eager to please his troops and display the spoils of his victory, Saul conveniently ignored God's command to destroy all Amalekites and their livestock (15:1–3, 7–18). He never learned one simple lesson: "to obey is better than sacrifice" (v. 22). So the prophet Samuel declared, "You have rejected the word of the LORD, and the LORD has rejected you from being king over Israel. . . .

The LORD has torn the kingdom of Israel from you this day and has given it to a neighbor of yours, who is better than you" (vv. 26, 28). That better "neighbor" was David.

The account of David's anointing in the home of his father, Jesse, emphasizes the contrast with Saul, who looked like a king, head and shoulders above others. When the prophet Samuel thought he could identify the next king by sight from among Jesse's sons, the Lord told him: "Do not look on his appearance or on the height of his stature . . . . For the LORD sees not as man sees: man looks on the outward appearance, but the LORD looks on the heart" (1 Sam. 16:7). David was an afterthought even to his father, mentioned only when Jesse had run out of other sons to present. He was ruddy and handsome (v. 12), but no one would have guessed that he was "royal material" by looking at him. As a royal warrior, however, David had what Saul lacked: trusting submission and fierce loyalty to God.

The confrontation with Goliath shows how far short Saul fell of what Israel's king was supposed to be, and introduces the "man after God's own heart" who was eager to wage war on behalf of God's people. The Israelites wanted a king to fight their battles for them, and this would have been the perfect opportunity for Saul to prove his mettle as their champion: representative, hand-to-hand combat, winner takes all (1 Sam. 17:8–11). Saul refused to fight for his people; but David, irate at the insults that the Philistine warrior lodged against the Lord and freshly anointed by God's Spirit, demanded the opportunity to avenge the contempt heaped on his God. Refusing King Saul's armor for protection, David advanced against the enemy with weaponry that he had tested and found reliable:

> You come to me with a sword and with a spear and with a javelin, but I come to you in the name of the LORD of hosts, the God of the armies of Israel, whom you have defied. This day the LORD will deliver you into my hand, and I will strike you down and cut off your head. And I will give the dead bodies of the host of the Philistines this day to the birds of the air and to the wild beasts of the earth, that all the earth may know that there is a God in Israel, and that all this assembly may know that the LORD saves not with sword and spear. For the battle is the LORD's, and he will give you into our hand. (1 Sam. 17:45–47)

The name of the Lord was David's royal armor, and in the Lord's strength he conquered that offspring of Satan, Goliath, who threatened to enslave

God's people. Although Psalm 118 is not attributed to David, it celebrates the Lord's victory over enemies through his anointed king, who recounts, "All nations surrounded me; in the name of the Lord I cut them off!" (Ps. 118:10). The warrior-singer knows where his strength lies and who gives him victory: "The Lord is my strength and my song; he has become my salvation. . . . The right hand of the Lord does valiantly" (vv. 14, 16). In the most explicit echo of David's words to the Philistine foe, as the king enters the gate of the Lord, the congregation greets him: "Blessed is he who comes in the name of the Lord! We bless you from the house of the Lord" (v. 26). Centuries later, as Jesus the Messiah rode into Jerusalem's gate, the crowds rightly welcomed him with these very words (Matt. 21:9; see Luke 19:38, where they call him the King). Yet they did not recognize the evil opponent that the King was coming to defeat and destroy, nor did they begin to perceive the personal price that the King would pay to secure his victory and his people's rescue.

As we read about David's successors, both in the southern kingdom that remained loyal to his dynasty and in the north, Israel, we find God's Word evaluating kings in terms of their resemblance to David, the faithful king.[1] David's devotion to the Lord served as the benchmark against which other rulers would be measured. Solomon's "heart was not wholly true to the Lord his God, as was the heart of David his father" (1 Kings 11:4). Concerning Solomon's grandson Abijam, the verdict is rendered:

> And he walked in all the sins that his father did before him, and his heart was not wholly true to the Lord his God, as the heart of David his father. Nevertheless, for David's sake the Lord his God gave him a lamp in Jerusalem, setting up his son after him, and establishing Jerusalem, because David did what was right in the eyes of the Lord and did not turn aside from anything that he commanded him all the days of his life, except in the matter of Uriah the Hittite. (1 Kings 15:3–5)

On the other hand, Abijam's son and successor "Asa did what was right in the eyes of the Lord, as David his father had done" (1 Kings 15:11).

Yet David himself fell short of the norm as the royal champion and defender of God's people. The standard for a true king is summed up in

---

1. By contrast, monarchs who ruled the northern kingdom "walked in the way of Jeroboam," the first king of the northern kingdom, "and in his sin" of leading those tribes into idolatry (1 Kings 15:26, 34; 16:19, 26; 22:52).

David's "last words," a prophetic oracle (2 Sam. 23:1–7). In this portrait of the perfect ruler, David clings to God's covenant promises to his royal house, but the biblical author does not let his readers imagine that David himself fits the description. David's last words are followed by a roster of David's great military champions, which closes with "Uriah the Hittite" (v. 39). That name is a stark reminder of David's darkest days on the throne. In the season "when kings go out to battle," David stayed in his royal palace, sending his troops to battle the Ammonites (11:1). The commander-in-chief's dereliction of his military duty led to David's adultery with the wife of the loyal Uriah and conspiracy to cover the sin by taking Uriah's life as an apparent casualty of war, grievous abuses of royal power that brought revolution and bloodshed into David's own house (2 Sam. 12–19). The last chapter of 2 Samuel again casts David in a negative light, showing him to be a king too much like those of the other nations. Against wise advice, he demanded a census to calculate the size of his army ("valiant men who drew the sword," 2 Sam. 24:9). Thus, the anointed warrior who had begun his tenure waging war "in the name of the LORD" (1 Sam. 17:45) almost ended up relying on the numbers of his troops, forgetting the motif of Psalm 118:8: "It is better to take refuge in the LORD than to trust in man." As a result, the Lord of hosts, the God of the armies of Israel, waged war against his own troops, inflicting a plague that decimated his people, making previous calculations of troop strength moot (2 Sam. 24:15). Clearly, David is not all that we need in a royal warrior, though in him we catch glimpses of the coming King who will conquer his enemies and defend his people.

Jesus, like his ancestor David, entered into combat on the very heels of his anointing by the Spirit. At his baptism, the Father's voice from heaven proclaimed him as the well-pleasing Son (Matt. 3:17) in words reminiscent of Psalm 2, in which the messianic King recounts his royal appointment by God:

> I will tell of the decree:
> The LORD said to me, "You are my Son;
>   today I have begotten you.
> Ask of me, and I will make the nations your heritage,
>   and the ends of the earth your possession.
> You shall break them with a rod of iron
>   and dash them in pieces like a potter's vessel." (Ps. 2:7–9)

As the Father spoke from heaven, the Holy Spirit descended upon Jesus, an event that Peter would later call his "anointing" for his royal office (Acts 10:38). In the power of God's Spirit, Christ immediately entered the wilderness to confront Satan, the tempter and accuser of God's people. The enemy challenged Jesus to prove his messianic identity by self-serving miracles: "If you are the Son of God" (Matt. 4:3, 6). Brazenly, the devil promised to give Jesus what God had promised his Messiah in Psalm 2, showing him all the world's kingdoms and offering, "All these I will give you, if you will fall down and worship me" (Matt. 4:9). God's royal Warrior, however, refused the proffered shortcut to global dominion at the price of idolatry, repelling the foe's assaults with the Word of God. As a result of his victory over the evil one in this initial skirmish, "Jesus returned in the power of the Spirit to Galilee" (Luke 4:14), and launched a campaign of liberation: "He went about doing good and healing all who were oppressed by the devil, for God was with him" (Acts 10:38). Demons cringed in terror, knowing that the arrival of God's Messiah spelled their defeat and demise: "What have you to do with us, O Son of God? Have you come here to torment us before the time?" (Matt. 8:29)

Christ triumphed over Satan and his demonic hosts not only at his temptation and through the exorcisms he performed, but also by his sacrificial death. Christ's death on the cross appeared to be the nadir of weakness to a world enamored of military might. In fact, however, that emblem of shame and seeming impotence was God's power (1 Cor. 1:18, 23–25). Enduring the just penalty for believers' sins, Christ wrested from Satan's hand the weapon by which he had tyrannized them. Thus, the letter to the Hebrews, which so often explores the priestly significance of Jesus' death, also characterizes it as royal combat:

> Since therefore the children share in flesh and blood, he himself likewise partook of the same things, that through death he might destroy the one who has the power of death, that is, the devil, and deliver all those who through fear of death were subject to lifelong slavery. (Heb. 2:14–15)

Writing to the Colossians, Paul also shows that the cross is the weapon by which our King has "disarmed the rulers and authorities and put them to open shame, by triumphing over them" (Col. 2:14–15). In the book of Revelation, John's vision shows "the great dragon . . . , that ancient serpent, . . . the devil and Satan," expelled from heaven, defeated and deprived of any and all grounds for accusing God's people. "And they have conquered him by the blood of the Lamb and by the word of their testimony, for they loved not their lives even unto death" (Rev. 12:9–11). The Lamb who conquered by enduring slaughter to rescue and procure people from every tribe, language, people, and nation (5:5–6, 9) has empowered those he redeemed to share in his victory.

King Jesus' warfare against God's enemies means nothing but destruction for Satan and his demonic forces, but the Messiah's triumph over human foes takes two very different forms. On the one hand, as Psalm 2 leads us to expect, those who stubbornly resist his reign to the end he will indeed "break . . . with a rod of iron and dash . . . in pieces like a potter's vessel" (Ps. 2:9). Later in Revelation, John reports:

> Then I saw heaven opened, and behold, a white horse! The one sitting on it is called Faithful and True, and in righteousness he judges and makes war. His eyes are like a flame of fire, and on his head are many diadems . . . . He is clothed in a robe dipped in blood, and the name by which he is called is The Word of God. And the armies of heaven, arrayed in fine linen, white and pure, were following him on white horses. From his mouth comes a sharp sword with which to strike down the nations, and he will rule them with a rod of iron. He will tread the winepress of the fury of the wrath of God the Almighty. On his robe and on his thigh he has a name written, King of kings and Lord of lords. (Rev. 19:11–16)

Men and women who persist in their rebellion against this conquering King of kings will, at last, suffer his righteous wrath. But before history's last battle, the New Testament shows the Anointed King waging war and vanquishing enemies with a very different outcome for those defeated foes. In Ephesians 4, for example, Paul invokes the imagery of a psalm, in which the Lord is portrayed as a triumphant monarch returning to his capital after defeating and capturing an opposing army, whose soldiers trudge behind their conqueror: "When he ascended on high he led a host of captives, and he gave gifts to men" (Eph. 4:8; see Ps. 68:18). As ancient kings distributed their captives, as spoils of war, to their loyal subjects, so Christ now gives to his church those whom he has captured in his sovereign grace: apostles, prophets, evangelists, pastors, and teachers (Eph. 4:11). In 2 Corinthians 2:14–16, when Paul evokes the image of the Roman triumphal procession following battle, it is uncertain whether he and other gospel heralds are to be viewed as the victorious troops or the captured enemies. Paul's likely point is that when Christ conquers by grace, enemies are reconciled and transformed into loyal soldiers, enlisted into the King's army (Rom. 5:10; Col. 1:21–22). Paul wrote from his own experience, for he had been Christ's enemy—"a blasphemer, persecutor, and insolent opponent" (1 Tim. 1:13)— but had received mercy from Christ, whom thereafter he gladly served as slave (Rom. 1:1).

Our triumphant King Jesus not only enlists us as his warriors but also arms us with his own weapons. In view of the hostile assaults we face from "the cosmic powers over this present darkness," Paul urged Christians to "put on the whole armor of God" (Eph. 6:10–12). He went on to list pieces of armor—belt, breastplate, footwear, shield, helmet, sword (vv. 13–17)—that were worn by the Messiah or by the Lord himself in various Old Testament texts (Ps. 144:1–2; Isa. 11:5; 49:2; 59:17). Elsewhere, Paul virtually equated "put on the armor of light" with "put on the Lord Jesus Christ" (Rom. 13:12, 14), reminding us of the contrast that David drew between Goliath's flimsy sword, spear, and shield, on the one hand, and "the name of the Lord of hosts" that constituted David's armor and weaponry, on the other (1 Sam. 17:45). As believers rest and take refuge in the King who conquered and now protects them, they wage spiritual warfare with weapons that "have divine power to destroy strongholds," that is, "every lofty opinion raised against the knowledge of God," and they "take every thought captive to obey Christ" (2 Cor. 10:3–5). The Heidelberg Catechism sums up the military dimension of Christians' royal calling because of our union with Christ, explaining that we share in his anointing as King "to strive with a free conscience against sin and the devil in this life" as well as "afterward to reign with Christ over all creation for eternity" (Lord's Day 12, answer 32).

So Christ the King wages war against his and our enemies. Through his death and resurrection, he has dealt the death blow to the greatest foe, Satan. And now, in surprising mercy, he is capturing people who were once his enemies and transforming them into his own loyal troops. He bestows on his soldiers his own armor for our protection and for our offensive assault on the strongholds of the evil one.

The King Leads in Accountable Authority

Kingship entails both power and authority. Authority is the right to exercise power, to receive both honor and obedience. The authority of

Israel's king rested on the fact that the Lord had anointed him, placed him on "Zion, my holy hill," and decreed that the king was "my Son" (Ps. 2:6–7). Rather than foolishly raging against the Lord and his anointed king or plotting their overthrow (vv. 1–2), the rulers of the earth would be wise to "serve the LORD with fear" and to "kiss the Son" in humble submission (vv. 10–12). Another royal psalm prays that the king will enjoy the submission of the surrounding nations, as befits the authority delegated to him by the Lord:

> May he have dominion from sea to sea,
> and from the River to the ends of the earth!
> May desert tribes bow down before him,
> and his enemies lick the dust!
> May the kings of Tarshish and of the coastlands
> render him tribute;
> may the kings of Sheba and Seba
> bring gifts!
> May all kings fall down before him,
> all nations serve him! (Ps. 72:8–11)

Subjects owe their Sovereign not only loyal obedience but also honor and respect. The authority of the royal office is vividly illustrated in David's refusing to kill King Saul when opportunities presented themselves, even though the king was unjustly seeking David's life (1 Sam. 24:1–16; 26:1–12). Though Saul's injustice and violence had dishonored his office, nonetheless out of respect for that royal office, since Saul was still the Lord's anointed (24:6), David refused to retaliate. The authority of the king to lead his people is illustrated positively in the devoted loyalty that bound the hearts of David's "mighty men" to him as their commander. His mere expression of longing (not demand) for water from the well in Bethlehem, his hometown, moved three of them to risk their lives to quench their captain's thirst (2 Sam. 23:13–17). During the reigns of David's successors, the kings' leadership, for good or ill, shaped the fluctuations in Israel's allegiance to the Lord. More faithful kings such as Hezekiah and Josiah took action to purify Israel's temple worship and to suppress the influences of pagan idolatry. Unfaithful kings led their people, by example and edict, into spiritual treason and resultant ruin. Although punctuated by occasional glimmers of light, the spiritual leadership of the royal houses of both Judah in the south and Israel in the north was largely shrouded in darkness and decadence. Where was the King who would rule God's people in righteousness and lead them in deepening covenant loyalty toward their divine Sovereign, the Ruler whose integrity of character would fit the dignity of his office?

David had looked forward to his own descendant—who would also be David's Lord—to whom God would say, "Sit at my right hand, until I make your enemies your footstool" (Ps. 110:1; see Matt. 22:41–45). That position of royal supremacy, the psalm continues (vv. 2–3), entails dominion over both enemies and willing subjects:

> The Lord sends forth from Zion
>   your mighty scepter.
> Rule in the midst of your enemies!
> Your people will offer themselves freely
>   on the day of your power.

In a later generation, the faithful Daniel, an exile forced to serve a pagan king, was granted a vision in which he saw God's court in heaven, into which "one like a son of man" entered to be installed as an eternal King: "And to him was given dominion and glory and a kingdom, that all peoples, nations, and languages should serve him; his dominion is an everlasting dominion, which shall not pass away, and his kingdom one that shall not be destroyed" (Dan. 7:13–14).

Any reader of the Gospels knows that Jesus often referred to himself as the "Son of Man." In doing so, he quietly claimed to be the Ruler promised in Daniel's vision, on whom the Ancient of Days would soon confer universal and endless dominion. The promised King, who could be trusted to wield royal authority with integrity, had come! Jesus even has the authority to forgive sins, a prerogative that belongs to God alone. Jesus healed the paralysis of a disabled man whose friends dug through the roof and ceiling to get him close to the Messiah. But before Jesus provided physical healing, he pronounced the paralytic's sins forgiven. The physical healing was a sign to demonstrate that Jesus, the Son of Man who would enter heaven on clouds to receive his eternal and universal kingdom, already had authority on earth—even before his ascent to the Ancient of Days—to pronounce sins forgiven (Mark 2:1–12).

243

The New Testament frequently says that when Jesus ascended to heaven after his death and resurrection, he sat down at God's right hand.[2] Jesus of Nazareth is the long-awaited King whose power subdues his enemies and whose authority leads his willing people into deepening allegiance to the Lord. Jesus' universal authority at God's right hand is the basis for the global expansion of God's kingdom through the proclamation of his gospel. The risen King's announcement, "All authority in heaven and on earth has been given to me" (Matt. 28:18), echoes the royal investiture of the Son of Man in Daniel 7:13–14. That universal authority is the grounds for his commission to his church to enlist disciples from all of earth's nationalities. Even after his resurrection, the apostles' conception of his messianic kingdom stayed snugly within Israel's boundaries (Acts 1:6), but his promise lifted their sights to glimpse the expansion of his domain to "the end of the earth" (v. 8). Forty days after rising from the dead, Jesus, David's royal heir, ascended and took his throne at God's right hand (2:30–32). From that position of supreme authority, he poured out the Holy Spirit in power on his waiting, willing servants (vv. 33–36). As a result, the peoples of the earth, each in their own tongue, heard the news of God's mighty works to establish his redemptive kingdom under his messianic King (vv. 6–11).

The King Judges in Wisdom and Equity

One extension of the king's responsibility to wage war on his people's behalf and to rule their otherwise unruly hearts is his role as their judge. The Israelites' demand for a king linked the functions of fighting and judging (1 Sam. 8:20). God delegates authority and power to the king so that he might protect his subjects not only from outside aggressors but also from one another. We recall that in Ezekiel 34 the Lord promised to come as Israel's true shepherd not only to rescue his sheep from wild beasts and exploitive shepherds (vv. 5–10), but also to "judge between the fat sheep and the lean sheep," between bullying rams and the weak who suffer abuse (Ezek. 34:16–22). In a fallen world, among fallen sinners, maintaining a just and peaceful community life demands that disputes must be arbitrated and resolved by those in authority.

For Israel in the wilderness, that task first fell to Moses, apparently virtually single-handedly, exhausting him and frustrating the Israelite liti-

---

2. Matt. 26:64 and parallels; Mark 12:36 and parallels; Acts 2:33–34; 5:31–32; see 7:55–56; Rom. 8:34; Eph. 1:20; Col. 3:1; Heb. 1:3, 13; 8:1; 10:12; 12:2; 1 Peter 3:22.

gants (Ex. 18:13–26; Deut. 1:9–18). Cadres of elders among the twelve tribes were appointed to assist him by rendering verdicts among their kinfolk. Seventy of those elders were set apart as an appellate court, so that Moses had to adjudicate only the most difficult cases (Num. 11:14–30). After Israel entered the Promised Land, the elders continued their judicial calling in cities and villages (Deut. 21:1–9, 18–21). God also raised up national leaders, judges. Although most judges were warriors fighting the pagan nations whom the Lord used to humble his people, the book that bears their name gives glimpses of some judges—Deborah, for example (Judg. 4:4–5)—as hearing disputes and rendering verdicts. Samuel, the last judge before the monarchy, had this judicial role also (1 Sam. 7:15–17).

The royal task that occupied Israel's first two kings, Saul and David, was largely military, since the era of the judges left Israel surrounded and beleaguered by national enemies. Finally, with the enthronement of David's son and successor, Solomon, whose name was derived from "peace" and whose reign was marked by peace, the role of the king as wise and just judge came to prominence. Soon after ascending the throne, Solomon begged God for wisdom to rule God's people and to resolve their disputes equitably: "Give your servant therefore an understanding mind to govern your people, that I may discern between good and evil, for who is able to govern this your great people?" (1 Kings 3:9). The Lord was delighted to grant the king's request, and 1 Kings immediately cites an example of the king's application of wisdom to two mothers' dispute over whose son had died and whose son still lived. In this "she said/she said" situation that seemed impenetrable, Solomon knew how to get to the truth, discerning that a mother's heart is willing to endure great loss in order to save her child's life (vv. 16–27). "And all Israel heard of the judgment that the king had rendered, and they stood in awe of the king, because they perceived that the wisdom of God was in him to do justice" (v. 28).

Solomon's royal wisdom extended beyond human psychology and jurisprudence. Solomon's wisdom and learning included literary production, musical artistry, botany and zoology, and other disciplines (1 Kings 4:29–33). Here is a royal sage whose insight across a wide spectrum of reality reflects the primeval kingship of Adam, who, in the naming of earth's animals, not only ruled them but also aptly categorized and characterized them (Gen. 2:19–20). Solomon was a student of virtually everything, and his wisdom won international renown: "And people of all nations came to hear the wisdom of Solomon, and from all the kings of the earth, who had heard of his wisdom" (1 Kings 4:34).

The close connection between the king's role as shepherd-judge and the biblical motif of wisdom, which is so vividly exemplified in Solomon, is confirmed when we compare two texts in the prophecy of Jeremiah. In Jeremiah 2:8, the Lord accuses three categories of leaders of dereliction in their official duties: priests, entrusted with God's law, failed to seek his presence; "shepherds" (that is, kings, Jer. 23:1–6), charged to uphold God's law, transgressed against him; and prophets spoke in the name of Baal. Therefore, God announced that he would bring shame on "the house of Israel[,] . . . their kings, their officials, their priests, and their prophets" (2:26; see 4:9). But neither the people nor their leaders believed God's threats through Jeremiah. They scoffed: "Come, let us make plots against Jeremiah, for the law shall not perish from the priest, nor counsel from the wise, nor the word from the prophet" (18:18). Whereas in 2:8 the three categories of leaders were priests, *shepherds*, and prophets, here they are priests, "*the wise*," and prophets. The royal image of *shepherds* is replaced here by *sages*, the circle of wise court advisers with the king at its center (see 2 Sam. 15:12; 16:23). The king was the chief justice in Israel's multilevel system of courts and appellate courts, from elders in tribes and cities on up; and for this task, as Solomon was well aware, the king needed great wisdom.

King Solomon's name is associated with the Old Testament's wisdom literature, especially Proverbs (1:1; 10:1; 25:1), Ecclesiastes (1:1, 12–13, 16; 2:1–9; see 1 Kings 10:23–24), and Song of Songs (1:1). The preface to Proverbs (1:1–7) implies that instruction in wisdom is needed because reality is often not as it appears to be on the surface. Among the figures who appear in Proverbs are the fool, who defies and ignores God, setting his sights on immediate gratification; the wise, who take the long view of things by trusting in God and living by faith; and the naive, who are vulnerable to deception and need to acquire wisdom. Proverbs inform royal heirs in their responsibility to administer "righteousness, justice, and equity," but they offer something to everyone:

> To know wisdom and instruction,
> to understand words of insight,
> to receive instruction in wise dealing,
> in righteousness, justice, and equity;

> to give prudence to the simple,
>> knowledge and discretion to the youth—
> Let the wise hear and increase in learning,
>> and the one who understands obtain guidance,
> to understand a proverb and a saying,
>> the words of the wise and their riddles.
>
> The fear of the LORD is the beginning of knowledge;
>> fools despise wisdom and instruction. (Prov. 1:2–7)

Kings such as Solomon issued proverbs to enable their sons and their subjects to see reality clearly and therefore to make wise and just decisions. But this takes work. That is the point of the imagery and analogy that compares gaining wisdom to mining in the earth for precious gems:

> If you seek [understanding] like silver
>> and search for it as for hidden treasures,
> then you will understand the fear of the LORD
>> and find the knowledge of God.
> For the LORD gives wisdom;
>> from his mouth come knowledge and understanding;
> he stores up sound wisdom for the upright;
>> he is a shield to those who walk in integrity. (Prov. 2:4–7)

Wisdom is God's gift, one of the many good gifts that come down from the Father of lights (James 1:5, 17). He lavishes wisdom not on the intellectually outstanding but on the humble who fear his name (Matt. 11:25–26). Yet wisdom is a treasure to be pursued with discipline and energy, and it is worth the effort!

Despite Solomon's fame as a sage, however, as his reign wore on, his own folly (and that of his son Rehoboam) deprived David's dynasty of authority over most of Israel's tribes. Solomon's foreign wives and concubines, numbering in the hundreds, "turned away his heart after other gods" (1 Kings 11:1–8). Worldly wisdom of the time commended such marriages as shrewd means to secure political alliances, and Solomon started early with his marriage to a daughter of the pharaoh of Egypt (3:1). But Israel's divine King had banned such liaisons as spiritually perilous (Ex. 34:11–16; 1 Kings 11:2). So they proved to be in the life of ancient Israel's wisest ruler. Solomon was not the ideal King described by the oracle in David's last words: "When one rules justly over men, ruling in the fear of God, he dawns on them like the morning light, like the sun shining forth on a cloudless morning, like rain that makes grass to sprout from the earth" (2 Sam. 23:3–4). Neither David nor his successors fit that portrait, yet God promised that just such a Ruler, a Judge distinguished by integrity and insight, would eventually spring from the almost-severed stump of David's dynasty:

> And the Spirit of the LORD shall rest upon him,
> > the Spirit of wisdom and understanding,
> > the Spirit of counsel and might,
> > the Spirit of knowledge and the fear of the LORD.
> And his delight shall be in the fear of the LORD.
> He shall not judge by what his eyes see,
> > or decide disputes by what his ears hear,
> but with righteousness he shall judge the poor,
> > and decide with equity for the meek of the earth;
> and he shall strike the earth with the rod of his mouth,
> > and with the breath of his lips he shall kill the wicked.
> Righteousness shall be the belt of his waist,
> > and faithfulness the belt of his loins. (Isa. 11:2–5)

Jesus was and is that long-anticipated royal Judge, who weighs human hearts with wisdom and justice. John the Baptist foretold his messianic mission as Judge, employing the agricultural metaphor of the winnowing process by which usable grain kernels are separated from useless husks: "His winnowing fork is in his hand, to clear his threshing floor and to gather the wheat into his barn, but the chaff he will burn with unquenchable fire" (Luke 3:17). Although he refused to be drawn into the role of arbitrator of petty disputes over ephemeral wealth (12:13–21), Jesus himself foretold the coming day when, as Son of Man, he would render judgment over all the peoples on the earth, as a shepherd divides sheep from goats (Matt. 25:31–46).

King Jesus was and is not only the royal Judge but also the royal Sage and, more than that, the ultimate source of God's own wisdom for those who humbly realize that they are clueless and confused about whom to believe and how to live. The wisdom of Jesus is displayed in three different ways in three successive chapters of Matthew's Gospel (chaps. 11, 12, 13). First, in Matthew 11, Jesus issued an invitation to the weary that echoed, in a general way, Wisdom's call to the simple (Prov. 9:1–6). Jesus' invitation was: "Come to me, all who labor and are heavy laden, and I will give you rest. Take my yoke upon you, and learn from me, for I am gentle and lowly in heart, and you will find rest for your souls. For my yoke is easy, and my burden is light" (Matt. 11:28–30). Jesus spoke not merely as a King wiser than Solomon, but as Wisdom itself.

Second, in Matthew 12, Jesus contrasted the Gentiles' humble response to God's spokesmen in the Old Testament to the resistance being mounted by his own Jewish countrymen. Cruel Ninevites had repented at God's warning through Jonah, a prophet who had been raised, in effect, from death in the sea. At the last judgment, those pagans will rightly condemn the contemporaries who refused to hear and heed Jesus, for in him "something greater than Jonah is here" (Matt. 12:41). Moreover, "The queen of the South will rise up at the judgment with this generation and condemn it, for she came from the ends of the earth to hear the wisdom of Solomon, and behold, something greater than Solomon is here" (v. 42). Jesus' wisdom exceeds that of Israel's wisest sage!

Third, because Jesus was the royal Sage par excellence, he spoke, as Solomon did, in proverbs—in comparisons or analogies or "parables." Matthew 13 is a collection of Jesus' instruction by analogy, drawing parallel patterns between everyday experiences and the realities of God's kingdom now come and coming with Jesus' arrival as Messiah. Matthew even calls attention to the linkage between Jesus' parabolic pedagogy and that of the Old Testament sages by quoting Psalm 78:2: "This was to fulfill what was spoken by the prophet: 'I will open my mouth in parables; I will utter what has been hidden since the foundation of the world'" (Matt. 13:35). The Hebrew word behind the Greek word *parable* is *mashal*, the same term used for Solomon's and other sages' many proverbs (Prov. 1:1). Many of Jesus' parables (though not all) are complete stories, in contrast to the concise comparisons that we find in Proverbs. But the principle of instruction—pointing out patterns that connect events in everyday life with spiritual realities—is the same.

The apostle Paul expanded on Matthew's revelation of Jesus as the royal Sage, carrying the theme of divine wisdom out from Israel to engage the healthy appetite for wisdom among the Gentiles of the Greco-Roman world. Writing to the church at Corinth, not far from the famous Greek intellectual center, Athens, Paul frankly acknowledged that the message of Christ crucified did not suit the taste of either the Jews or the Greeks:

249

> For Jews demand signs and Greeks seek wisdom, but we preach Christ crucified, a stumbling block to Jews and folly to Gentiles, but to those who are called, both Jews and Greeks, Christ the power of God and the wisdom of God. For the foolishness of God is wiser than men, and the weakness of God is stronger than men. (1 Cor. 1:22–25)

Paul knew that Christ the Crucified One alone could deal with the depth of our human problem, our sinful rebellion against and alienation from the all-wise and all-holy Creator of all things. Although Christ's cross appeared to the power-hungry to be the depth of weakness and to the academically sophisticated as the height of folly, it was in fact the remedy that we need above all others, provided by the sovereign grace of God, whose "folly" infinitely surpasses the best of human wisdom. Across the Aegean Sea to the east, in the Roman province of Asia, the church at Colossae was being influenced by other claims to hidden religious knowledge through mystical experience. To that church Paul described Jesus Christ in words that echoed Proverbs' summons to search out divine wisdom like precious hidden ore. The ancient sage commended the strenuous pursuit of wisdom "like silver" and searching "for it as for hidden treasures" (Prov. 2:4). Paul knew the divine-human person who is the source of such fabulous wealth and preached Christ with the goal that his hearers would "reach all the riches of full assurance of understanding and the knowledge of God's mystery, which is Christ, in whom are hidden all the treasures of wisdom and knowledge" (Col. 2:2–3).

Recognizing that the Bible's wide array of themes concerning the king's role as wise judge converge in the long-awaited Messiah will alert us to royal landmarks embedded throughout the Old and New Testaments, both in records of justice and in aphorisms of wisdom. All those landmarks direct our paths toward the person of Jesus the King of kings, the Wisdom of God in flesh and blood.

Conclusion

Kings were anointed to defend, to rule, and to judge. Although the Israelites were wrong to want a king "like all the nations," they understood the king's task rightly: to "judge us and go out before us and fight our battles" (1 Sam. 8:20). At first they had such a champion in Saul (1 Sam. 11). Later, the newly anointed David succeeded him in this role, single-handedly defeating the Philistine Goliath (1 Sam. 16–17). But only Jesus Christ is the Champion who has defeated and disarmed his people's ultimate enemy. He is the offspring of the woman who struck the serpent's head, as his own heel was struck (Gen. 3:15). Yet the Heidelberg Catechism (answer 32) is also right to say that spiritual warfare still rages and that every Christian, sharing Jesus' royal anointing, participates in the combat against Satan's evil empire (Eph. 6:10–20). Wherever in Scripture we glimpse battles or skirmishes in the war between God's king and kingdom, on the one hand, and Satan's domain of darkness on the other, we are catching sight of landmarks that point the way to Christ, our Warrior-King.

Wisdom and justice are also indispensable to the king's mission. Jesus is the wise, just, and mighty Ruler par excellence. The close association of Israel's wisdom tradition with Solomon, the preeminent sage, suggests the connection that links Proverbs, Job, Ecclesiastes, and the Song of Songs into God's new-creation project, to renew individuals as kings in the divine image to create a kingdom community characterized by orderly peace with justice and mercy, Christ's church. Ultimately, of course, the destruction of the last enemy and emergence of the peaceable kingdom in its fullness awaits the return of the King. Yet his kingdom has begun, and the King's transforming grace enables his grateful subjects and assistant rulers to display the King's wisdom and justice even in a decomposing world. Wherever in the Bible we see justice administered and hear words of wisdom, we are encountering landmarks that direct us to Jesus the Judge of all, in whom all the treasures of God's wisdom reside.

Putting It into Practice: Starting Well and Ending Badly (2 Kings 12; 2 Chronicles 23–24)

The sad life trajectory of King Joash, descendant of David, illustrates a sobering lesson: Receiving a superior theological education does not immunize the heart from apostasy. Of the three kings of Judah who are omitted from the genealogy of Jesus the Messiah in the first chapter of Matthew's Gospel (cf. 1 Chron. 3:11–12; Matt. 1:8), the most surprising omission is Joash. Joash occupied Judah's throne for forty years, and four chapters of Scripture are devoted to him (2 Kings 11–12; 2 Chron. 23–24). He had been rescued from slaughter in infancy by the courageous and godly priest Jehoiada and his wife. His story echoes the rescue of the infant Moses from Pharaoh's genocidal edict, and it previews the deliverance of the infant

Jesus from the rage of King Herod. In childhood, Joash was instructed in God's law by Jehoiada, receiving the finest theological education available from the high priest himself. Jehoiada had not only the official authority to teach the Torah but also the personal integrity and faith to explain and apply it rightly. Protected from the violent designs of his ruthlessly pagan grandmother Athaliah, for his first six years Joash grew up hidden in the house of the Lord and instructed in his law (2 Kings 11:2–3).

When he came to the throne at the tender age of seven, Joash started strong. At his coronation, the high priest Jehoiada had placed "the testimony"—the covenant law of the Lord—into Joash's hands, heeding Moses' command that Israel's future kings keep a copy of the law and consult it constantly as they ruled (Deut. 17:18–20). Then Joash, a faithful son of David, showed his zeal to repair and restore the house of the Lord after it had been plundered under the illegitimate tyranny of his evil grandmother (2 Kings 12:4–16). Zeal for God's house moved Joash to urge the priests to collect offerings for the temple's repair and refurnishing. When other priorities delayed the repairs, Joash even confronted Jehoiada, his beloved mentor, and negotiated a new strategy to move the project forward. Early on, the king's subjects might have wondered: Could Joash be the long-promised offspring of the woman, destined to crush Satan's power? Could he be the ideal King of David's last words, ruling "justly over men, ruling in the fear of God" (2 Sam. 23:3)?

Joash's beginning certainly seems to confirm what we read in 2 Kings 12:2: "Jehoash [Joash] did what was right in the eyes of the LORD all his days, because Jehoiada the priest instructed him." But the Hebrew text is more ambiguous than the ESV leads us to believe. The New International Version renders the same verse this way: "Joash [Jehoash] did what was right in the eyes of the LORD all the years Jehoiada the priest instructed him." The difference is slight but significant: Did Joash remain faithful *as long as he lived* ("all his days") because he had been instructed by Jehoiada in his childhood (ESV), or did he remain faithful only *as long as Jehoiada was teaching him* (NIV)? The Hebrew conjunction (*asher*) could support either "all his days *because* Jehoiada taught him" or "all his days *that* Jehoiada taught him." Only the rest of the story reveals which alternative is right. Sadly, the rest of the story makes it plain that Joash's faithfulness did not long outlive his protector and mentor, Jehoiada the priest. So the author of 2 Chronicles made this point unambiguously: "And Joash did what was right in the eyes of the LORD *all the days of Jehoiada the priest*" (2 Chron. 24:2). And the Jewish people who first read and heard Joash's story, *as they went into exile in Babylon*, knew the truth: They needed a King far more faithful than Joash, a King whose integrity lasts a lifetime.

Even in Joash's early "wonder years," all was not well with the king and his subjects. However we understand 2 Kings 12:2, the very next verse casts a dark shadow: "Nevertheless, the high places were not taken away; the people continued to sacrifice and make offerings on the high places." It seems that the people, not the king, were succumbing to the attraction of the old Canaanite paganism. But where was the king as his subjects went whoring after the hollow gods who had collapsed before the Lord's triumphant hosts under Joshua centuries before? Of all the kings in David's dynasty, only Hezekiah and Josiah exercised their royal authority rightly, removing the pagan high places in God's land (2 Kings 18:4; 23:5–15).

Second Kings 12:17–21 answers our question about the state of the king's heart, or rather the drift of the king's heart. In 2 Kings, the end of Joash's reign and life is summed up in two events. First, when the king of Syria invaded Judah and besieged Jerusalem, Joash bought political peace at the price of plundering and defiling the Lord's temple, the very sanctuary that he had once insisted on restoring. Second, Joash was assassinated by his own servants. What a sad ending to a life begun with such promise!

Yet behind this disappointing story lies an even uglier chain of events, recorded in 2 Chronicles 24:17–27. The plotline spiraling behind the scenes into spiritual ruin runs like this: Joash stayed "on the rails" spiritually until Jehoiada's death (v. 17). After the death of his godly spiritual mentor, however, the king was seduced by the flattery of his aristocrats and began to endorse the people's dabbling with idolatry. Like Rehoboam before him, Joash gladly heeded his peers' flattery and misguided counsel (10:6–16), so his royal influence for good in the hearts of his subjects dissipated. The Lord, in his jealous love and faithful patience, sent prophets to bring Joash and Judah back from the brink of destruction, especially by sending his Spirit upon the son of Jehoiada, Zechariah, to prophesy against the unfaithful king (24:19–20). Zechariah's prophetic boldness and indicting message posed Joash's "moment of truth": Would he heed Zechariah for the sake of his father Jehoiada, Joash's bold protector and godly teacher? Would Joash show himself to be a spiritual son of David, the king who had remembered the covenant loyalty of his friend Jonathan and showed corresponding kindness to Jonathan's son Mephibosheth (2 Sam. 9)? Most importantly, would Joash hear in Zechariah's voice the voice of God? But Joash put out a contract on the life of God's prophet, Jehoiada's son. The king's henchmen murdered Zechariah "in the court of the house of the LORD," staining God's sanctuary with his blood as the dying Zechariah issued one final indictment: "May the LORD see and avenge!" Joash had forgotten the covenant loyalty (ESV "kindness") of Jehoiada, Zechariah's father (2 Chron. 24:22).

This was the apostasy that left Joash and Judah vulnerable to invasion from their Syrian neighbors to the northeast, and again Chronicles fills in additional details. The Syrian invasion force was small, and Judah's defensive army was "very great" (2 Chron. 24:24). In the past, God's people had been in the reverse situation, vastly outnumbered—Gideon and his three hundred, and Jonathan with his armor-bearer, who routed a Philistine garrison, killing twenty. They had seen the truth of Jonathan's confidence: "Nothing can hinder the LORD from saving by many or by few" (1 Sam. 14:6). Here that scenario was turned upside down, as the Lord "executed judgment on Joash" by handing a vast host of his own people over to a tiny band of pagans. Finally, Chronicles reveals that Joash's payoff to the Syrian king was precipitated by this humiliating military defeat, which left Joash gravely wounded and vulnerable to assault by his treacherous servants. A king incapable of remembering steadfast love and showing steadfast love could hardly expect his own subordinates to show him loyalty.

What is to be learned from the trajectory leading from Joash's hopeful beginning to his despicable end? Recall the last words of David at the literary "hinge" that ties together the books of Samuel and of Kings (2 Sam. 23:1–7). In one sense, the kings in the books of Kings are judged by the standard of David. Are their hearts true to the Lord, like David's, or not? But in another sense, 2 Samuel has shown that David himself is not the righteous Ruler of whom he sings in his oracle, the coming King who will bring a bright sunrise of joy. The King we need is the One who not only held the Lord's law in his hand at his coronation as Joash did, but also embraced it in his heart his whole life long. Hebrews 10:5–10 tells us that Jesus spoke words from Psalm 40 as he entered the world to accomplish his mission, gladly confessing, "I delight to do your will, O my God; your law is within my heart" (40:8). Jesus is the King we need, rescued from slaughter in infancy like Joash, zealous for the building of God's house like Joash—but, unlike

Joash, a King who maintains steadfast love and loyalty straight through to the finish line, fulfilling obedience even to the death, even death on the cross.

But we should take something more away from the tragic downward trajectory of Joash: we need Jesus not only to obey for us (actively in commandment-keeping, passively in curse-bearing), but also to write his Word into our hearts. That is one of the promises of the new covenant: "I will put my law within them, and I will write it on their hearts" (Jer. 31:33, quoted in Heb. 8:10). Believers who share in Jesus' messianic anointing by God's Spirit execute our royal office not merely by holding the royal law in our hands but also by embedding it in our hearts.

Joash did not have Jehoiada forever, and when his pastoral mentor was out of the picture, Joash's allegiance to the law that had once been placed in his hands as a boy faded. If you have been blessed with godly shepherds, you will not have them forever either. Hebrews 13:7 exhorted its first audience: "Remember your leaders, those who spoke to you the word of God. Consider the outcome of their way of life, and imitate their faith." If you want to last, lifelong, in God's covenant communion and grace, the Word has to get down deep into you, drawing you close to Jesus, who is "the same yesterday and today and forever" (v. 8), the King who never forgets his covenant commitments.

Questions for Reflection and Discussion

1. How did ancient kingdoms differ from the "separation of powers" in modern representative democracies? What made the ancient form of government a more fitting illustration of God's kingship than our modern system? On the other hand, how did the division of labor among prophets, priests, and kings in ancient Israel underscore the limitations of authority wielded by all human leaders? (For example, what could priests do that kings could not?)

2. When Israel approached the prophet-judge Samuel to demand a king, "that we also may be like all the nations" (1 Sam. 8:19–20), what tasks did Israel expect the king to perform?

3. What royal themes are associated with Adam and Eve's authority and tasks as those created in the image of God? How do these royal dimensions of every human being's identity as God's image-bearer help us to discover the significance of biblical passages about people who are *not* (at least officially) kings or queens or judges? How do the Bible's

royal themes apply to us, though we might not be (at least officially) rulers or rescuers of others?

4. How were Israel's first two kings, Saul and David, *alike* and *different*: in appearance, in the beginning of their royal careers after being anointed, in the long-term trajectory of their responses to God and their reigns? How do their resemblances and contrasts illustrate the qualities of the ultimate King whose rule and rescue we need?

5. How does Psalm 118 link David's victory over Goliath to the combat for which Jesus would enter Jerusalem?

6. How did the author of 2 Samuel hint that David himself was not the ideal Ruler portrayed in his "last words" (2 Sam. 23:1–7)? In what ways was David a faithful preview of his coming messianic heir, and how did David fall short as king?

7. What royal themes are associated with the accounts of Jesus' baptism, his temptation in the wilderness, his casting out of demons, his death on the cross, his resurrection, his ascension, and his second coming?

8. What should be our response to the accountable authority that Jesus wields over his people, in submission to God the Father? In what situations or areas of life do you resist the specific rule of Christ, balking at the obligation to "offer [yourself] freely on the day of [his] power" (Ps. 110:3)?

9. How should we understand the meaning of *wisdom* in the Bible? Why is it related to the tasks of the king? How does God's wisdom inform the priorities and decisions of everyone who bears God's image as we seek to act with discernment in everyday life?

10. Where does the New Testament reveal that Jesus Christ is the fulfillment of the royal wisdom motif in Scripture? What feature of Jesus' teaching methodology shows him to be "the royal Sage par excellence"? What aspect of Jesus' mission most fully displayed God's wisdom, though it seemed utter foolishness to the world's intellectuals? Why was that "foolishness of God" actually the focal point of God's astonishing wisdom?

PART 6

"Are We There Yet?"

10

How Walking with Jesus through His Word Changes Us

WE HAVE COMPARED reading the Bible to taking a journey. We began with a brief trek from Jerusalem to the village of Emmaus. During that journey, two downcast disciples with dashed hopes became men whose hearts flamed with joy as their mysterious traveling Companion showed them from the Scriptures God's plan to lead his Messiah through suffering into glory and, through that Messiah, to lead others out of spiritual death into eternal life. As they traveled those miles, their conversation traversed millennia: from the garden of God to the still-future New Jerusalem, from Adam and Eve's exile at history's dawn to God's embrace through grace at history's destination.

We have surveyed the ways that God has marked out the paths and avenues that lead through the Bible's various territories and terrains to Jesus, that long-promised Messiah who was showing those two disciples that he and his saving mission are the themes that unify the writings of Moses, the prophets, the Psalms, and other Scriptures. As this book comes to a close, I hope your and my journey with Jesus through his Word will continue for the rest of your days and mine.

What will this Christ-focused way of exploring the Bible do to us and in us? When the two disciples and their unrecognized Teacher reached Emmaus, they offered him hospitality over supper. Surprisingly, he took the host's role, breaking the bread. Suddenly their eyes were opened and they saw Jesus for who he is. Afterward they recalled, "Did not our hearts burn within us while he talked to us on the road, while he opened to us the Scriptures?" (Luke 24:32). Some weeks later, Jesus' followers were no longer hiding in secrecy and cringing in fear but rather announcing, publicly and boldly, the meaning of Jesus' death and the reality of his resurrection. When the authorities "saw the boldness of Peter and John, and perceived that they were uneducated, common men, they were astonished. And they recognized that they had been with Jesus" (Acts 4:13). Can "being with Jesus" still make such a radical change in our lives that others notice the difference? If so, how can we spend such transformative time with this Lord of glory?

On the evening before his crucifixion, Jesus prepared his closest disciples for his imminent departure—not just his death, but his ascent to heaven after his resurrection from the dead. Though he would soon be absent from them physically, he nevertheless promised that he would continue to keep God's "Immanuel" ("God with us") commitment in another way. "I will not leave you as orphans; I will come to you" (John 14:18). How would he come? He had just told them: "I will ask the Father, and he will give you another Helper, to be with you forever, even the Spirit of truth, whom the world cannot receive, because it neither sees him nor knows him. You know him, for he dwells with you and will be in you" (vv. 16–17). Through the personal presence of the Holy Spirit and the abiding of Jesus' words in their hearts, the triune God would continue to be with those who believe in the Son:

> Whoever has my commandments and keeps them, he it is who loves me. And he who loves me will be loved by my Father, and I will love him and manifest myself to him. . . . If anyone loves me, he will keep my word, and my Father will love him, and *we will come to him and make our home with him.* (John 14:21–23)

Through the Spirit who indwells us and the Word of Jesus that stays with us, God the Father and Jesus the Son take up residence with and in us. Though he has ascended bodily to God's right hand in heaven, the risen Christ is still our traveling Companion on earth, keeping his promise, "I will never leave you nor forsake you" (Heb. 13:5). Because "Jesus Christ is the same yesterday and today and forever" (v. 8), we can and must approach the Bible, whenever we read and study it, expecting that Paul's prayer for the Ephesians will be answered for us as well: that God will "give you [the Spirit] of wisdom and of revelation in the knowledge of him, having the eyes of your hearts enlightened" to "know . . . the hope to which he has called you, . . . the riches of his glorious inheritance in the saints, and . . . the immeasurable greatness of his power toward us who believe, according to the working of his great might that he worked in Christ" (Eph. 1:17–20).

As we walk through God's Word in the company of Christ's Spirit, with our minds and hearts attuned to the perspectives that the risen Lord Jesus imparted to his first followers as he led them through the Scriptures, we will find that our living Savior is moving us to marvel and worship, to hope and trust, and to become more like himself.

Walking with Jesus Moves Us to Marvel and Worship

The interconnections throughout the Bible—a collection of documents written over a millennium and a half, through dozens of authors to audiences in a variety of living situations—should move us to marvel at the wisdom and sovereign power of God. All the characters who populate the drama of the Bible's history of redemption, all the plots and subplots, are bound together into one unified story of conflict and triumph by one Hero, Jesus the Messiah, Son of God and Son of Man.

If we were dealing with a work of fiction composed by a single author in a single generation, we might not be surprised to encounter a consistent and coherent plotline in which every detail finally falls into place at the story's finale. But the Bible's plotline focuses on actual persons and historical events, not the products of a human imagination. To be able to weave so many real people, flaws and all, and their various actions, good and bad, into a single narrative tapestry that reaches its focal point and fulfillment in one Galilean who is Savior of the world, the Author of the story would have to be none other than the Sovereign Planner and Orchestrator of everything that happens everywhere, over the whole span of human history and cosmic time.

This is, in fact, exactly what the Scriptures claim about their divine Author: he has a purpose for everything that he has created (which is everything other than himself, the Creator), and he "works all things according to the counsel of his will" (Eph. 1:11). At the center of God's invincible agenda for cosmic history is "his purpose, which he set forth in Christ as a plan for the fullness of time, to unite all things in him, things in heaven and things on earth" (vv. 9–10). It is no wonder, then, that we find these words of Paul in the midst of an outpouring of astonished adoration that begins, "Blessed be the God and Father of our Lord Jesus Christ, who has blessed us in Christ with every spiritual blessing in the heavenly places" (v. 3). Later in the letter, Paul marveled over the divine grace that granted to him, "the very least of all the saints," the privilege to preach "the unsearchable riches of Christ, and to bring to light for everyone what is the plan of the mystery hidden for ages in God who created all things, so that through the church the manifold wisdom of God might now be made known . . . according to the eternal purpose that he has realized in Christ Jesus our Lord" (3:8–11). God's one eternal plan, brought to fruition in one person, "Christ Jesus our Lord," displays the splendor of his multifaceted wisdom.

Nebuchadnezzar, a powerful pagan monarch accustomed to getting his own way, endured abject humiliation for his preening arrogance. When he finally came to his senses, he had caught a glimpse of the true Sovereign whose will cannot be thwarted, so he confessed in wonder and in worship:

> I blessed the Most High, and praised and honored him who lives forever,
>
> for his dominion is an everlasting dominion,
>   and his kingdom endures from generation to generation;
> all the inhabitants of the earth are accounted as nothing,
>   and he does according to his will among the host of heaven
>   and among the inhabitants of the earth;
> and none can stay his hand
>   or say to him, "What have you done?" (Dan. 4:34–35)

You and I have far more reason to marvel and to bow in adoration as we walk, page by page, through God's Word, discovering vista after vista of his power, purity, faithfulness, and mercy. We watch him patiently guide the passing generations and unfolding ages toward the arrival of Jesus, the promised offspring of the woman, descendant of Abraham, final and faithful Israel, perfect Priest and Sacrifice, royal son of David, last and best Word from God the Father. The road signs, landmarks, and lay of the land that reveal the paths that finally converge in Christ are not given merely to intrigue our minds with tantalizing, unexpected connections across the centuries. They move our hearts to marvel over God's manifold wisdom, to adore him for his surprising concern for rebels like us, for his astounding skill in devising the plan for our rescue, and for the astonishing price he paid to execute that plan. Walking with Jesus through his Word, we find ourselves blending our voices with Paul's outburst of praise:

Oh, the depth of the riches and wisdom and knowledge of God! How unsearchable are his judgments and how inscrutable his ways!

"For who has known the mind of the Lord,
    or who has been his counselor?"
"Or who has given a gift to him
    that he might be repaid?"

For from him and through him and to him are all things. To him be glory forever. Amen. (Rom. 11:33–36)

Walking with Jesus Moves Us to Hope and Trust

Writing about the purpose of the Old Testament, the apostle Paul told the Christians in Rome: "For whatever was written in former days was written for our instruction, that through endurance and through the encouragement of the Scriptures we might have hope" (Rom. 15:4). He wrote those words immediately after quoting Psalm 69:9 ("The reproaches of those who reproached you fell on me") as illustrating the commitment of Christ not to please himself but to please his Father and serve our needs (Rom. 15:3). In fact, it is only because those ancient Scriptures, as well as the New Testament books, bear witness to the person and redeeming mission of Jesus the Messiah that they can bring us encouragement and hope.

Apart from the golden thread woven through the tapestry of biblical history, glistening with the glory of Christ, the Scriptures would present only a dark record of dashed and hollow hopes. Repeatedly across the ages, the Bible brings into view individuals who seem heroic at first glance, but in time prove to be disappointments. *Adam and Eve*, created in God's likeness and image, were placed in a lush and fruitful garden on an earth and in a universe that was all "very good." But they believed Satan's lie, disobeyed their good Creator, and brought guilt and death on all their children down through the generations and a curse on the very earth that sustained them. Yet God spoke a word of promise, a shaft of light, into the midnight of their shame: someday a woman's Son would come to shatter the father of lies and his lethal venom, and the Son would win that victory as he himself would be wounded.

As generations passed, *Noah* was named by his father in the hope that he, at last, would bring relief from that curse for toiling, weary humanity (Gen. 5:28–29). Noah was "a righteous man, blameless in his generation," and "found favor in the eyes of the LORD" (6:8–9). Trusting God's word, Noah built an ark. His family survived as God's floodwaters washed the earth clean from human pollutants. Yet even Noah subsequently abused the Creator's good gifts from the earth, and in his drunken stupor he was shamed by his own son. Noah was not the son destined to bring relief from the curse.

Abraham left family and homeland, trusting in God's promise. Yet his faith faltered when he feared that powerful pagan rulers would take his life in order to take his beautiful wife. The half-lie that he urged the lovely Sarah to tell could have compromised the purity of the wife and mother through whom God planned to give Abraham countless descendants, bringing blessing to all nations. Yet the promise-keeping God protected Sarah's dignity and Abraham's life, despite the patriarch's flinching, fluctuating faith. Their doubting efforts to "help" God keep his promise by using Sarah's slave Hagar as her reproductive surrogate only bred conflict within the household immediately and for countless generations to come. Though blessing would come to all of earth's peoples through Abraham's family, the man himself disappoints us if we look to him to vanquish evil altogether.

Where shall we look for the offspring of the woman? On whom can our hopes for rescue rest? *Jacob*? The name given to him at birth, as he grabbed his brother's heel, forecast his cheating character. He would mature into a shrewd trader—a birthright for a bowl of lentil stew—and cunning trickster, deceiving his blind father. *Joseph*? Resented by his brothers, he endured great suffering in patient faith and was finally exalted to power, to become those same brothers' rescuer from death by starvation. But Joseph died outside God's land, clinging to the promise that the Lord would one day bring his kinfolk home. *Moses*? After a privileged upbringing, the adopted grandson of the Egyptian pharaoh got off to a rocky start as his fellow Israelites' rescuer. Taking matters into his own hands, he imagined that a violent murder, committed in secret (as he thought), could start the movement that would set God's people free. But there was a witness, and when Moses' secret emerged, he fled Egypt in fear for his life. Later, when Israel's fiery Lord commissioned and commanded him to return, Moses marshaled every excuse he could come up with to evade the divine call. One moment strong in courageous faith and the next fearful and complaining, one moment meeker than anyone on earth (Num. 12:3) and the next exploding in frustration and arrogant disobedience (20:10–13), Moses was not the one in whom hopes would find fulfillment. Could *Israel as a people* be the hope of the world? The Israelites' immediate response to the Lord's book of the covenant was just what it should have been: "All that the LORD has spoken we will do, and we will be obedient" (Ex. 24:7). Yet when Moses went back up the mountain to receive the Lord's design for his dwelling place with his people, they turned their backs on him and worshiped a statue of a calf, cast in gold (32:1–10). If hopes were vested in Israel, they would be disappointed not just once but repeatedly over the centuries, as the sad narrative leading from exodus to exile demonstrates.

How about *David*? In his youth, when anointed as king, the man after God's own heart (1 Sam. 13:14) killed the champion of God's enemies with the weapon that he knew to be trustworthy, "the name of the LORD of hosts, the God of the armies of Israel" (17:45). But later, on the throne, David used God's enemies as weapons to eliminate a loyal soldier, Uriah, in a futile attempt to cover up his own immorality. David falls tragically short of the royal benchmark that God announced in David's own final oracle: "When one rules justly over men, ruling in the fear of God, he dawns on them like the morning light" (2 Sam. 23:3–4).

What about *Solomon*, wisest of ancient Israel's sages and sovereigns? Sadly, his wily political alliances, secured by marriages to multiple wives belonging to pagan royalty, stole his heart away from the God who had given Solomon wisdom. He played the fool and served the idols to the point that God announced that he would wrest most of Israel from the hands of the dynasty of David and Solomon (1 Kings 11:9–13). And so it goes, even among the heirs of the beloved David. King *Joash* started well, under the spiritual mentoring of the faithful priest Jehoiada; but he ended very badly, slaughtering Jehoiada's son for speaking God's prophetic indictment against the king (2 Chron. 24). *Hezekiah* "did what was right in the eyes of the LORD, according to all that David his father had done" (2 Kings 18:3). But he plundered God's temple to buy off Assyria and foolishly opened his treasuries to envoys from Babylon. *Josiah* instigated an even more radical purging of the land from its idolatry and restoration of the Lord's true worship in the temple. Yet he, too, resisted God's word at one crucial juncture, and so died in battle (2 Chron. 35:20–24). Neither David himself nor any of his royal descendants fit the profile of the utterly righteous Ruler for whom David himself hoped—not until that final son of David, the One whom David described mysteriously as "my Lord" (Ps. 110:1; see Matt. 22:41–45).

The pages of the Old Testament teem with historical figures who evoke our admiration in many ways, yet not one of them has the integrity, much less the eternity of life, to bear the weight of our hopes for rescue from sin and reconciliation with God. The same can be said of the prominent individuals in the New Testament accounts—Mary, Peter, James and John, Stephen, Paul, and others. Only Jesus himself can sustain our hopes and bring us encouragement amid life's disillusionments, discouragements, despair, and even death itself. As we notice the clay feet on which even the best of the Bible's merely human heroes stand, we discover that our gaze cannot be fixed on them but must rather look up to the Redeemer to whom they looked forward in hopeful faith. As those admirable but flawed figures give us glimpses of the faithfulness, compassion, and holiness of Jesus, those glimpses are designed to point us to the Messiah himself. As we walk through the Word with Jesus as our Companion and Guide, pointing out to us the previews of his glorious person and his gracious mission, his Spirit encourages our hearts and fortifies our hope.

Walking with Jesus Makes Us More like Him

The New Testament authors frankly acknowledge that because Jesus has ascended bodily to God's right hand in heaven, we who trust him now do not see him with our physical eyes. To be sure, Stephen was granted a vision of Jesus standing in heaven (Acts 7:55–56), and his persecutor Saul (Paul) would later behold the blinding splendor of Jesus' glory (9:3–9). But most Christians "walk by faith, not by sight" (2 Cor. 5:6–7). Peter had been among the "eyewitnesses of [Jesus'] majesty" on the mountain of transfiguration (2 Peter 1:16–18); but Peter also stressed that others' faith, apart from sight, was no less effective in uniting them to Jesus the Savior: "Though you have not seen him, you love him. Though you do not now see him, you believe in him and rejoice with joy that is inexpressible and filled with glory" (1 Peter 1:8).

In another sense, however, even though we do not now see Jesus as his apostles did, we do see Jesus. Paul reminded the Gentile Christians of Galatia: "It was before your eyes that Jesus Christ was publicly portrayed as crucified" (Gal. 3:1). That presentation of Jesus "before your eyes" took place not through visions or visual aids, but rather through Paul's preaching: "Did you receive the Spirit by works of the law or by *hearing with faith*?" (v. 2). The Galatians "saw" Jesus by hearing the message that Paul preached and by believing it.

Writing to the Christians at Corinth, Paul drew lines of connection and contrast between Moses' privilege of beholding God's glory on Mount Sinai and our privilege of beholding God's glory in the face of Christ (2 Cor. 3:7–18). Moses' face apparently absorbed glorious light from his meeting with the Lord and then reflected that light to the Israelites when he descended the mountain to deliver the law (Ex. 34:29–35). That radiance was visible to their physical eyes, and so terrifying that Moses covered it with a veil, which he removed when he returned to meet with God again (2 Cor. 3:13). But that glory also faded over time, signifying that the covenant mediated by Moses would eventually give way to a new and better covenant (vv. 6–11). What makes the new covenant better than the old is that the law mediated through Moses brought condemnation and death through the Israelites' violation of its commands, whereas the new covenant brings us righteousness and life through Christ's redeeming work and his Spirit's presence (vv. 7–9). But there is another amazing difference between Moses' ministry and new covenant ministry: Moses alone entered God's presence, so Moses' face alone shone with God's glory. Now, through "the light of the gospel of the glory of Christ," proclaimed by Paul and others (4:4–5), "we *all*, with unveiled face, beholding the glory of the Lord, are being transformed into the same image from one degree of glory to another. For this comes from the Lord who is the Spirit" (3:18).

Pause a moment to ponder that parallel between Moses, on the one hand, and *every believer in Jesus* today, on the other. Both for Moses and for you, to behold the glory of the Lord is to be transformed to resemble that glory. But then stop to consider the contrast: on Sinai and in the tent of meeting, Moses alone experienced that wonderful and terrifying privilege of approaching the resplendent presence of the living God. Now, Paul stresses, "we *all*" share in that life-transforming sight (2 Cor. 3:18). And the glory that "has shone in our hearts to give the light of the knowledge of the glory of God in the face of Jesus Christ" (4:6) does not diminish over time, as the gleam on Moses' face did. Instead, it *increases* "from one degree of glory to another" (3:18). Seeing Jesus through the Word makes us more and more like Jesus in love, purity, compassion, faithfulness, kindness, and truth.

Over the centuries, countless people have read the Bible in a passionate pursuit of personal transformation in their desires and character and behavior. Not surprisingly, many have focused on the Bible's many commands and prohibitions. What better way to change than to listen carefully to God's directions, and then to muster up the willpower to obey what God has said? Paul himself, before Christ's grace and glory conquered and captured him, had practiced this way of reading and responding to Scripture. In fact, he had achieved as much as was humanly possible through this approach: "as to righteousness under the law, blameless" (Phil. 3:6). Coming face to face with the risen Lord Jesus, however, made Paul realize that "a righteousness of my own that comes from the law" (v. 9) would never evoke an approving smile from the holy God. Paul the law-observant Jew, no less than the most idolatrous and sensual pagan, was "dead in . . . trespasses and sins," deserving divine wrath "like the rest of mankind" (Eph. 2:1–3). His stone-dead heart needed to be raised up to vibrant, gladly obedient life; but God had given no law—no set of commands and expectations—that could give such life (Gal. 3:21).

As the ancient prophets had seen, only God's Sovereign Spirit could make dead people live again and turn stony hearts tender toward the Lord (Ezek. 36:25–27; 37:8–14; see Isa. 44:3–5). The new covenant that God had promised through the prophet Jeremiah would bring about both forgiveness for sins and the inscribing of God's law right into his people's hearts (Jer. 31:31–34). That is exactly what the Holy Spirit now does as he uses God's Word, written and preached, to turn us around and open our eyes to see God's glory in Jesus' face. After describing the anguished frustration of recognizing how right God's law is and finding oneself utterly unable to meet its standard, Paul exulted in the new way of deep transformation opened up by the redemptive work of Jesus, applied by the life-giving power of his Spirit:

> For the law of the Spirit of life has set you free in Christ Jesus from the law of sin and death. For God has done what the law, weakened by the flesh, could not do. By sending his own Son in the likeness of sinful flesh and for sin, he condemned sin in the flesh, in order that the righteous requirement of the law might be fulfilled in us, who walk not according to the flesh but according to the Spirit. (Rom. 8:2–4)

As you read your Bible, then, be on the alert to catch glimpses of Jesus, for as you fix your heart's gaze on him, the Holy Spirit will carry on his mysterious project to make you more like your Savior—a good work that he is committed to "bring . . . to completion at the day of Jesus Christ" (Phil. 1:6). Should you pay attention to the Bible's many commands? Of course you should, since every command shows, somehow or other, what it means to love God above all and your neighbor as yourself (Matt. 22:37–40). In other words, every command casts light on the loving heart and deeds of Jesus, who gladly kept the law's every command out of sheer love for his Father and for us. But the *living power* to keep God's commands is conveyed by God's Spirit as he fixes our heart's gaze on the beauty of God's Son. See him, and be transformed!

Questions for Reflection and Discussion

1. As you reflect on your prior experience of reading the Bible, what has made the difference between the times when your "heart burned within you" and other times when the words of Scripture, though you knew them to be true, did not move you to marvel and worship?

2. As we consider the way in which the living Lord Jesus came in person and taught people how the Old Testament foretold his sufferings and glory, can we expect Jesus to come to us still today to open our minds to the Scriptures, and to open the Scriptures to our understanding? How does he do this now?

3. According to Ephesians 1:3–14, what is the focal point of God's overarching purpose for history? How should God's purpose for history influence the way we read the Bible, in which he has revealed his plan?

4. Think over major figures in Old Testament history—Adam and Eve, Noah, Abraham, Jacob, Moses, David—one by one, asking this question about each one: How does this individual's story exemplify the ways in which hope in God's promise transforms lives?

5. Think over major figures in Old Testament history—Adam and Eve, Noah, Abraham, Jacob, Moses, David—one by one, asking this question about each one: How does this individual's life story demonstrate that this individual *cannot* bear the weight of our hopes for redemption?

6. Think over major figures in Old Testament history—Adam and Eve, Noah, Abraham, Jacob, Moses, David—one by one, asking this question about each one: How does Jesus exceed and excel this "hero" who preceded him (as well as each one who came after him)? How does his flawless faithfulness as Lord and Servant of the covenant place our hopes for rescue and re-creation on a firm, eternal foundation?

7. When Paul affirms in 2 Corinthians 3:18 that believers, by *beholding the glory of the Lord*, "are being transformed into the same image," he

is not implying that our physical eyes take in the visible light of God's radiance as Moses' eyes did on Mount Sinai. So how do Christians today "behold the Lord's glory"?

8. When Paul affirms in 2 Corinthians 3:18 that believers, by beholding the glory of the Lord, "are being *transformed into the same image*," he is not implying that our physical appearance will glow as Moses' face did when he descended from Mount Sinai. So what does it look like for Christians today to be transformed into the image of Christ? What aspects of your affections, attitudes, and actions are most in need of this transformation?

9. Which way of reading the Bible is more practical and powerful in changing our character and behavior: to focus our attention on the Scriptures' commands and prohibitions, or to focus on how it reveals Christ and his redemptive mission? Why?

10. What insight or reading strategy that you encountered in *Walking with Jesus through his Word* is going to change the way you read the Bible? Where do you plan to start?

Appendix:
Themes Linked to the
Three Theocratic Offices

Prophet

Westminster Shorter Catechism (WSC) 24: "Christ executeth the office of a prophet, in revealing to us, by his word and Spirit, the will of God for our salvation."

Brought into the **heavenly council** of God to receive commission, **word** of the Lord
    to be delivered to God's people (Moses, Isaiah, Ezekiel)

Covenant **treaty** (Moses as covenant mediator, historical prologue, stipulations, etc.)

Covenant **history** (= "former prophets") narrates the Lord's faithfulness and grace,
    and the servant's unfaithfulness

Covenant **lawsuit**—prosecution of the servant, guilty of covenant treason

Covenant **curse** (Deut. 28)—word of God carries out sanctions

Promise of eschatological **restoration** (rain on dry ground)—word of God effects a
    new creation when the last days come, just as God first created by speaking

Signs to attest the prophet's ministry (Moses, Elijah/Elisha, Jesus, apostles) function
    as *God's testimony* that they indeed speak on his behalf

Testing of prophets for orthodoxy as well as fulfillment of predictions

Priest

WSC 25: "Christ executeth the office of a priest, in his once offering up of himself a sacrifice to satisfy divine justice, and reconcile us to God; and in making continual intercession for us."

Presence of God—seeing and serving God before his face

Sanctuary (holy place)—city, land

Holiness and purification (moral and ceremonial)

Separation (kosher, grains in field, clothing, Sabbath/weekdays, people of God from the unclean nations, etc.)

Instruction in Torah, **advice** to judges

Consecration—devotion to worship for the glory and delight of God—creation consumed in praise of the Creator

Atonement—cleansing and covering of sin's defilement, which makes God's consuming holiness lethal to the sinner

Sacrifice—substitutionary suffering and death as the means of atonement

Prayer—intercession for others

Compassion/mercy and **relief from want** for the widow, orphan, alien from the treasury of God's sanctuary

King

WSC 26: "Christ executeth the office of a king, in subduing us to himself, in ruling and defending us, and in restraining and conquering all his and our enemies."

Warrior, champion
> **Liberator** from slavery

Defender from enemies
> **Conquest** of and **security** in homeland (inheritance)

Builder of God's house, city

Kinsman-redeemer (combines familial connection with themes of liberation, defense from injustice, and provision of inheritance/homeland)

Judge and ruler
> **Justice/righteousness**—equity in adjudicating disputes

Wisdom—discerning reality, discriminating and categorizing difference, weighing words, observing patterns and paradigms and drawing parallels (parables). Punishment of injustice within the community, too

Responsible to the Lord's Word, brought by the prophet and taught by the priest

For Further Reading

More Accessible

Barrett, Michael P. V. *Love Divine and Unfailing: The Gospel According to Hosea.* GAOT.[1] Phillipsburg, NJ: P&R Publishing, 2008.

Boda, Mark J. *After God's Own Heart: The Gospel According to David.* GAOT. Phillipsburg, NJ: P&R Publishing, 2007.

Clowney, Edmund P. *The Unfolding Mystery: Discovering Christ in the Old Testament.* 2nd ed. Phillipsburg, NJ: P&R Publishing, 2013.

Dillard, Raymond B. *Faith in the Face of Apostasy: The Gospel According to Elijah and Elisha.* GAOT. Phillipsburg, NJ: P&R Publishing, 1999.

Drew, Charles D. *Ancient Love Song: Finding Christ in the Old Testament.* Phillipsburg, NJ: P&R Publishing, 2000.

Duguid, Iain M. *Living in the Gap between Promise and Reality: The Gospel According to Abraham.* GAOT. Phillipsburg, NJ: P&R Publishing, 1999.

———. *Living in the Grip of Relentless Grace: The Gospel According to Isaac and Jacob.* GAOT. Phillipsburg, NJ: P&R Publishing, 2002.

Duguid, Iain M., and Matthew P. Harmon. *Living in the Light of Inextinguishable Hope: The Gospel According to Joseph.* GAOT. Phillipsburg, NJ: P&R Publishing, 2013.

Estelle, Bryan D. *Salvation through Judgment and Mercy: The Gospel According to Jonah.* GAOT. Phillipsburg, NJ: P&R Publishing, 2005.

Eswine, Zachary W. *Recovering Eden: The Gospel According to Ecclesiastes.* GAOT. Phillipsburg, NJ: P&R Publishing, 2014.

Ferguson, Sinclair. *Preaching Christ from the Old Testament.* London: Proclamation Trust, 2002. Available for download at http://old.proctrust.org.uk/dls/christ_paper.pdf.

Goldsworthy, Graeme. *According to Plan: The Unfolding Revelation of God in the Bible.* Downers Grove, IL: IVP Academic, 2002.

---

1. *GAOT* is an acronym for Gospel According to the Old Testament, a series published by P&R Publishing.

273

Gregory, Bryan. *Longing for God in an Age of Discouragement: The Gospel According to Zechariah*. GAOT. Phillipsburg, NJ: P&R Publishing, 2010.

Jackson, David R. *Crying Out for Vindication: The Gospel According to Job*. GAOT. Phillipsburg, NJ: P&R Publishing, 2007.

Longman, Tremper, III. *Immanuel in Our Place: Seeing Christ in Israel's Worship*. GAOT. Phillipsburg, NJ: P&R Publishing, 2001.

Murray, David. *Jesus on Every Page: Ten Simple Ways to Seek and Find Christ in the Old Testament*. Nashville, TN: Thomas Nelson, 2013.

Schwab, George M. *Hope in the Midst of a Hostile World: The Gospel According to Daniel*. GAOT. Phillipsburg, NJ: P&R Publishing, 2006.

———. *Right in Their Own Eyes: The Gospel According to Judges*. GAOT. Phillipsburg, NJ: P&R Publishing, 2011.

Selvaggio, Anthony T. *From Bondage to Liberty: The Gospel According to Moses*. GAOT. Phillipsburg, NJ: P&R Publishing, 2014.

Ulrich, Dean R. *From Famine to Fullness: The Gospel According to Ruth*. GAOT. Phillipsburg, NJ: P&R Publishing, 2007.

Wright, Christopher J. H. *Knowing Jesus through the Old Testament*. Downers Grove, IL: IVP Academic, 1995.

More Advanced

Beale, G. K. *Handbook on the New Testament Use of the Old Testament: Exegesis and Interpretation*. Grand Rapids: Baker Academic, 2012.

Goldsworthy, Graeme. *Gospel-Centered Hermeneutics: Foundations and Principles of Evangelical Biblical Interpretation*. Downers Grove, IL: InterVarsity Press, 2010.

———. *Preaching the Whole Bible as Christian Scripture: The Application of Biblical Theology to Expository Preaching*. Grand Rapids: Eerdmans, 2000.

Horton, Michael. *Introducing Covenant Theology*. Grand Rapids: Baker, 2009.

Johnson, Dennis E. *Him We Proclaim: Preaching Christ from All the Scriptures*. Phillipsburg, NJ: P&R Publishing, 2007.

Robertson, O. Palmer. *The Christ of the Covenants*. Phillipsburg, NJ: P&R Publishing, 1981.

Index of Scripture

283

Index of Subjects and Names